Social Security Reform in Advanced Countries

Increasingly ageing populations and a slowing rate of growth in the macro-economy are forcing advanced countries to reconsider their social security programmes. The need for detailed examination of the possible reforms and initiatives has never been greater.

This book brings together internationally-renowned scholars to evaluate the effect of recent social security reforms in advanced countries (pension programmes in particular) and to suggest policy reforms for the future.

Considering both theoretical and empirical aspects, the contributors evaluate three different policy reforms in order to address the problems common in developed nations:

- The shift from pay-as-you-go to funded systems
- The privatization of public pension systems
- The contribution of tax revenues to social security benefits is suggested.

Including detailed studies of countries including Australia, Germany, Japan, Scandinavia, the UK and the USA, this book will be of essential interest to economists and policy-makers working in pension financing reform, and public economics more generally.

Toshihiro Ihori is Professor of Economics at the University of Tokyo. His previous publications include *Public Finance in an Overlapping Generations Economy* (1996) and (in Japanese) *Right Ideas on Government Deficit* (2000).

Toshiaki Tachibanaki is Professor of Economics at the University of Kyoto. His previous publications include *Public Policies and Japanese Economy* (1996) and *Wage Determination and Distribution in Japan* (1996).

Routledge Contemporary Economic Policy Issues
Series Editor Kanhaya Gupta

This series is dedicated to new works that focus directly on contemporary economic policy issues. It aims to include case studies from around the world on the most pressing questions facing economists and policy makers at both a national and international level.

1 Regionalism and Globalization
Theory and practice
Edited by Sajal Lahiri

2 The Political Economy of Corruption
Edited by Arvind K. Jain

3 International Migration
Trends, policies and economic impact
Edited by Slobodan Djajić

4 Social Security Reform in Advanced Countries
Evaluating pension finance
Edited by Toshihiro Ihori and Toshiaki Tachibanaki

Social Security Reform in Advanced Countries

Evaluating pension finance

**Edited by Toshihiro Ihori
and Toshiaki Tachibanaki**

London and New York

First published 2002 by Routledge
11 New Fetter Lane, London EC4P 4EE

Simultaneously published in the USA and Canada
by Routledge
29 West 35th Street, New York, NY 10001

Routledge is an imprint of the Taylor & Francis Group

Typeset in Times New Roman by Wearset Ltd, Boldon, Tyne and
Wear
Printed and bound in Great Britain by Antony Rowe Ltd,
Chippenham, Wiltshire

British Library Cataloguing in Publication Data
A catalogue record for this book is available from the British Library

Library of Congress Cataloging in Publication Data
Social security reform in advanced countries : evaluating pension finance / edited by
Toshihiro Ihori and Toshiaki Tachibanaki.
    p. cm.
  Papers presented at the conference at the University of Tokyo in September, 1998.
  Includes bibliographical references and index.
  1. Social security—Finance—Congresses. 2. Social security—Finance—Case
studies—Congresses. 3. Privatization—Congresses. 4. Pension trusts—Congresses. I.
Ihori, Toshihiro, 1952– II. Tachibanaki, Toshiaki, 1943–

  HD7091 .S626 2002
  368.4'3—dc21

2002068158

ISBN 0–415–28278–0

Contents

Figures

Tables

Contributors

Hazel Bateman, School of Economics, University of New South Wales, Australia

Gary Burtless, The Brookings Institution, Washington DC, USA

Suzanne Doyle, School of Economics, University of New South Wales, Australia

Tatsuo Hatta, Center for Spatial Information Science, University of Tokyo, Japan

Fredrik Haugen, The Ragnar Frisch Center for Economic Research, Norway

Erik Hernæs, The Ragnar Frisch Center for Economic Research, Norway

Toshihiro Ihori, Faculty of Economics, University of Tokyo, Japan

Hideki Konishi, Faculty of Economics, Gakushuin University, Japan

Kai A. Konrad, Department of Economics, Free University of Berlin, Germany

Ashwin Kumar, Department of Social Security, UK

Olivia S. Mitchell, Wharton School, University of Pennsylvania, USA

Noriyoshi Oguchi, Department of Commerce, Senshu University, Japan

Akira Okamoto, Department of Economics, Okayama University, Japan

Mats Persson, Institute of International Economic Studies, Stockholm University, Sweden

John Piggott, School of Economics, University of New South Wales, Australia

Steinar Strøm, University of Oslo and The Ragnar Frisch Center for Economic Research, Norway

Toshiaki Tachibanaki, Institute for Economic Research, Kyoto University, Japan

G. Wagner, Europa-Universität Viadrina, Germany

Preface

Both advanced and developing countries suffer from the problem of social security, in particular old-age pension programmes for various reasons. Typical reasons for advanced countries are an ageing trend in the age-population structure, and a slower rate of economic growth in the macro-economy. These changes suggest the necessity of policy reforms in advanced countries.

This book attempts to evaluate the effect of recent social security reforms in many advanced countries, in particular pension programmes, and to show several desirable policy recommendations.

This book evaluates three different policy reforms in order to solve problems common to developed nations. First, a shift from a pay-as-you-go system to a funded system is recommended. Second, privatization of the public pension system is proposed in several countries. Third, the contribution of tax revenues (i.e. tax financing) to social security benefits is suggested.

This book also considers both the theoretical and empirical aspects. 'Theoretical' implies that an evaluation is made based on both efficiency and equity grounds. 'Empirical' implies that countries like Australia, Germany, Japan, Scandinavia, the UK, and the US are evaluated empirically.

Both theoretical and empirical chapters help to recognize the present status of social security reforms in advanced countries.

All chapters in this book were presented as papers at a conference at the University of Tokyo in September 1998, which was organized by the present editors. The conference was sponsored by the Center for International Research on the Japanese Economy at the University of Tokyo. We are much indebted to the center both financially and logistically, and are grateful for their support.

Toshihiro Ihori
Toshiaki Tachibanaki

1   Introduction

Toshihiro Ihori and Toshiaki Tachibanaki

1.1 Reason for this book

A large number of advanced countries have problems with their social security systems, in particular public pension systems. One of the most important causes of this problem is that many countries face an ageing trend in age–population structure. The number of people who contribute financially to the system is decreasing. The problem is serious particularly when the system is either a pay-as you-go scheme or an unfunded scheme.

There are, of course, several other factors such as the decrease in the participation of men in the labour force, the slow increase in female participation, the policy of early retirement to offset youth unemployment, which cause serious problems in social security. In several industrialized countries the following can be added: the weak performance in the macroeconomy which reduces the amount of contributions, and the low rate of interest which lowers the rate of return on asset management.

There are several studies which show projections of the fiscal liabilities of public pensions programmes and serious financial deficits, and present incapabilities of paying a sufficient amount of pension benefits continuously, when the current pay-as-you-go or the unfunded scheme is kept below the ageing trend. See, for example, OECD (1996) and Disney (2000) for advanced countries, specifically the OECD countries. If we look at studies for particular individual countries, we should be looking at an extremely large field.

Many countries contemplate policy reforms to modify public pension systems in order that the government can sustain the system without reducing the benefit level drastically and/or increasing the contributions level considerably.

Several countries have contemplated such reforms, and other countries have already finished implementing them. This book intends to investigate reasons for introducing policy reform, and outcomes derived from its introduction. The method for investigating these issues is both theoretical and empirical.

'Theoretical' implies that an evaluation is made by theoretical papers based on both efficiency and equity grounds. Efficiency means economic efficiency such as optimal resource allocation, higher economic growth, lower cost performance, while equity means that income is distributed without producing both desperately poor people and extremely rich people. 'Empirical' implies that an evaluation is made by empirical models which propose policy reforms for a particular country, and investigate the outcome induced by them.

Policy reforms in public pension programmes are not the only issues in advanced countries. A large number of developing countries also face serious problems. Several countries have committed themselves to drastic reforms. The famous example is the Chilean one which initiated privatization of social security, and then, several other South American countries followed Chile's example regarding the privatization of social security. See, for example, Edwards and Edwards (1991). Even advanced countries have been influenced by similar privatization experiences.

This book is concerned only with advanced and industrialized countries for the following reasons. First, the social and economic conditions, and the degree of development in public pension programmes between developing countries and advanced countries are so different that it is difficult to put the case for policy reforms based on common concepts and implementation methods.

Second, old age pension programmes are not the only means of supporting income after retirement in developing countries, because families and other institutions support the economic life of the elderly in these countries. Families are crucial in these countries, particularly many Asian countries. Thus, we have to take into account the role of families and other arrangements, even when the role of public pension programmes is evaluated. In other words, investigating only public pensions gives only part of the story.

Third, political instability is frequently observed in these countries. One example was Chile where a drastic change in the political system enabled Chile to introduce privatization. A drastic reform in advanced and democratic countries may be difficult for implementation for various reasons.

The key concept which characterizes policy reform in advanced countries is the pay-as-you-go (unfunded) scheme versus the funded scheme. Retaining an unfunded component was called a 'parametric' reform strategy by Chand and Jaeger (1996), and a funded component is called an 'actuarially fair' system. Disney (2000) classified the latter into two parts: a 'clean break' privatization and a 'partial' privatization.

Disney separated the current reform strategies into four parts based on the above two classification criteria: (1) a parametric reform of the unfunded programme, (2) an actuarially fair unfunded programme, (3) clean break privatization, and (4) partial privatization.

The crucial distinction appears between unfunded schemes (normally defined benefit plan: DB plan) and funded schemes (normally defined contribution plan: DC plan), and a shift from the former to the latter is often proposed in order to solve the current social security problem. A further shift may be called privatization. We can see such strong propositions by many economists in the US such as Feldstein (1998), Kotlikoff (1996), Mitchell and Zeldes (1996), and others. This idea influenced economists in a large number of advanced countries, and the received wisdom is that a shift to fully funded is the best solution.

It is, nevertheless, important to note three different views in this received wisdom. First, several studies do not accept such a shift even in the US as given by Aaron (1999) and Diamon (1999), who prefer unfunded schemes. The reasons for disliking the funded scheme are that they are too high a risk on the rate of return and have high administration costs. Second, several European studies, in particular Continental European ones, also provide critical evaluations of funded schemes as shown by Boldrin, Dolado, Jimeno and Peracci (1999), and Miles and Timmermann (1999), for various reasons. Of course, there is non-negligible number of studies which prefer funded to unfunded schemes even in continental Europe. Third, we tend to ignore one idea and proposition in the discussion of financing social security, a shift from insurance financing to tax financing. Several authors propose that general tax revenues rather than social insurance contributions should be used to finance old-age pensions. In fact, there are several countries such as Canada, Denmark, and some others where general tax revenues are used to finance social security.

The present book attempts to investigate these controversial issues such as: (1) unfunded versus funded, (2) American (or Anglo-American) versus continental Europe, (3) the role of tax financing, which is common in many advanced countries. Several additional issues are, (4) the relationship between the labour supply of the elderly and penions benefits, (5) the risk aspect of pension fund and administration costs in managing funded scheme.

It is emphasized, again, that this book investigates these issues both theoretically and empirically. Theoretical chapters present useful propositions under reasonable assumptions and behavioural actions regarding the working of social security, and empirical ones show evaluations of policy reforms in social security on whether such reforms are useful or not for several countries. Suggestions for social security reforms are presented based on these theoretical and empirical works.

1.2 Summary of the content

The content of each chapter will be summarized below. Because the defined contribution (DC) pension model is as yet new to Japan, it is likely that the experience of other countries who have previously adopted this approach to pensions may be useful in designing the required investment and governance frameworks to support these plans. Chapter 2, which is written by Olivia S. Mitchell, intends to highlight global innovations in the design, structure, and governance of pensions, so as to emphasize those points that will require special attention in the Japanese context as the pension system continues to evolve. She first outlines the legacy of defined benefit plans and explains what has motivated the global transition to defined contribution pensions. This movement to DC plans occurred in two waves, with a first followed by a second wave of DC plan growth. This second phase was spurred on in the US by the passage of legislation allowing for the development of 401(k) pensions. She shows that these plans pose new challenges to the pension market, and to the government seeking to regulate them to ensure that they deliver a reasonable retirement income. She concludes with an overview of the most important governance and regulatory implications of the new pension model, lessons for Japan.

Chapter 3, which is written by Mats Persson, investigates five fallacies in the social security debate which are as follows:

1   The present problems in the social security systems are due to demography.
2   A pay-as-you-go system is inferior to a funded system since it has a lower rate of return.
3   In a riskless world, a low-return PAYG system is dominated by a high-return funded system.
4   The social security system is a suitable instrument for intergenerational risk sharing.
5   The government is a safe provider of social security.

He points out that the first step of a reform should be to make the benefit rules actuarial. After then, the gains from proceeding further, into a funded system, are not due to the fact such a system has a higher yield. The gift to the first PAYG generation has already been given, and a funded system cannot remove that cost. What we can accomplish by means of government debt management, is to shift it over the generations. The main reason for funding the system seems to be that it can thus be privatized. And the main reason for privatization is that of transparency and safety; competition will guarantee that the rules remain actuarial and the political risk may thus be reduced.

Chapter 4, which is written by Gary Burtless, surveys the relative advantages of public and private systems. More important, he assesses the financial market risks facing contributions in a private system based on individual retirement accounts. The first part of the chapter describes the difference between public and private systems and considers the main economic and political arguments for privatization. A principal claim is that private plans can provide better returns to contributors. If this were true, it seems appropriate to weigh possible risks associated with the improved returns. Some of the most important risks are those associated with financial market fluctuations. The second part of the chapter provides evidence for these risks by considering the hypothetical pensions US workers would have obtained between 1911 and 1999 if they had accumulated retirement savings in individual accounts. He shows that the financial market risks in a private retirement system are empirically quite large. Although some of these risks are also present in a public retirement system, a public system has one important advantage over private ones. Because a public system is supported by the taxing and borrowing authority of the state, it can spread risks over a much larger population of potential contributors and beneficiaries. This makes the risks more manageable for active and retired workers, many of whom have little ability to insure themselves privately against financial market risk.

Chapter 5, which is written by Hazel Bateman, Suzanne Doyle and John Piggott, addresses two important questions: administrative charges and payout design and market structure by drawing on Australian and Chilean experience. Their chapter also aims to relate to a generic economy in which private mandatory retirement provision is being implemented or considered. In 1992 Australia introduced the Superannuation Guarantee, the first private mandatory retirement saving policy in the English-speaking world. At that time the only country to have adopted a policy of this type was Chile, in 1981. Private mandatory policies require either employers or employees to invest some fraction of the employee's wages with a private sector organization, with the aim of eventually helping to finance the employee's retirement. Typically, these worker accumulations are defined contribution DC, fully funded, and kept in individual accounts. In the eight years since 1992 more than a dozen countries, mostly in Latin America and the transition economies of Central Europe, have either mandated private retirement provision or have stated their intention to reform their pension policies along these lines. Further, a number of developed countries have either reformed their pension systems in this direction (for example, the UK) or have debated doing so (the US). Rarely has a novel policy design spread so swiftly across disparate nations. This chapter suggests that administrative cost and retirement income stream policy will be critical areas of policy design within the mandatory private paradigm, and that this is borne out by Australian and international experience. It is these questions which have proved the most controversial in the policy debate, and which have been the most challenging in terms of policy design.

Chapter 6, which is written by Tatsuo Hatta and Noriyoshi Oguchi, investigates the plausibility of switching the Japanese social system from pay-as-you-go to actuarially fair. Under the current Japanese pension system the lifetime pension benefit of an average salaried man born in 1935 is greater than his lifetime pension contributions by $500,000. If he had been faced with the contribution and benefit schedules that a person born in 2000 faces, his lifetime benefit would be less than his lifetime contributions by $250,000. This means that the net pension benefit is different between the two cohorts by $750,000 even under the assumption that their lifetime incomes are equal. Such extreme disparity between different cohorts is caused by the fact that Japan's public pension system is essentially a pay-as-you-go one. This chapter outlines the '23 per cent Reform Plan' and shows its effects both on the public fund accumulation and on the net benefits of different cohorts. This chapter briefly outlines the current structure of Japan's public pension system and examines its redistributional effects. The pay-as-you-go scheme and the actuarially fair scheme will be compared. Then they analyse the 23 per cent reform plan. Finally, privatization is discussed. If we privatize the system now, the government still must continue to financially support pensions for an extended period. Privatization does not reduce the financial burden of the government by itself. This chapter points out that whether the system is privatized or not, it is necessary to make the pension system actuarially fair, and spread the net burden of pensions evenly among generations.

Chapter 7, written by Akira Okamoto and Toshiaki Tachibanaki, studies the integration of the social security and tax systems. The essence of their proposal includes the following two ideas. First, the social security and the tax systems should be integrated. In other words, social security contributions should be replaced by the general tax revenue. Second, a progressive consumption tax is recommended to raise a major part of the general tax revenue. A progressive consumption tax is a direct tax, which falls on consumers, namely, an expenditure tax. Their proposal is to introduce a progressive consumption tax and to substitute it for other taxes such as a labour income tax or an interest income tax. There are four reasons why integration is desirable. First, integration facilitates an introduction of the idea of a minimum contribution for all people in the field of social security because a universal minimum level which guarantees the necessary payment of public pensions and medical costs to all people can be covered from the general tax revenue more efficiently and equitably. Second, the integration can eliminate the concept 'who gained and who lost from the both intergenerational and intragenerational aspects' under the social insurance system where cost is covered by social insurance contributions. Third, a minimum subsistence guarantee from general tax revenue is consistent with the principle of social security, which intends to produce no desperately poor individuals. Fourth, the integration of the social security and the tax systems reduces considerably administration costs of the revenue side because only one institution collects revenue from the private sector. There is a potentially difficult problem in the implementation of a progressive expenditure tax in the real world. It is indicated that the savings figure can be consolidated by using an individual tax number and an electrictronic collection system.

Chapter 8, which is written by Ashwin Kumar, reviews pension reform in the UK from contribution to participation. This chapter seeks to draw out the implications of the reform proposals, over time and across the earnings distribution and to place them in the wider context of the concepts behind pension provision. The UK government's main proposal was a new contract for welfare, *Partnership in Pensions*, which was published in December 1998. The proposals contained within this document represented a fundamental shift in the concept behind state second tier pension provision in the UK. This shift was from the contributory and earnings-related principle of the 1970s to the wider entitlement of a participatory principle and to the flat rate benefit principle enshrined in the Beveridge Report of 1942. The UK government identified guaranteeing a minimum standard as a more important goal than the provision of earnings replacement. This chapter concludes that its mechanism for achieving this goal, however, is not rooted in either the citizenship principle or the means-tested principle. Instead, it sits somewhere between, although closer to the citizenship principle. As such, it provides enough nourishment to the adherents of both camps that the one thing we can be sure of is that unemployment is not a danger for the pensions pundits of the future.

Chapter 9, written by Kai Konrad and G. Wagner, studies the current crisis in the German pension system and discusses the various reform proposals. The demographic trend of shrinking population size in Germany reduces the internal rate of return of the pay-as-you-go pension system far below the market rate of interest. At the same time the system has grown to a size at which contributions become a major share of workers' budgets. Accordingly, there will be growing labour market disincentives of the implicit tax which make reform of the system inevitable. This chapter highlights that reform of pension systems is mainly a matter of redistribution between the currently retired generation, the current workforce and their children, between high income earners and low income earners, between those currently paying into the system and those who do not, and between families with many children and families with few children. Political economy aspects will be essential in predicting and understanding the reform outcome.

Chapter 10, by Fredrik Haugen, Erik Hernæs, and Steinar Strøm, gives an overview of the structure of the pension system in Denmark, Finland, Norway and Sweden, and the most important of the recent changes in these systems. In all the Nordic countries, the public pension component plays an important role. These public pension systems are the pay-as-you-go type, and are in all countries set to encounter financial problems in the not-so-distant future. Some recent changes aimed at meeting this problem are described, but the chapter includes no discussion of the financial situation of the public pension systems. The emphasis in the chapter is on the institutional arrangements and the ensuing labour force incentives for older persons. The chapter also includes a brief overview of labour force participation of older pensioners in the Nordic countries. The situation in Norway has been treated most extensively. For Norway, the result of two recent analyses of the impact of an early retirement system, which was introduced in 1989 is also discussed.

Chapter 11, which is written by Hideki Konishi, examines the welfare effects of public pension reforms, changing a public pension programme from pay-as-you-go to a fully funded one, privatizing a public pension programme, and mandating a minimum coverage limit on private annuity contracts, within a model of a small open economy with adverse selection. Under a mild condition, the premium charged for private annuities increases in response to both the level of public pension benefits and contributions. When taking into account the externalities caused on the annuity market, the

Golden-Rule criterion is found to be valid with regard to financing a fixed public pension benefit, though this is not the case for introducing a public pension programme. It is shown that first the benefit levels affect the long-term economic welfare as well as the relative cost advantage of public pensions; second a public pension programme must provide a sufficiently large level of benefit if it is to be introduced in at all, and third implementing mandatory participation in private annuity plans will improve efficiency in cases where a public programme is abolished.

Chapter 12, by Toshihiro Ihori, investigates dynamic implications of pension contributions and intergenerational transfers under modified funded systems. By incorporating interest groups' contributions to social security funds into the conventional overlapping generations model, the chapter explores a long-term policy of public spending, social security fund and economic growth. Favourable economic conditions will not necessarily lead to high growth in pension funds. The pension fund is too little in terms of the static efficiency (or compared with private consumption) but may be too much or too little in terms of dynamic efficiency (or as the steady state level). This chapter finally examines the normative role of taxes on consumption and pension contributions. It is shown that consumption taxes or a subsidy to social security contributions would always be desirable even if the pension fund is overaccumulated. If a government can control the replacement ratio so as to realize the modified Golden Rule, it would attain dynamic efficiency.

References

Aaron, H. J. (1999) 'Social security: tune it up, don't trade it in,' in H. J. Aaron and J. B. Shoven (eds) *Should The United States Privatizee Social Security?* Cambridge: MIT Press, pp. 55–112.

Boldrin, M., Dolado, J. J., Jimeno, J. F. and Peracchi, F. (1999) 'The future of pensions in Europe,' *Economic Policy*, October, 289–320.

Chand, S. K. and Jaeger, A. (1996) *Aging Populations and Public Pension Schemes*, Occasional Paper No. 147, IMF.

Diamond, P. (ed.) (1999) *Issues in Privatizing Social Security*, Cambridge: MIT Press.

Disney, R. (2000) 'Crisis in public pension programmes in OECD: what are the reform options?' *Economic Journal*, 110, 461, F1–F23.

Edwards, S. and Edwards, A. (1991) *Monetarism and Liberalization: The Chilean Experiment*, Chicago: University of Chicago.

Feldstein, M. (ed.) (1998) *Privatizing Social Security*, Chicago: University of Chicago Press.

Kotlikoff, L. (1996) 'Privatizing social security at home and abroad,' *American Economic Review*, 86, 2, 368–372.

Miles, D. and Timmermann, A. (1999) 'Risk sharing and transition costs in the reform of pension systems in Europe,' *Economic Policy*, October, 253–285.

Mitchell, O. and Zeldes, S. (1996) 'Social security privatization: a structure for analysis,' *American Economic Review*, 86, 2, 363–367.

OECD (1996) *Aging in OECD Countries: A Critical Policy Challenge*, Social Policy Studies, No. 20.

2 Managing pensions in the twenty-first century

Global lessons and implications for Japan[1]

Olivia S. Mitchell

As the twenty-first century dawns, global changes in pension structures are attracting keen interest from economists, demographers, and politicians. These pension changes are driven in part by rapidly-growing numbers of people aged 65 and older, an aging phenomenon that will have numerous positive as well as negative economic and social consequences. Nowhere is this set of economic and social challenges more salient than in Japan. This nation leads the globe in world aging, with its population recording the longest life expectancy patterns and among the lowest fertility rates in the OECD. This aging phenomenon, combined with recent economic stagnation, has begun to lead many to question how retirement can be financed in the future. Testament to this concern is a recent survey showing that over 90 percent of Japanese consumers were worried about the inadequacy of their own saving for retirement (Business Wire 1999).

New institutions must be developed to meet and cope with the challenges of population aging in Japan as elsewhere.[2] The task is difficult in Japan due to widespread corporate defined benefit pension plan underfunding problems[3] as well as national public pension cash-flow insolvency projected to occur before 2020 since the system has projected unfunded liabilities estimated at US$3.5 trillion.[4] Also contributing to this challenging environment are recent developments in financial accounting requirements that now require pension underfunding to be shown in accounting reports,[5] and the slow deregulation of the Japanese financial system.[6] But perhaps most interesting to retirement experts is the fact that these pressures are creating an environment favorable to the development of defined contribution pensions in Japan.[7] Thus the government of Japan recently announced that employees may contribute to defined contribution pensions in funded, invested accounts. Taking the lead, two large Japanese firms have allied to launch US-style 401(k) pensions giving participants choice over investments and access to international mutual funds.[8]

Because the defined contribution (DC) pension model is new to Japan, other countries' experiences in the DC pension environment may be informative in illustrating the investment and governance frameworks needed to support such pension plans. For instance, several of Japan's East Asian neighbors have had national DC pensions known as provident funds for some years and even decades. Experience with these plans has been decidedly mixed, as we illustrate below. In the Americas and in the UK, workers have had access to both company-based and individual-style DC pensions for more than a decade. This experience indicates that certain plan features are extremely valuable to employers and employees, while others may require supervisory and regulatory attention.[9] Accordingly, the goal of the present study is to note global innovations in the design, structure, and governance of defined contribution pensions, with a view to emphasizing those issues that may require special attention as the Japanese pension system evolves to meet the challenges of an aging society. The fact that Japan is adopting this new pension model in the twenty-first century affords citizens, their employers, and the government, an opportunity to take advantage of some of the lessons other nations have recently learned.

In what follows we first outline the legacy of defined benefit plans and explain what has motivated the global transition to defined contribution pensions. As we shall show, these plans pose new challenges to the pension market, and to the government seeking to regulate these plans to ensure that they deliver a reasonable retirement income. We then provide an overview of the most important governance and regulatory implications of the new pension model, which we link to the Japanese context.

2.1 The defined benefit legacy

In recent years, governments and taxpayers throughout the developed world have slowly awakened to the painful fact that many of their defined benefit (DB) retirement systems are going bankrupt. While some countries have problems sooner and others face them later, actual or prospective insolvency in DB pension systems concerns virtually every developed nation. This particularly plagues public sector pension systems throughout the developed world, as depicted in Figure 2.1. For example, in Japan as well as Germany and France, the projected unfunded liability of benefit promises to retirees under the national DB pension system currently exceeds the entire nation's GDP.

Evidently, new revenue sources and/or ways to cut benefit will have to be found to return these large PAYGO defined benefit plans to viability. One possibility is to raise taxes substantially to meet retirees' expectations. However it is not clear that younger workers and indeed unborn generations will concur with the future tax increases that would be required, which produces substantial uncertainty regarding the security of future old-age consumption. In Japan for instance, it is estimated that the payroll tax must rise by over 3.5 percent of GDP if promised benefits are to be paid. Payroll taxes in the US must rise by around 1 percent of GDP (Figure 2.2). The burden of these additional taxes will be exacerbated, of

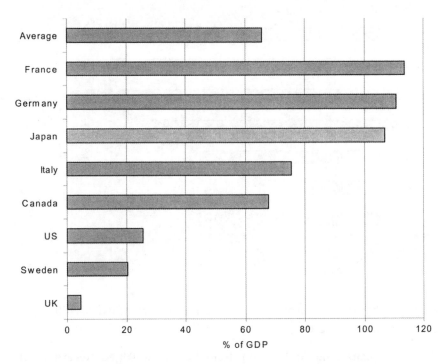

Figure 2.1 Projected public pension liability: percent of GDP to 2050

Source: Chand and Jaeger (1996).

course, by unemployment and economic recession such as experienced in Japan of late.

A different way to cover projected DB plan shortfalls would be for pension managers to earn more on plan assets, an outcome that is possible only if the pension system in fact has some assets to invest. However, in practice, many developed-country DB plans have no invested assets backing their promises, instead running on a pay-as-you-go (PAYGO) basis. In a PAYGO plan, workers' taxes are channeled immediately to pay retiree benefits, without generating any investment buildup. Such an approach traditionally was the hallmark of national retirement plans, and in some countries it has characterized employer-provided pensions as well. In Japan, for instance, Japanese firms have only recently been asked to recognize the promised but not funded pension benefit offerings made to employees. Current evidence indicates that needed reserves are far less than those required according to international accounting standards, producing a PAYGO private pension system alongside the public one (Takahasi 1999; Watson Wyatt 1999).

While company-sponsored pensions in some countries do hold assets in their DB plans, they have sometimes earned very low and even negative returns, as illustrated in Figure 2.3. This has been due, in part, to the fact

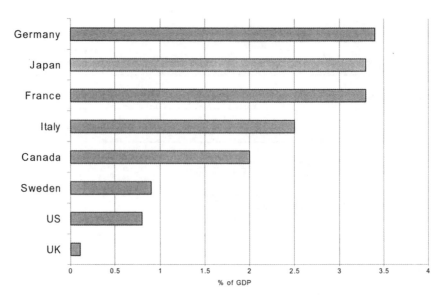

Figure 2.2 Projected annual public pension tax gap: percent of GDP to 2050

Source: Chand and Jaeger (1996).

that such plans tend to hold portfolio heavily weighted toward fixed income assets and government bonds. In many country cases, these assets fail to hold their value due to lack of inflation protection.

In the Japanese context, the country's first tier program, known as the Basic National Pension, has no assets inasmuch as it is a PAYGO defined benefit. Underfunding also affects the second and third-tier plans, with the second layer involving a DB pension promise for private employees under the Employees' Pension Fund system, and Mutual Aid Associations for public sector workers, teachers, and some other smaller occupations (JETRO, nd). Though in some cases these second-tier plans do control some assets, they have been traditionally managed by trust banks (60 percent) and life insurers (about 40 percent) and returns have not been high (JETRO, nd). The third tier of the Japanese pension system is made up of private pension plans that some corporations offer their workers; here assets have again been managed conservatively by trust banks and life insurers (58 percent and 38 percent respectively, as of 1994; JETRO, nd). Recent reforms in reporting standards will clarify the extent of DB underfunding in the near future.

In the past, private saving tended to earn low returns in Japan because of regulatory caps termed the "5-3-3-2" limits. These were government regulations that required trust banks to hold no more than 50 percent of the assets in guaranteed assets (bonds), a maximum of 30 percent in domestic stocks, 30 percent in foreign assets, and 20 percent in real estate

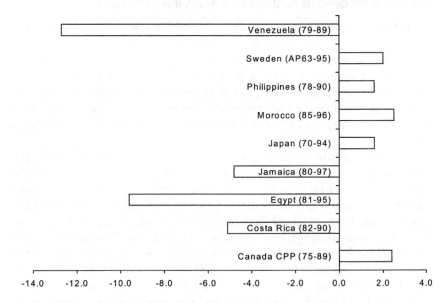

Figure 2.3 National defined benefit plans produced poor returns: percent real, per annum

Source: Iglesias and Palacios (1999).

(insurers were held to the 3-3-2 limits; JETRO, nd). The result of these policies was that many pensions in Japan experienced low real returns over the years (Takahasi 1999). This is a partial explanation for today's corporate pension underfunding problems, estimated at around half a trillion US dollars (Kono 1999; McDonald 1998). These rules have been changed recently, but historically they produced a concentration of pension assets in low-return fixed income domestic holdings.

Low investment returns have also been an issue in many other countries as well, in part because few if any of the plans were diversified on the international market. In Japan this was the result of government policy, but it has also occurred in the US, despite the lack of similar restrictive regulation. It is indeed a puzzle that few investors appear to take full advantage of the diversification potential resulting from holding a globally diversified portfolio (Lewis 1999). For example, Griffin (1997) reports that US pension plans had only 9 percent of their total portfolio in non-US investments, and insurers held under 1 percent. The fact that US plans earned high returns over the twenty years, in contrast to the Japanese plans, is attributable to the strong US stock market, rather than international diversification.

2.2 What do defined contribution plans have to offer?

In the light of current and projected problems with DB plans, some observers have proposed that defined contribution (DC) pension plans are the better alternative. They point out that plan assets may be invested more professionally, assets can be better protected against malfeasance and political pressures, and plan participants' risk preferences can be better matched than in the traditional DB context. To the extent these predictions are true, a DC plan may offer more retirement security than a DB alternative.

Whether and when such claims are true depends on which type of DC plan one has in mind. Several variants have developed over time, with the first generation of DC plans seen by some as "mystery pensions" because they were designed by employers or governments and were poorly understood by participants. These first-generation DC plans include many from East Asia such as Singapore and Malaysia, and also corporate DC pensions offered in the US and the UK for many years. In these plans, a DC sponsor typically designed, implemented, and serviced plan participants with little input from employees. Investment options were few; assets were rarely marked to market; employees had few chances to select investment portfolios, and opportunities to transfer investments across asset types were rare. National provident plan managers established by governments throughout East Asia, as in Malaysia and Singapore, also have sometimes had to follow government wishes in terms of investments, inasmuch as governments were usually a major stakeholder. Sensitivity to political influence resulted from permitting politicians to select and impose asset limits on pension investment options, neglecting reporting to covered workers regarding investment performance, and lack of interest in tracking pension management expenses and investment returns. Plan operations were generally far from transparent and employee understanding was low (Asher 1999; Hurt 1998). As a result of this lack of transparency, the first-generation DC plans generally turned in a disappointing level of investment performance when they did accumulate assets (see Figure 2.4). During the most recent financial crisis, provident fund investment outcomes suffered particularly from government restrictions prohibiting diversification into international capital markets (Asher 1998).

In contrast to this top-down approach to DC pensions, a second generation of DC plans has emerged in the last decade or so that has had a profoundly energizing impact on pensions and pension management throughout the world. This second-generation approach is characterized by individual accounts (IA), taking hold first in the UK and then in Chile, and later spreading to the rest of Latin America. The US variant is the very popular 401(k) pension plan: as is shown in Figure 2.5, DC plans claim more active participants and more assets than their DB counterparts.[10]

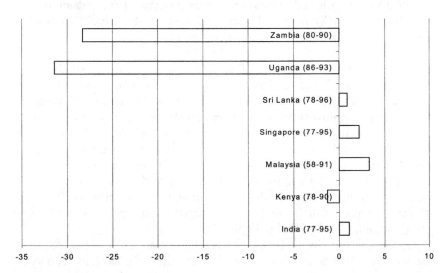

Figure 2.4 Global provident plans provided poor returns: percent real, per annum

Source: Iglesias and Palacios (1999).

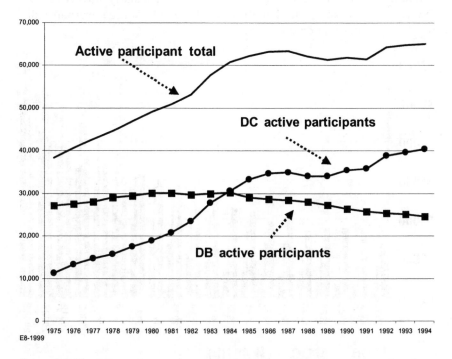

Figure 2.5 The US pension environment: defined contribution pension plans have more active participants than defined benefit plans

Source: US Department of Labor, PWBA (1999).

One frequently-asked question posed by observers from outside the US is "what is a 401(k) plan and what makes it so attractive?" In brief, a 401(k) is an employer-sponsored pension plan, which gives employees extensive choice and flexibility regarding their contributions, their pension investments, and the structure of benefits (McGill *et al.* 1996). Its name refers to the particular section of the Internal Revenue Code making it possible to establish these pension plans on a "tax-qualified" basis. In other words, employers and employees may make pre-tax contributions to the pension plan (up to an annual limit); this tax-protected status has also been granted to the investment earnings as long as they remain in the plan. At retirement, plan withdrawals are subject to income tax but participants are allowed to take their money out under a variety of payout options, ranging from lump sum withdrawals to minimum distributions (Brown *et al.* 2000). These plans have become extraordinarily popular, with rapid growth in assets as depicted in Figure 2.6.

One might ask why 401(k) plans have grown so rapidly in the US, given the fact that "first generation," more traditional, DC plans had been available for many years. The fact is the 401(k) structure offers stakeholders a number of features that the first-generation DC plans did not. We next elaborate on the features that make these particularly attractive to a modern labor market, and then turn to a discussion of the governance and regulatory issues that emerge.

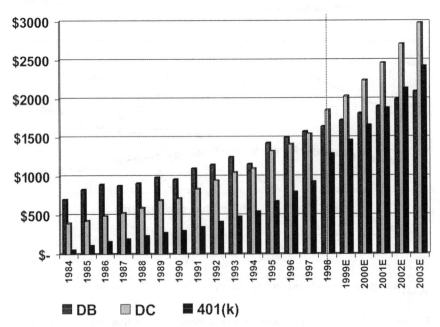

Figure 2.6 DC surpass DB assets (US corporate, B$)

Source: Cerulli Associates (1999).

2.2.1 Many employees favor 401(k) plans

A major difference between the second-generation plans and the first-generation DC pensions is that the newer 401(k) plans are tailored to individual participants tastes in a variety of ways. An employer sponsoring such a plan provides each worker with an opportunity to voluntarily contribute to retirement savings out of pre-tax income if he or she chooses, up to a taxable limit.[11] As a result, employees tend to look on these pensions as retirement plans with particularly appealing features, because the contributions are treated attractively by the tax code and because of the employer match.

In this sense, the fundamental difference between the first- and the second-generation DC plans becomes one of ownership and control. Participants in 401(k) plans tend to see themselves as "in the driver's seat," rather than relying on their employer to design, maintain, and direct the pension plan. As a consequence, employees tend to pay closer attention to their plan's investments, comparing them with other types of financial assets. Employees also ask for, and often get, multiple investment options in their 401(k) plan, which permits them to allocate their pension assets in conformity with personal risk preferences. This is particularly evident in the US context, where the last few years have brought marked increases in the number of investment choices permitted. For example, 401(k) plans offered an average of 5 investment choices as of 1994, but now the average stands at 12 choices (Siegel 1999). Some firms go even farther: Ford Motor Company offers automakers some 60 investment options in its plan, and at American Stores employees have 182 choices.

2.2.2 Employers like 401(k) plans

Some might imagine that an employer would be indifferent to whether its company pension takes the form of a DB or a DC plan, since economic theory implies that workers "pay" for their retirement benefits in reduced earnings one way or another (Lumsdaine and Mitchell 1999). Nevertheless, economists have noted that companies might prefer 401(k)-style DC plans over the DB alternatives, because of their behavioral impacts. One is that DC plans permit employee mobility across firms quite flexibly, whereas traditional, back-loaded DB plans discourage employees from changing companies (Gustman *et al.* 1994). This results from the fact that each worker knows how much he or she has accumulated under the individual-account approach and can move these assets from one investment pool to another. By contrast, in the DB world, workers do not "own" a specified portion of the pooled assets and generally cannot move their accumulations to a new plan when they change jobs. Pension portability is therefore appealing where the workforce is mobile and must expand or contract with economic circumstances.

Another behavioral effect of 401(k) plans is that these plans can be designed to attract and retain a particular kind of worker, while simultaneously penalizing other sorts of employees. For example, the employer 401(k) match rate might be relatively generous but be limited to workers who remain at the firm for a relatively long vesting period (which is typically five years, but can be as long as seven years). Thus the additional employer match would be limited to longer-term workers, a method of rewarding loyalty. Further, the match aspect of the plan implies that an employee receives his full pension accumulation only if he or she contributes to the plan out of his own salary. Anyone choosing not to contribute effectively receives lower total compensation, while participants receive higher compensation when the match is taken into account. This differentiation could be desirable when an employer wishes to select in favor of workers with a long time horizon (i.e. they have a low discount rate): these are more likely to contribute voluntarily to the plan and hence receive the match (Ippolito 1999). On the assumption that low discount rates are correlated with employee productivity, the match aspect permits a company to structure its compensation system so as to differentially reward the most productive.

While US employers are generally positively inclined toward these second-generation DC plans, a few concerns about 401(k)s have emerged. One pertains to the possibility of employer liability under a 401(k) plan. This might arise because employers are responsible for choosing which investment options are permitted in their retirement plan portfolios, and which financial institutions are selected to manage the plans. As a result, corporate pension sponsors are considered to be a legal fiduciary, and in the US, they may potentially be held liable for pension mismanagement. This possibility becomes a delicate matter when individual participants have free access within the plan to a wide range of investment choices, each with different risk-return characteristics. In a recent court case, employees sought to shift investment burden onto an employer that had offered a 401(k) plan, arguing that the "prudent man rule" required Unisys Corporation, the plan sponsor, to make participants whole when one pension asset lost money (Ortelere 1998). The legal opinion upheld Unisys, in finding that the pension investment risks and potential for losses had been widely reported in the financial press, and that participants could have moved their funds to safer investments if they had wanted to. Further testing of the limits on employer liability under 401(k) pensions will no doubt emerge, in the future.

2.3 Market impacts of second-generation DC pension plans

Evolution in the form and structure of DC pensions has been felt in many ways, in the global pension market. Most critically, as pension sponsors find they must offer covered workers the chance to choose their pension

investments, this places new demands on plan recordkeeping and investment management skills. As a result, financial institutions have had to
undertake massive investments in computer, recordkeeping, and investment
systems to modernize their investment practices (Carter 1999). Participants,
along with their plan administrators, now see their plans as facilitating "total
participant interaction facilitated by technology" (Hurt 1998). The pension
plan market of the twenty-first century is therefore spurring a very different
financial marketplace as compared to the rather slow-moving institutional
environment characteristic of first-wave DC plans.

A related development is that workers and their employers are beginning to require more transparency regarding plan expenses, greater cost
containment and efficacy in recordkeeping, and improved service regarding reliability in deposits and payouts. Most importantly, 401(k) participants demand customized service over the telephone and Internet, in a
24-hour per day and 7-day per week on-demand model. In this new
environment, plan participants tend to think of themselves rather than
financial intermediaries as the account managers. Consequently, employers are more often asked to report and justify investment costs, recordkeeping expenses, and net investment performance. This move is also
driving financial institutions to develop new products such as the new
tiering approach being offered by many mutual fund organizations. For
example, a 401(k) plan might provide a participant with access to a small
investment choice set initially, with a more sophisticated and wealthy
investor gaining access to a second and more complex range of offerings.
Participants desiring yet additional flexibility can increasingly obtain
access to more complex investment options including brokerage accounts
(Siegel 1999). At the same time, the move toward increased complexity
has been paired with improved awareness of fees and expenses, and there
is more competitive pressure than ever before on costs associated
with pension management. In the US, the government has sought to set

Type of fund	Annual management charge in basis points
Stock	40
Global equities	46
Growth	42
Equity index	36
Social choice	38
Bond market	38
Inflation-linked bond	39
Money market	34
Real estate	64

Figure 2.7 Annual TIAA-CREFF expenses (in hundredths of a percent, or basis
pts): 2001

Source: www.tiaa-cref.org

standards for reporting and disclosing plan administrative costs (see Appendix 1). Accordingly, investment costs for pension portfolios have declined for some providers, with the lower-fee firms in the US now charging 40 basis points for a stock indexed fund, and sometimes less for indexed bond funds (see also Mitchell 1998).

Another aspect of the dynamic pension marketplace has to do with the role of financial planning advice and investment education. Under US law, a consultant providing a pension participant with financial advice could be sued if the investments perform poorly. On the other hand, investors in a DC pension plan tend not to be very sophisticated about financial matters, and many want investment advice. The difficulty people have understanding risk and return was recently highlighted in an experimental study prepared by Bernartzi and Thaler (1999), where they provided pension plan participants information regarding stock and bond returns in two different formats. The goal was to observe how different ways of presenting financial information influenced 401(k) participant investment choices. In their first scenario, they depicted the distribution of 1-year returns from an indexed stock and an indexed bond portfolio over the last several decades. The stock fund stood a higher chance of larger losses than did the bond index fund. The second scenario showed historical risk and return patterns that would have resulted from holding the same stock and bond returns over a 30-year period. In this second case the stock return graph typically dominated the bond return graph. Interestingly, when plan participants were shown the 1-year risk and return information, they elected to invest only 40 percent of their pension assets in the stock fund. By contrast when they were shown the 30-year risk/return data, participants chose to invest 90 percent of their money in the stock fund.

Clearly, it matters how risk and return is explained to 401(k) plan participants, if they are to make informed decisions consistent with their underlying risk preferences. And as might be anticipated, the market for financial advice is expanding rapidly. A recent survey found that almost one-quarter of all US firms offers employees investment advice, and another third was seriously considering offering it (Management Library 1999). Most of this advice is being provided by financial institutions managing the pension plans, rather than by employers directly. Further, when advice is offered, it can be influential – and potentially less costly to employers – than offering costly employer plan contributions matching worker contributions, as Clark and Schieber (1998) point out. The result of all this has been that there has been a dramatic shift in DC plan asset mix over time, with the plans today holding 60–70 percent equities, as compared to the majority in bonds and stable value funds two decades ago.

2.4 Regulatory and oversight implications of the second-generation DC pension market

As features of the pension environment are changing, this in turn suggests the need for new government oversight and regulation functions in the pension arena. There are four areas where governments must establish standards for "best practice," so as to ensure that the new pension models can meet the needs of plan participants. These pertain to the four key functions of pension systems, namely collecting contributions (or taxes), managing pension assets, recordkeeping, and benefit payouts.

2.4.1 Streamlining the environment for contributions

In the area of pension contributions, some countries use a mandatory structure, while others permit employees to decide how much they will pay for their pensions voluntarily. As a rule, if a pension system is national in scope, it typically requires that some (or all) of the workforce be included on a mandatory basis. In this instance, it might be thought that incentives for pension payments might not be terribly important, but this is in fact not true since workers and their employers may evade contributions if they do not perceive participation in the national pension system to be worthwhile (Manchester 1999). Hence governments must carefully structure policy regarding the tax deductibility of pension contributions to increase pension participation. Even in a mandatory plan, then, tax preferences for contributions and pension investment buildup are likely to increase participation; in a voluntary system, tax preferences are obviously even more important.

Other ways to induce participation in a national DC pension system might be to provide government or employer *matches*, possibly matches that are greater for the low-wage employees so as to increase perceived value to those with little ability to save. It is also important to have governments play a role in making sure that pension contributions are made in a timely fashion and are deposited rapidly with their intended investment managers. In Mexico, for instance, the government requires that deposits to the national individual accounts system be invested in no more than 9 business days $(t+9)$, a turnaround time that should fall in the future to ensure that workers' funds are taken to market instead of left idle. These steps are important in building confidence in the system, and in increasing workers' willingness to contribute or pay taxes.

2.4.2 Improving the investment environment

As pension plans move toward building up substantial assets to invest, governments have found it necessary to re-evaluate and in many cases change their old rules regarding how pension funds may be managed. Under the old DB model, it was common to have governments regulate the inputs to pension funds, where such limits were tied to specific asset classes, caps or prohibitions were set on foreign assets, certain types of investments were outlawed, and so forth. One danger of such an "inputs-based" focus is that it distorts asset management patterns and restricts the opportunity for pension plan diversification (Reisen 1997; Iglesias and Palacios 1999). These rules have sometimes been imposed in DC plans as well: in Mexico, for example, pension fund investments initially were restricted to government bonds, this limiting participants' access to global diversification. Over time, these restrictions are often relaxed; for example in Chile, pension funds can own at most 7 percent of any one company, and the extent of foreign assets is capped as well.

It should not be surprising that these pension investment limits have been found to be deleterious to participants. For example, Srinivas and Yermo (1998) evaluate pension systems in Chile, Argentina, and Peru, where no worker choice was permitted in pension fund portfolios for many years. After computing risk-adjusted returns in each country, the authors compare these to other financial instruments within these same countries and conclude that the pension fund investments performed worse than the alternatives. Thus if Chileans had been permitted to hold their pension money in a national indexed mutual fund, they would have earned a risk-adjusted 2.3 percentage points over returns actually earned by Chilean pension funds. These limitations thus curtail pensions payable at retirement and replacement rates as well. The critical point is, of course, that it is "not enough to say that a country's pension funds did well because they returned 6.4 percent in real terms net of fees over the last fifteen years. The key question is how well did pension funds do relative to other investments in the market" (p. 24).

It is encouraging that pension systems in developed nations have, over time, moved away from such strict asset limits. For instance, DB pension plans in the US can now select their portfolios as a function of Board decisions rather statutory limits,[12] and of course DC plans offer particip-ants multiple investment choices, usually with some international mix. These changes have required governments to develop a different supervi-sory model, one that focuses on the investment decision-making process rather than the asset mix. In the US, this approach finds expression in the so-called "prudent person" policy, codified in the US with the Employee Retirement Income Security Act of 1974 (ERISA) and adopted by many state pensions as well. The prudent person rule requires only that pension plan fiduciaries manage the money in the best interests of plan particip-ants, showing that they have appropriately diversified the pension portfo-lio as to risk and return, ensuring that individual assets make sense within the overall investment strategy, avoiding all but arms'-length transactions, and doing all this at low levels of administrative cost. Plan managers can be held personally liable for mismanagement or party-in-interest transac-tions, and plan participants may file suit against nonperforming fiduciaries.

In turn, putting more emphasis on Board decision-making highlights the increasing importance of making pension Boards responsive to and sometimes directly representative of participants.[13]

Having access to a global capital market is likely to move pension managers away from "herding behavior" often seen where money managers gravitate toward identical portfolios. As government regulation of pension investments becomes more flexible, pension managers in many countries including Japan will begin to take advantage of global diversification in pension holdings (Lewis 1999). This is likely to substantially improve participants' risk/return tradeoff in DB and DC pensions alike. For instance, Figure 2.8 represents the risk and return frontier for several countries – Japan, the UK, Germany, and the US – as well as an Asia-Pacific ex Japan index. This figure confirms that Japanese pension plan participants would have benefited from holding a more diversified global portfolio over the last decade, and the same may well be true for the future.

2.4.3 Enhancing the environment for pension recordkeeping, reporting, and disclosure

As pension participants are increasingly allowed to select different contribution levels, investment portfolios, and payout options, it becomes more complex to maintain participant records and to do a good job of providing information on plan status. As a result, many financial institutions managing pension plans have had to invest substantial sums to ensure that contributions are properly tracked and assets are marked to market frequently. This is particularly important in the DC individual-account environment,

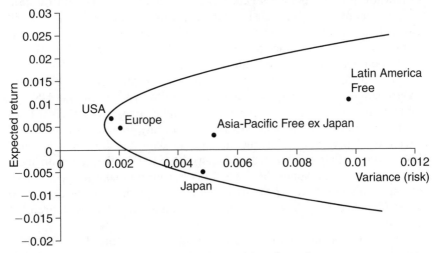

Figure 2.8 Estimated efficient frontier for world stock markets

Source: MS Total Return Indices, Real $US, continuously compounded monthly returns. 1/88–8/02 (assumes normal returns).

so that participants can accurately assess account balances and transfer assets from one portfolio to another. Such flexibility has been less common in East Asia, to date, so there will no doubt be substantial need for investment in the technology needed to make flexible access feasible (Asher 1998). In addition, it appears that participants must be educated about risk, return, investment, and other issues to protect against excessive churning of accounts and high expenses.

These developments lead, in turn, to a new role for government oversight, namely establishing disclosure standards for pension system fees and commissions. For example, the recent mis-selling scandal in the UK highlighted problems that can arise when sales agents collect commissions for pension participants who lacked understanding of their pension system's structure. In the US, the Department of Labor has recently issued a "Fee Disclosure Form" recommended for use by employers establishing 401(k) plans, to ensure that investment and other fees be fully disclosed and benchmarked (see Appendix 1). In Mexico a similar strategy has been taken, where the national pension supervisory agency has provided a spreadsheet that converts disparate fee and commission structures into a single common format (Mitchell 1998b). This implies that the government's role in pension regulation is evolving into one where it provides information and establishes disclosure criteria, thus ensuring that participants are informed enough to decide whether they want to pay for additional services, and what the costs of these services might be.

2.4.4 Structuring the pension plan payout environment

As pension plan participants gain more autonomy over the contribution and investment phases of their retirement saving, it is natural that they will also seek autonomy over the payout phase of their retirement assets. This raises a series of additional questions regarding the appropriate role for government oversight and regulation.

Deciding how to provide access to pension savings is an area where government policy and oversight can be quite critical. In the US, for instance, active workers are permitted to take loans from their 401(k) pension accounts, and this has become increasingly popular with almost 20 percent of all participants having outstanding loans. In addition, when they leave a job, participants are currently permitted to take their pension accumulations in a lump sum. Though US tax incentives make it appealing to roll the funds into another tax-qualified account, many people do not do this, and hence they lose substantial accumulations in their retirement accounts.

A related issue has to do with how retirees manage their DC accumulations during the retirement phase of life. If, as in Japan, a retiring worker can take a lump sum at retirement rather than buying a life annuity, he or she runs a substantial risk of outliving these assets. A similar pattern has emerged in the US where it appears that only a tiny fraction of retirees with 401(k) plans converts pension accumulations to annuities. By contrast, in the UK, retirees must use their pension accruals to purchase a minimum annuity that is protected against inflation (Brown *et al.* 1999, 2000).

It is clear that there is a role for government oversight in ensuring that the retirement payout process from second-generation DC accounts is handled sensibly. For one thing, it will be useful to standardize reporting regarding annuity fees and commissions, so that participants can compare different annuity products. There is also some question about the nature of the risk pool included in the set of annuity purchasers. As noted by Brown *et al.* (2001), adverse selection among annuity purchasers in a voluntary market means that those who anticipate living longer than average will buy an annuity, while those expecting shorter-than-average mortality will not. This makes pricing of annuity products less attractive for anyone anticipating an average life expectancy, and it also raises questions about whether governments should mandate some minimum amount of risk pooling for all pension participants.

A related role for government in the pension payout arena has to do with how retirement funds are treated from a tax perspective. As illustrated by Brown *et al.* (1999), tax law handles different types of pension payouts differently, depending on whether the pension participant takes a lump sum, a minimum distribution payout, or buys an annuity. Furthermore, pension accruals are treated differentially by tax law depending on whether the payouts are to a living plan participant or paid after he or she dies. Having a coherent tax policy toward pension plan payouts will become increasingly important, as these second-generation DC plans accumulate substantial levels of assets.

2.5 Conclusions

In the next decade, as the Japanese population ages and then moves into retirement, this nation will confront many challenges. Like many of its developed nation counterparts, it has inherited a defined benefit pay-as-you-go retirement system that faces impending insolvency, exacerbated by an underfunded defined benefit corporate pension system. Whether defined contribution pensions will play an important role in reforming the Japanese retirement system will depend critically on how they are designed, where the funds are invested, and how well they are managed.

Our historical review has established that defined contribution pensions experienced two growth phases, with the first wave involving centrally-managed plans that failed to invest particularly well and that were operated without much transparency. This experience taught that participants do better if permitted to diversify their fund investments internationally, and also the importance of reducing administrative and investment expenses. A second phase of DC plan development has been spurred by individual account plans, such as 401(k) pensions in the US. Here, pension participants are given incentives to contribute in a tax-protected manner; their investment preferences can be implemented individually, and withdrawal provisions are relatively flexible.

Looking ahead, these sweeping pension changes will continue to pose challenges to financial intermediaries and plan sponsors, to covered employees and retirees, and to government regulatory agencies seeking to ensure that these funds are saved for retirement. Pension participants will continue demanding more flexibility, investment choices that meet their risk preferences, up-to-the-minute reporting and disclosure, and educational and investment advice services. These developments have motivated many financial institutions to invest heavily in technology, and they further imply that regulators of these new and nimble pension institutions must also be at the technological frontier if they are to successfully oversee and protect participants. Another implication of the new pension environment is that cost pressures on financial institutions are increasing, which is probably appropriate toward the goal of enhancing plan participants' retirement saving. At the same time, there is increasing interest in the opportunity for global asset diversification, to take advantage of the better risk/return tradeoff prior to as well as after retirement.

As Japan moves to implement its own approach to pension reform, those charged with plan design would do well to examine international "best practice" standards. Only by meeting and exceeding these criteria will pension plans in Japan be able to do what is required in order to strengthen prospects for old-age economic security.

Appendix 1

US Department of Labor Suggested Fee Disclosure Form
ABC PLAN: 401(k) PLAN FEE DISCLOSURE FORM For
Services Provided by XYZ Company: Overview

The Employee Retirement Income Security Act of 1974, as amended (ERISA) requires employee benefit plan fiduciaries to act solely in the interests of, and for the exclusive benefit of, plan participants and beneficiaries. As part of that obligation, plan fiduciaries should consider cost, among other things, when choosing investment options for the plan and selecting plan service providers. This 401(k) plan fee disclosure form may assist you in making informed cost-benefit decisions with respect to your plan. The purpose of this form is to help you determine the total cost of the plan. It is also intended to provide you with a means to compare investment product fees and plan administration expenses charged by competing service providers, regardless of how a particular service provider structures its fees. The 401(k) plan fees included in this disclosure form represent the following: _____ actual 401(k) plan expenses for the period X/XX/XX through X/XX/XX or _____ estimated 401(k) plan expenses for the period X/XX/XX through X/XX/XX. Additional investment product information regarding fees may be obtained from the product prospectus, annuity contract or other similar documents. Additional information relating to plan administration services and expenses is contained in documentation provided by the service provider, including the contract for plan services. Others plan expenses may include legal fees for initial plan design and ongoing amendments resulting from changes in pension law or plan design and the cost of a mandatory annual audit. You need to contact your legal advisor or accountant to determine these charges.

Selecting a service provider requires that you evaluate and differentiate services offered by competing companies. Cost is one of the criteria, but not the only criterion, for making this evaluation. Other factors of equal or greater importance to consider include the quality and type of services provided, the anticipated performance of competing providers and their investment products and other factors specific to your plan's needs. The service provider offering the lowest cost services is not necessarily the best choice for your plan.

Calculation of fees

In general, fees are calculated in four ways:

- Asset-based: expenses are based on the amount of assets in the plan and generally are expressed as percentages or basis points.
- Per-person: expenses are based upon the number of eligible employees or actual participants in the plan.
- Transaction-based: expenses are based on the execution of a particular plan service or transaction.
- Flat rate: fixed charge that does not vary, regardless of plan size.

Fees may be calculated using one or any combination of these methods. Plan administration-related expenses can also be charged as one-time fees or ongoing expenses. One-time fees are typically related to start-ups, conversions (moving from one provider to another) and terminations of service.

Ongoing fees are recurring expenses relating to continuing plan operation:

1   There may be plan expenses incurred by other providers, other than the company completing this form. For a complete list of expenses charged to your plan, please contact all plan service providers with

whom you contract or may contract and request fee information with respect to their services.

2   If you are considering a conversion from an existing plan service provider to a new service provider, you will need to provide the service provider(s) with certain information about the plan, including the number of plan participants, the number of eligible participants and the amount of plan assets in order for the service provider(s) to be able to complete this form. Similarly, if you are considering starting a plan, you will need to provide the service provider(s) with estimates of plan participants and plan assets.

When providing potential service providers with information regarding your plan, it is critical that you provide identical information to all of the competing companies in order to ensure equivalent comparisons.

401(k) PLAN FEE DISCLOSURE FORM Institution For Services Provided by XYZ Company

Total Plan Expenses
I. Investment Product Fees (See Schedule A)

		Amount/Estimate
A.	Collective Investment Fund(s)	$_____
B.	Insurance/Annuity Product(s)	$_____
C.	Mutual Fund(s)	$_____
D.	Individually Managed Account(s)	$_____
E.	Brokerage Window	$_____
F.	Other Product(s) (Specify)	$_____
	Total Investment Product Fees	$_____

II. Plan Administration Expenses (See Schedule B)
Total Plan Administration Expenses $_____

III. Plan Start-Up or Conversion Related Charges (See Schedule C)
One Time Start-Up/Conversion expenses $_____

IV. Service Provider Termination Related Charges (See Schedule D)
Service Provider Termination expenses $_____
Total Plan Expenses $_____
For definitions of terms used throughout this disclosure form, see Schedule E.

Amounts are calculated based on rates charged, which are identified in attached schedules as applied to relevant information (for example amount of assets or number of participants). Certain calculations may be estimates based on information provided by you, the plan sponsor, and may vary as circumstances change.

ABC PLAN: 401(k) PLAN FEE DISCLOSURE FORM For
Services Provided by XYZ Company
Schedule A: Investment Product Fees/Estimates

Collective Investment Fund

	Assets (X/X/XX)	Management Fee	Other* (Specify)	Total Cost
Fund 1				
Fund 2				
Fund 3				
Fund 4				
TOTAL				

Insurance/Annuity Product

	Assets (X/X/XX)	Management Fee	Mortality Risk & Admin. Expense	Other* (Specify)	Total Cost
Fund 1					
Fund 2					
Separate Account 1					
Separate Account 2					
TOTAL					

Mutual Fund Assets

	Assets (X/X/XX)	Expense Ratio**	Front-End Load	Other* (Specify)	Total Cost
Fund 1					
Fund 2					
Fund 3					
Fund 4					
TOTAL					

Individually-Managed Account

	Assets (X/X/XX)	Management Fee	Other* (Specify)	Total Cost
Product 1				
Product 2				
Product 3				
Product 4				
TOTAL				

Brokerage Window***

	Assets (X/X/XX)	Commission (Range)	Transaction Fee (Range)	Other* (Specify)	Total Cost

Total Transactions

Other Product****

	Assets (X/X/XX)	Management Fee	Other* (Specify)	Total Cost
Product 1				
Product 2				
Product 3				
Product 4				

Total Investment Product Fees $_____

Notes:
*   Fees represent product-related charges paid by the plan. Fees associated with participants' transfer of account balances between investment options, including investment transfer expenses and any contingent back-end loads, redemption fees and surrender charges should be included in "other" expenses. In addition, any wrap fees or pricing charges for non-publicly traded assets should be included in the "other" expenses column. For investment product termination fees associated with plan termination or conversion, see Schedule D. Insurance companies incur marketing and distribution costs, which are recouped through charges assessed against the plan.
**   Includes 12b-1 fee and management fee. (See fee table in fund prospectus.)
***   When providing potential service providers with information/assumptions regarding the brokerage window plan feature, it is critical that you provide identical information to all of the competing companies in order to ensure equivalent comparisons.
****Other products could include investment vehicles such as REITs and limited partnerships.

ABC PLAN: 401(k) PLAN FEE DISCLOSURE FORM For Services Provided by XYZ Company
Schedule B: PLAN ADMINISTRATION EXPENSES

Expense Type	Rate Estimate*	Bundled Service Arrangement**	Total Cost***
Administration/Recordkeeping Fees:			
Daily valuation	$_____		$_____
Payroll processing	$_____		$_____
Balance inquiry	$_____		$_____
Investment transfer	$_____		$_____
Contract administration charge	$_____		$_____
Distribution processing	$_____		$_____
QDRO processing	$_____		$_____
Participant statements	$_____		$_____
Plan sponsor reports	$_____		$_____
VRU/Internet services	$_____		$_____
Other (specify)	$_____		$_____
Subtotal	$_____		

Participant Education/Advice:

Participation education materials/distribution	$_____		$_____
Education meetings (frequency _____)	$_____		$_____
Investment advice programs	$_____		$_____
Other (specify)	$_____		$_____
	Subtotal	$_____	

Trustee/Custodial Services:

Certified annual trust statement	$_____		$_____
Safekeeping of plan assets	$_____		$_____
Other (specify)	$_____		$_____
	Subtotal	$_____	

Compliance Services:

Nondiscrimination testing	$_____		$_____
Signature ready form 5500	$_____		$_____
Annual audit	$_____		$_____
Other (specify)	$_____		$_____
	Subtotal	$_____	

Plan Amendment Fee:

Plan amendment fee	$_____		$_____
Plan document/determination letter fee	$_____		$_____
Other (specify)	$_____		$_____
	Subtotal	$_____	

Loan Administration:

Loan origination fee	$_____		$_____
Loan processing fee	$_____		$_____
Loan maintenance/repayment fee	$_____		$_____
Other (specify)	$_____		$_____
	Subtotal	$_____	
Total separate charges		$_____	
Total bundled services		$_____	
(Less offsets/credits paid to plan)		$(_____)	
	Total Plan Administration Expenses	$_____	

Notes:
* Amounts represent the method by which the fee is calculated, for example as a percentage of plan assets under management, based upon number of participants or based upon number of transactions. For start-up or take-over situations, fees are based upon estimates and/or certain assumptions, i.e. regarding assets under management and number of participants. When providing potential service providers with information/assumptions regarding your plan, it is critical that you provide identical information to all of the competing companies in order to ensure equivalent comparisons. Without a standardized set of assumptions, service providers will certainly use differing assumptions, defeating the intended purpose of clarifying fee comparisons among service providers.
** Services provided under a bundled services arrangement are indicated by a check mark next to the specific service.
*** Amounts represent flat dollar amount charges or total charges based upon the particular method of calculation. In some instances, these amounts represent estimates based on assumptions provided by you, the plan sponsor.

ABC PLAN: 401(k) PLAN FEE DISCLOSURE FORM For
Services Provided by XYZ Company
Schedule C: ONE TIME START-UP/CONVERSION EXPENSES

Expense Type	Rate/Estimate*	Total Cost**
Start-up/conversion education program	$_____	$_____
Start-up/conversion enrollment expense	$_____	$_____
Installation fee	$_____	$_____
Start-up/conversion plan document fee/filing fee	$_____	$_____
Other (specify)	$_____	$_____
Total Start-up/Conversion expenses	$_____	

Notes:
* Amounts represent the method by which the fee is calculated, for example as a percentage of plan assets under management, based upon number of participants or based upon number of transactions. For start-up or take-over situations, fees are based upon estimates and/or certain assumptions, i.e. regarding assets under management and number of participants. When providing potential service providers with information/assumptions regarding your plan, it is critical that you provide identical information to all of the competing companies in order to ensure equivalent comparisons. Without a standardized set of assumptions, service providers will certainly use differing assumptions, defeating the intended purpose of clarifying fee comparisons among service providers.
** Amounts represent flat dollar amount charges or total charges based upon the particular method of calculation. In some instances, these amounts represent estimates based on assumptions provided by you, the plan sponsor.

ABC PLAN: 401(k) PLAN FEE DISCLOSURE FORM For
Services Provided by XYZ Company
Schedule D: SERVICE PROVIDER TERMINATION EXPENSES

Expense Type	Rate/Estimate*	Total Cost**
Investment Product Expenses		
Contract termination charges	$_____	$_____
Back-end load	$_____	$_____
Product termination fee	$_____	$_____
Other (specify)	$_____	$_____
Total $_____		
Plan Administration Expenses		
Service provider termination charge	$_____	$_____
Service contract termination charge	$_____	$_____
Other (specify)	$_____	$_____

Total Termination Expenses $_____

Notes:
* Amounts represent the method by which the fee is calculated, for example as a percentage of plan assets under management, based upon number of participants or based upon number of transactions. For start-up or take-over situations, fees are based

upon estimates and/or certain assumptions, i.e. regarding assets under management and number of participants. When providing potential service providers with information/assumptions regarding your plan, it is critical that you provide identical information to all of the competing companies in order to ensure equivalent comparisons. Without a standardized set of assumptions, service providers will certainly use differing assumptions, defeating the intended purpose of clarifying fee comparisons among service providers.

**   Amounts represent flat dollar amount charges or total charges based upon the particular method of calculation. In some instances, these amounts represent estimates based on assumptions provided by you, the plan sponsor.

ABC PLAN: 401(k) PLAN FEE DISCLOSURE FORM For Services Provided by XYZ Company
Schedule E: Definition of Terms

Administration/Recordkeeping Fee: Fee for providing recordkeeping and other plan participant administrative type services. For start-up or takeover plans, these fees typically include charges for contacting and processing information from the prior service provider and "matching up" or mapping participant information. Use of this term is not meant to identify any ERISA Section 3(16)(A) obligations.

Annual Audit: Federal law requires that all ERISA-covered plans with more than 100 participants be audited by an independent auditor. It is also common to refer to a DOL or IRS examination of a plan as a plan audit. Any charge imposed by a service provider in connection with this audit is reflected on Schedule B.

Back-End Load: Sales charges due upon the sale or transfer of mutual funds, insurance/annuity products or other investments, which may be reduced and/or eliminated over time.

Balance Inquiry: Fee that may be charged each time a participant inquires about his or her balance.

Brokerage Commission: A fee paid to a broker or other intermediary for executing a trade.

Brokerage Window: A plan investment option allowing a participant to establish a self-directed brokerage account.

Bundled Services: Arrangements whereby plan service providers offer 401(k) plan establishment, investment services and administration for an all-inclusive fee. Bundled services by their nature are priced as a package and cannot be priced on a per service basis.

Collective Investment Fund: A tax-exempt pooled fund operated by a bank or trust company that commingles the assets of trust accounts for which the bank provides fiduciary services.

Contract Administration Charge: An omnibus charge for costs of administering the insurance/annuity contract, including costs associated with the maintenance of participant accounts and all investment related transactions initiated by participants.

Contract Termination Charge: A charge to the plan for "surrendering" or "terminating" its insurance/annuity contract prior to the end of a stated time period. The charge typically decreases over time.

Conversion: The process of changing from one service provider to another.

Distribution Expense: The costs typically associated with processing paperwork and issuing a check for a distribution of plan assets to a participant. May include the generation of IRS Form 1099R. This fee may apply to hardship and other in-service withdrawals as well as to separation-from-service or retirement distributions.

Eligible Employee: Any employee who is eligible to participate in and receive benefits from a plan.

Expense Ratio: The cost of investing and administering assets, including management fees, in a mutual fund or other collective fund expressed as a percentage of total assets.

Product Termination Fee: Investment-product charges associated with terminating one or all of a service provider's investment products.

QDRO (Qualified Domestic Relations Order): A judgement, decree or order that creates or recognizes an alternate payee's (such as former spouse, child, etc.) right to receive all or a portion of a participant's retirement plan benefits.

Separate Account: An asset account established by a life insurance company, separate from other funds of the life insurance company, offering investment funding options for pension plans.

Service Provider Termination Charge: Plan administrative costs associated with terminating a relationship with a service provider, with the permanent termination of a plan, or with the termination of specific plan services. These may be termed "surrender" or "transfer" charges.

Signature Ready Form 5500: Fee to prepare Form 5500, a form which all qualified retirement plans (excluding SEPs and SIMPLE IRAs) must file annually with the IRS.

Start-up/Enrollment Expense: Costs associated with providing materials to educate employees about the plan, and enrolling employees in the plan. This may be part of, or included in, the education programs. There may be a one time cost associated with implementing a new plan, as well as ongoing enrollment costs.

Trustee Services: Fees charged by the individual, bank or trust company with fiduciary responsibility for holding plan assets.

VRU: Voice Response Unit.

Wrap Fee: An inclusive fee generally based on the percentage of assets in an investment program, which typically provides asset allocation, execution of transactions and other administrative services.

12b-1 Fee: A charge to shareholders to cover a mutual fund's shareholder servicing, distribution and marketing costs.

Source: US Department of Labor (1999)

Notes

1 The author acknowledges support for this study from the Pension Research Council at the University of Pennsylvania and the ESRI in connection with the International Collaboration Project on Aging at the National Bureau of Economic Research. Helpful research assistance was provided by David McCarthy and data were kindly supplied by Morgan Stanley. Useful suggestions were provided by Robert Clark. Opinions are solely those of the author and not of any organization with which she may be affiliated.
2 See for instance Clark (1996), Curuby *et al.* (1998), Murakami (1996), and Takahashi (1999).
3 See Curuby *et al.* (1998) and Harney (1999).
4 See Kono (1999) and Curuby *et al.* (1998).
5 For further information see Kono (1999).
6 The extent of corporate pension underfunding is not well known since most firms in Japan do not yet fully follow IASB accounting conventions; see Choy (1999) and Takahasi (1999).
7 A survey of the recent developments in Japanese public and private pensions is contained in Takayama (2001).

 8 See Tett (1999) and Dow Jones (1999).
 9 See Clark (1999) on pensions in East Asia; Mitchell *et al.* (2000) and Barreto and Mitchell (1997) discuss Latin American pensions.
10 Public sector employees are, as yet, less likely to have defined contribution pensions than are private sector workers in the US, though a few states have recently moved to a DC model and some cities and one state (Nebraska) have had a DC plan for many years (Mitchell *et al.* 2000). The slower growth of DC pensions in the public sector is in part attributable to the high rate of unionization among public sector workers, and unions have tended to favor DB plans as a rule. In addition, until recently, public sector workers were unlikely to leave government employ prior to retirement, making the portability advantage of a DC plan less appealing. Nevertheless government "downsizing" as well as the potential for stock market investment has awakened US public sector employees' interest in DC plans of late.
11 This limit was recently changed by legislation passed in 2001, from its cap of US$10,000 to a higher level that will henceforth be indexed to inflation; in many cases employers also provide those who contribute out of their own salary a match amount, up to a cap.
12 Some US public pensions still face limits or caps on stocks and derivatives (Mitchell *et al.* 2000).
13 Pension governance issues are considered by Useem and Hess (2000), and Useem and Mitchell (2000).

References

Asher, Mukul (1998) "Investment policies and performance of provident funds in southeast Asia," paper prepared for the Economic Development Institute of the World Bank, Workshop in Beijing, China.

Asher, Mukul G. (1999) "The pension system in Singapore," paper prepared for Poverty Reduction and Economic Management (PREM) and Human Development (HD) units of the World Bank.

Barreto, Flavio A. and Mitchell, Olivia S. (1997) "Privatizing Latin American retirement systems," *Benefits Quarterly* 13(3): 83–5.

Bernartzi, Shlomo, and Thaler, Richard (1999) "Risk aversion or myopia? Choices in repeated gambles and retirement investments," *Management Science* 45(3): 364–81.

Brown, Jeffrey, Mitchell, Olivia S., Poterba, James, and Warshawsky, Mark (1999) "Taxing retirement income: nonqualified annuities and distributions from qualified accounts," *National Tax Journal*.

Brown, Jeffrey, Mitchell, Olivia S., Poterba, James, Warshawsky, Mark (2001) *The Role of Annuity Markets in Financing Retirement*, Cambridge, MA: MIT Press.

Brown, Jeffrey, Mitchell, Olivia S., and Poterba, James (2000) "The role of real annuities and indexed bonds in an individual accounts retirement program," in John Y. Campbell and Martin Feldstein (eds), *Risk Aspects of Investment-Based Social Security Reform*, 321–60.

Business Wire (1999) "Japanese consumers fear inadequate retirement income: prudential survey signals possible shift in Japanese retirement confidence."

Carter, Marshal N. (1999) "How technology is forging a revolution in financial markets," Speech before Tokyo Executive Group, Tokyo, Japan, June 25.

Cerulli Associates (1997) *The State of the Defined Contribution/401(k) Market, 1996*, Boston, MA: Cerulli Associates.

Chand and Jaeger (1996) "Aging populations and public pension schemes," IMF Occasional Paper No. 147, December.

Choy, Jon (1999) "Japan's securities industry: from big bank to e-boom," Japan Economic Institute Report 22A. Washington, DC: JEI, July 11.

Clark, Robert L. (1999) "Ageing policies in East Asia," paper presented at the National University of Singapore, Conference on Perspectives on Public Policy in the Twenty-First Century , September.

Clark, Robert L. (1996) "Japanese pension plans in transition," *Benefits Quarterly*, first quarter.

Clark, Robert and Schieber, Sylvester (1998) "Factors affecting participation rates and contribution levels in 401(k) plans," in Olivia S. Mitchell and Sylvester Schieber (eds), *Living with Defined Contribution Pensions: Remaking the Responsibility for Retirement*. Pension Research Council, Philadelphia, University of Pennsylvania Press, 69–97.

Curuby, George N., Uwamori, Nobuyuki, and Yamauchi, Itsuko (1998) *Japan's Pension Market to 2005: a capital report*, Hong Kong: ISI Publications, Curuby and Company.

Dow Jones (1999) "Japan prepares for pensions, American-style," *Asian Wall Street Journal*, February 1, 7.

Griffin, Mark W. (1997) "Why do pension and insurance portfolios hold so few international assets?," *Journal of Portfolio Management*, Summer: 45–50.

Gustman, Alan S., Mitchell, Olivia S., and Steinmeier, Thomas (1994) "The role of pensions in the labor market," *Industrial and Labor Relations Review* 47(3): 417–38.

Harney, Alexandra (1999) "Japanese pension chiefs peer into a bottomless pit," *Financial Times*, 7/16/99.

Hsin, Ping Lung and Mitchell, Olivia S. (1997) "Public pension plan efficiency," in M. Gordon, O. S. Mitchell, and M. Twinney (eds), *Positioning Pensions for the 21st Century*, Pension Research Council, Philadelphia, PA: University of Pennsylvania Press, 187–208.

Hurt, Ron (1998) "The changing paradigm of 401(k) plan servicing," in Olivia S. Mitchell and Sylvester Schieber (eds), *Living with Defined Contribution Plans: Remaking Responsibility for Retirement*, Pension Research Council, Philadelphia: University of Pennsylvania Press, 193–207.

Iglesias, Augusto and Palacios, Robert (1999) "Managing Public Pension Reserves," *Pension Primer Paper*, World Bank, May.

Ippolito, Richard (1999) "Using defined contributions to sift for higher quality workers," *Benefits Quarterly*, third quarter: 40–6.

Japan Social Insurance Agency (1998) *Outline of Social Insurance in Japan*.

JETRO, Ministry of Health and Welfare of Japan, nd, *An Introduction to the Japanese Pension System*, New York: JETRO.

Kono, Yoshinobu (1999) "Unfunded liabilities of Japanese corporate pensions," Report from Goldman Sachs Pension Services Group, May 20.

Lewis, Karen (1999) "Trying to explain home bias in equities and consumption," *Journal of Economic Literature* 37(2), June.

Lumsdaine, Robin and Mitchell, Olivia S. (1999) "New developments in the economics of retirement," in Orley Ashenfelter and David Card (eds), *Handbook of Labor Economics*, Amsterdam: North Holland, 3261–308.

Management Library (1999) "Managing 401(k) plans: BARRA Rogers-Casey/IOMA 1999 DC plan survey: who's using and paying for investment advice?," May. www.ioma.com/nls/9905/401k.shtml

Manchester, Joyce (1999) "Compliance in social security systems around the world," in Olivia S. Mitchell, Robert Myers, and Howard Young (eds), *Prospects for Social Security Reform*, Pension Research Council. Philadelphia: University of Pennsylvania Press.

McDonald, James (1998) "Japanese face $457 billion shortfall: remedy could be higher returns through more investment in foreign assets," *Pensions and Investments*, September, 15.

McGill, Dan, Brown, Kyle, Haley, John, and Schieber, Sylvester (1996) *Fundamentals of Private Pensions*, Pension Research Council. Philadelphia, PA: University of Pennsylvania Press.

Mitchell, Olivia S. (1998a) "Administrative costs of public and private pension plans," in Martin Feldstein (ed.), *Privatizing Social Security*, NBER, Chicago: University of Chicago Press, 403456.

Mitchell, Olivia S. (1998b) "Evaluating administrative costs in Mexico's AFORES system," WB-LCSF, Pension Research Council Working Paper 98-1. http://prc.wharton.upenn.edu/prc/prc.html

Mitchell, Olivia S. (2000) "Developments in pensions," in Georges Dionne (ed.) *Handbook of Insurance*.

Mitchell, Olivia S. and Hsin, Ping-Lung (1997) "Public sector pension governance and performance," in Salvador Valdes Prieto (ed.), *The Economics of Pensions: Principles, Policies, and International Experiences*, Cambridge: Cambridge University Press, 92–126.

Mitchell, Olivia S., McCarthy, David, Wisniewski, Stanley C., and Zorn, Paul (2000) "Developments in state and local pension plans," in Olivia S. Mitchell and Edwin Hustead (eds), *Pensions for the Public Sector*, Pension Research Council, Philadelphia, PA: University of Pennsylvania Press, 11-40.

Mitchell, Olivia S., Poterba, James, Warshawsky, Mark, and Brown, Jeffrey (1999) "New evidence on the money's worth of individual annuities," *American Economic Review*.

Murakami, Kiyoshi (1996) "The 1994 pension reform in Japan and future issues," *Benefits and Compensation International* 24(8): 2–8.

Ortelere, Brian (1998) "Emerging problems of fiduciary liability," in Olivia S. Mitchell and Sylvester Schieber (eds), *Living with Defined Contribution Plans: Remaking Responsibility for Retirement*, Pension Research Council, Philadelphia: University of Pennsylvania Press, 178–92.

Reisen, Helmut (1997) "Liberalizing foreign investment by pension funds: positive and normative aspects," *World Development* 25(7): 1173–82.

Siegel, Matt (1999) "Can you have too many 401(k) choices?," *Fortune Investor*, 139(8). www.pathfinder.com/fortune/investor/1990/04/26/str8.html

Srinivas, P. S. and Yermo, Juan (1998) "Do investment regulations compromise pension fund performance?," *Pension Primer Paper*, The World Bank. Washington, DC.

Takahashi, Hiroyuki (1999) "Trends in Japan's corporate pension system," *Japan Economic Institute Report* No. 11A. Washington, DC: JEI.

Takayama, Noriyuki (2001) "Reform of public and private pensions in Japan," paper presented at the 9th Annual Colloquium of Superannuation Researchers, UNSW Sydney, Australia.

Tett, Gillian (1999) "Spotlight shifts to underfunding," *Financial Times*, 21 March.

US Department of Labor, Pension and Welfare Benefits Administration (PWBA), "Suggested fee disclosure form." www.dol.gov

Useem, Michael and Mitchell, Olivia S. (2000) "Holders of the purse strings: governance and performance of public retirement systems," *Social Science Quarterly*: 489–506.

Useem, Michael and Hess, David (2000) "Governance and investment of public pensions," in Olivia S. Mitchell and Edwin Hustead (eds) *Pensions in the Public Sector*, Pension Research Council, Philadelphia: University of Pennsylvania Press.

Vanderhei, Jack, Galer, Russell, Quick, Carol, and Rea, John (1999) "401(k) Plan Asset Allocation, Account Balances, and Loan Activity," *ICI Perspective* 5(1): Investment Company Institute: Washington, DC.

Watson, Wyatt (1999) "Pension shortfall in Japan hits company balance sheets," *Watson Wyatt Insider* 9(6): 1–2.

3   Five fallacies in the social security debate[1]

Mats Persson

Abstract

This chapter discusses five examples of the conventional wisdom that has often been expressed in the social security debate, even among academic economists. These are:

1   The major problem in most social security systems is that of demography: people simply live too long.
2   Disregarding the issue of demography, a pay-as-you-go system is inferior to a fully funded system since the former usually has a lower rate of return.
3   Disregarding the portfolio aspect (which might favor a PAYG system), a funded system dominates a PAYG system in a world of certainty.
4   The social security system is a suitable instrument for intergenerational risk-sharing.
5   The government is a safe and reliable provider of insurance.

Social security, dealing with intertemporal and intergenerational issues, is a difficult field. Therefore, the basic economic mechanisms are often obscured by technical complications, and even academic economists might yield to conventional wisdom when those basic mechanisms are concerned. In this chapter, I will discuss five cases where the conventional wisdom, although containing a grain of truth, could be challenged.

These five points are not new. Still, I think it is useful to have them collected in one chapter, instead of seeing them scattered in various publications – sometimes only mentioned implicitly, in quite a different context.

3.1 The present problems in the social security systems are due to demography

By demography, this argument usually refers to longevity, people simply live for too long.[2] The argument sounds quite convincing, and almost all

papers discussing social security begin with a section on ageing populations. These sections are very similar for most countries, showing diagrams
of how the dependency ratios (i.e. the number of retired persons relative
to the size of the active population) have increased over the decades.

There is however a snag in the argument. In most countries, the problems of social security are confined to government-run systems. Private
pension schemes – at least those sold in competitive markets – seem to be
thriving, with no discernible difficulty in coping with an ageing population.
This is surprising, since demography should be the same in both cases.

The enigma has a simple solution, however. Private pension systems are
in principle rather simple. Knowing the expected remaining lifetime of
each cohort, and having a fair idea of the expected yield of the portfolio,
the actuaries at the insurance companies can easily compute the fees to be
paid during the active years that are necessary for a particular person to
receive a given pension during retirement.

Assume now that the population is ageing, i.e. the expected remaining
lifetime increases. Such a change would cause no problem to the actuaries,
as soon as they have observed this new demographic feature in their data.
It only means that the (correctly computed) fees should be somewhat
higher, in order for the funds to cover a longer period of retirement. And
the buyers of these pension schemes will gladly pay these higher fees, since
they know that a longer expected retirement period makes higher fees – or
correspondingly lower pensions – necessary for the pension scheme to
break even. Thus a rational individual will not regard a longer life
expectancy as a problem (as some social security analysts seem to do) but
as a blessing. The corollary is that a private pension scheme, with actuarially fair contributions and benefits, will be able to handle even large
anticipated changes in demography.[3]

Why does the same not apply to public schemes? The answer is that in
most such schemes the benefit rules are not actuarially fair; there is only a
weak link between what the individual pays to the system during the active
years and what he or she later receives as a pension. From the individual's
point of view, most of the contribution is merely a tax on earned income.[4]
Note that this tax is not due to the fact that the individual is forced to
"save" in a system with a return that is lower than the market rate of interest. That particular tax – which is the one criticized in many papers on
social security, e.g. Feldstein (1996) – will be discussed in Section 2 below.
Here, the tax derives instead from the fact that, regardless of the rate of
return, the pension system performs a considerable amount of intra-cohort
income redistribution. If this redistribution benefited low-income earners
at the expense of high-income earners, the tax would be like an ordinary
progressive income tax and could perhaps be justified as a form of intragenerational risk sharing. Since the benefit rules are often rather complicated, and have evolved over the years as the result of several political
compromises, there is however no such egalitarian twist to the system in

general. For most countries, the redistribution is quite arbitrary; in some cases, it has even been shown to benefit high-income earners at the expense of low-income earners.[5]

Regardless of whether the actual redistribution taking place can be justified on egalitarian grounds or not, the contributions are thus to a large extent to be regarded as income taxes. And income taxes have tax wedges that distort the economy. As life expectancy increases, it is problematic to raise the fees of non-actuarial systems, since this will be equivalent to a tax increase. Thus, with non-actuarial rules, an ageing population will mean larger tax wedges and thereby more distortions to the economy. This is, I think, the main reason why public systems run into problems as demography changes, while private systems do not.

Thus demography should not bear all the blame for the present problems of social security all over the world. Rather, the combination of demography and non-actuarial benefit rules is the main problem. And since demography is not a policy instrument, the first step towards a reform should be the introduction of actuarial rules.[6] After that, one could start dealing with the more subtle issue of a pay-as-you-go system versus a funded system.

3.2 A pay-as-you-go system is inferior to a funded system, since it has a lower rate of return

This is the most common argument against pay-as-you-go (PAYG) systems. It is the basis for the view expressed by e.g. Feldstein (1996) of the PAYG system as a tax, with a distortive tax wedge. There is some evidence supporting it. For example, the average yearly increase in the US real wage sum over the period 1960–95 was 2.6 percent, according to Feldstein. Forcing individuals to save at such a low rate of return, the average real yield on equity over the same period was 9.3 percent, implies a rather high tax indeed. I will not argue that this view is wrong, but I will argue that a lower rate of return of the PAYG system does not necessarily imply that we ought to change into a funded system. There are two ways of arguing, one that will be discussed here, and one that will be discussed in Section 3 below.

The fact that asset *A* has a higher average yield than asset *B* does not mean that the latter should be banned from the rational investor's portfolio. Not even if *B* has both a lower average yield and a higher risk should it be automatically excluded. It all depends on the covariances; maybe the low-yielding asset can be used as a hedge to reduce total portfolio risk.

Let us take an example involving three assets. In Sweden, the average yearly real yield on equity (the change in the SOX stock market index) was 5.6 percent over the period 1963–97. Over the same period, the average yearly yield on an index of Swedish nominal bonds was 2.6 percent,[7] while the yearly increase in the wage sum was 2.2 percent. From

Table 3.1 Covariance matrix for Swedish stocks, bonds and the wage sum, 1963–97

	Stocks	*Bonds*	*PAYG*
Stocks	0.04959	0.00275	0.00005
Bonds		0.00246	−0.00022
PAYG			0.00099

a casual glance at these figures, one would be tempted to exclude the third "asset" from one's portfolio. An example of the covariance matrix is given in Table 3.1.

Using these data, we can compute the efficient frontier for these three assets. This is shown in Figure 3.1, which illustrates the importance of the PAYG "asset." The minimum risk portfolio consists of 32 percent bonds and 68 percent PAYG. As we move up along the frontier, the share of PAYG falls and the share of stocks increases. At a standard deviation of 0.012 (corresponding to an expected return of 0.04), the PAYG ceases to be an interesting "asset," at that point, the efficient portfolio consists of 56 percent bonds and 44 percent stocks. Needless to say, the underlying data are highly unreliable, and this example serves as an illustration only.

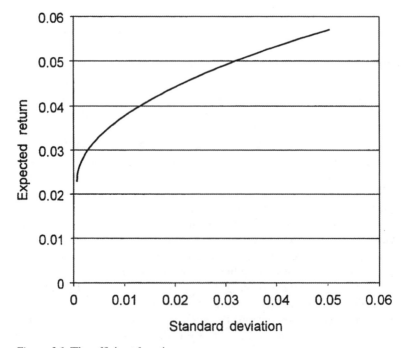

Figure 3.1 The efficient frontier

A PAYG system can thus be justified on welfare grounds; it introduces a new "asset" and spans a wider space for the investor. There is a lot to be said about this, and I will briefly touch upon some problems. First, the variances and covariances in Table 3.1 are computed from yearly data and it is not self-evident that yearly returns are relevant to a pension plan having an investment horizon of maybe half a century. Since reliable data are not available on a semi-centennial basis, however, I use the yearly data only to illustrate my point.[8] In fact, the proper investment horizon, and thus the covariances relevant for portfolio analysis, is still an unsolved issue in pension fund management.

Let us finally note that the view of a PAYG system as an "asset" to be included in investor portfolios raises an interesting issue in terms of capital market equilibrium. From the CAPM we know that asset prices will be determined endogenously, the only exogenous variable being the risk-free rate of interest. The data, on expected yields and covariances of Swedish stocks and bonds, used in my numerical example above were taken from a period when Sweden had a PAYG system, and the asset prices are thus likely to have been affected by that fact.

An alternative would have been to take data from a period prior to the introduction of a PAYG system. The question is then whether the expected yields and the covariance matrix of the financial assets, prior to the introduction of the PAYG system, should be used to assess the desirability of introducing such a system. After the introduction of the PAYG system, the asset prices might have adjusted in such a fashion that the PAYG "asset" should always be included in the portfolio, in the same way as the CAPM determines the prices of all existing assets so that all of them become included in the market portfolio. The problem is complicated by the fact that the PAYG "asset" is not traded on any market; its price can be considered as exogenously given and not affected by capital market equilibrium considerations.[9] In fact, the view of the PAYG as an asset seems to generate several interesting questions that have not yet been satisfactorily dealt with in the literature.

3.3 In a riskless world, a low-return PAYG system is dominated by a high-return funded system

The argument in Section 2 above is based on the possibility of reducing total portfolio risk. But in the absence of risk, would a PAYG system with a (risk-free) yield of, say, 2.6 percent not be dominated by a funded system with a (risk-free) yield of, say, 9.3 percent?

The answer is, not necessarily. As has been pointed out recently by Robert Shiller (1998), the yield differential is not to be regarded as a sign of the PAYG system being inferior to the funded system, but rather as a form of payment for the gift to the first PAYG generation. If we switch back to a funded system, this gift still has to be paid somehow.

How it is paid, and who pays it, depends on how we design the new system.

The simplest kind of reform is to privatize the PAYG system by letting the first generation of the reformed system bear the cost in the form of a "double contribution." The members of that generation thus both pay the pensions of the previous generation and buy bonds in the market to place in its own pension fund. Then we would really have a funded system in the true meaning of the word.

Another way would be for the government to privatize the PAYG system by explicitly recognizing the existing pension claims and backing them by issuing new government bonds. These bonds are then placed in the new pension fund. From a legal point of view, we would thus have a funded system. From a macroeconomic point of view, however, the system would still be PAYG since the pensions of the present retired generation (which are paid from the interest earned by the bonds in the fund) are actually paid by the present active generation, being the taxpayers servicing the newly issued government debt. In the old PAYG system, the active generation received a low return on its contributions. In the reformed system, the active generation receives a high return, but has also to pay higher taxes to pay for the higher return on the contributions of the earlier generation. In principle, the two systems are thus equivalent, although they look quite different from a formal point of view.

Reforming the system by explicitly recognizing the pension claims and issuing new government bonds is perhaps more fair – or at least more egalitarian – since it does not place the entire burden of paying the gift on the first generation of the reformed system. Rather, it makes it possible to distribute the burden over an arbitrary number of future generations of taxpayers.

The choice of whether – and how – to reform the system is thus not a question of whether to avoid the cost of the gift to the first generation of the PAYG system. That cost cannot be avoided, the gift having already been given. The choice is instead, as usually in economies, a question of distribution and a question of efficiency. The distributional question is who should pay the gift. If we do not reform the system, but hold on to the PAYG system, the cost is borne by all future generations in the form of a lower yield on their contributions; if we reform the system, the cost could be shifted to the first generation of the new system (the "double contribution" or to an arbitrary number of future generations (the government debt approach).

The efficiency question is a matter of optimal taxation. If we do not reform the system, the gift to the first generation of the PAYG system is financed by a tax (in the form of a forced saving at a low yield, of a given fraction of labor income) on all future generations. If we reform the system, and apply the government debt approach, the gift is probably financed by a tax on the incomes of future generations. Since the former alternative could be regarded as a tax on labor income only, while the latter could be regarded as a tax on all income (including capital income), not reforming the system seems to be preferred from an optimal taxation point of view.

The view of the yield differential as a payment for the gift raises a host of new questions. For most countries, and for most time periods, the rate of growth of the wage sum has been lower than the rate of return on financial assets. But this does not always have to be the case. Assume, for instance, that the opposite holds. Does this mean that the gift to the first generation is a free lunch? The answer is, yes. This is an application of the Golden Rule in neo-classical growth theory: if the rate of growth of the economy is higher than the interest rate, this is a sign of dynamic inefficiency.[10] The capital stock is simply too large, and we could thus consume part of it without having to reduce steady-state consumption. This reduction of the capital stock could take the form of introducing a PAYG system with a corresponding gift to the first generation. Another option – which might be more fair – would be to sell off part of the capital stock in order to reduce national debt, which would increase consumption of all future, debt-serving generations.

Another question is the following. Assume an economy with several risky assets, i.e. the portfolio model of Section 2 above is relevant. Assume further that there is no dynamic inefficiency, i.e. no over-accumulation of capital, in the economy.[11] If we introduce a PAYG system we give a gift to the first generation, but if this "asset" also turns out to be a desirable item in the representative investor's portfolio, there seems to be a free lunch in this case, too. In fact, there is. The free lunch of the first generation in this case illustrates the welfare gain to society from creating a wider space of assets for the investor.

3.4 The social security system is a suitable instrument for intergenerational risk-sharing

In a small but growing literature, social security is analyzed as an instrument for sharing risk across generations.[12] The idea is very reasonable; since generations are linked via the contributions to a PAYG system, a real-wage shock to one generation is transmitted as a shock in the yield to the social security "savings" of the next generation. In a general equilibrium model, this also holds for a funded system; a wage shock then affects (the endogenously determined) interest rate, and thus the benefits of the retired generation are affected.

The basic PAYG setup is the following. In a two-period overlapping-generations model, each individual receives an income Y_y when young and Y_o when old. If labor supply is modeled as endogenous, $Y_y = wl$, where w is the wage rate. Using a time index t for the cohort that is young at time t, we see that there are two cohorts alive at that time: the young generation, with an income Y_{yt}, and the old generation, with an income $Y_{o,t-1}$. The net income of the young is $Y_{yt}(1-\tau_t)$, where τ_t is the tax rate (which could vary over time). Similarly, the net income of the old is $Y_{o,t-1} = \rho_t \cdot Y_{y,t-1} = n \cdot Y_{yt} \cdot (1-\tau_t)$, where ρ_t is the replacement rate and n is the growth rate of the wage sum.

This setup can be exploited in a number of ways. The simplest solution is that, at each point in time, the incomes of the young and the old are pooled. Thereby the income uncertainty for both cohorts can be reduced. This pooling can take many different forms. For example, Thøgersen (1998) shows that a system with a fixed replacement rate $\rho_t = \rho$ (and thereby a variable tax rate, to ensure government budget balance) will increase income uncertainty; while a system with a fixed tax rate $\tau_t = \tau$ (and thereby a variable replacement rate) will provide intergenerational risk-sharing, reducing the variance in net income for each generation.

The surprising thing with these studies, however, is that they only allow for risk sharing over two generations. Thus uncertainty regarding Y_{yt} (or w_t, in the case of endogenous labor supply) is pooled over the two generations alive at time t. Limiting the number of risk-pooling generations to two is rather inefficient; if one could pool income risk over three or four generations, the risk for each individual generation would be correspondingly lower. In fact, there is a vehicle for achieving risk pooling over an infinite number of generations, namely government debt. Since the organization of a PAYG program requires the existence of a government in the first place, and since all papers on risk-sharing also assume the existence of government debt (namely, to deal with the gift to the first generation of the PAYG system; see Section 3 above), there is no reason to limit the management of income risk to the social security system only. In fact, I think the reason why all writers have limited themselves to two generations can be explained by the setup of the two-period OLG model; it makes it natural to think of only two generations at the time, and thus limits one's thinking of the actual scope for risk sharing.

If exogenous income (or, with endogenous labor supply, the wage rate) follows a stationary process, government debt can be used to remove virtually all income uncertainty for each generation.[13] I write "virtually all" since there are some technical problems involved. For example, if income is exogenous and follows an i.i.d. process, and if government debt is used to achieve complete smoothing, government debt will follow a unit root process. Thus the government's solvency constraint might not be satisfied, and the actual amount of smoothing would therefore have to be conditional on, e.g. the previous period's stock of government debt.

Even disregarding such technical issues, I am not claiming that all uncertainty should be ("virtually") removed, only that it could be removed. Incidentally, eliminating all income uncertainty also means that the uncertainty with respect to the yield of the PAYG system disappears, which may not be desirable from a portfolio point of view (cf. Section 2 above). Also, letting intergenerational risk sharing be a primary goal of government debt management is in conflict with the traditional goal of debt management, which is tax smoothing.[14] In a more realistic setting, debt management should be used to some extent for both purposes, the optimal mix being an empirical matter. Third, using government debt to smooth wage variability might not be desirable from an allocational point of view. If wages suddenly increase dramatically, this probably reflects an increase in labor productivity, and the optimal response to such a situation is to increase labor supply by intertemporal substitution. Artificially trying to reduce the wage level in such a situation might not at all be welfare enhancing. The optimal mix of risk reduction (in the form of wage rate smoothing) and allocation (in the form of intertemporal substitution) is yet to be worked out by means of an OLG model with heterogeneous agents.

I thus do not claim that all risk should be eliminated. What I claim is that limiting the risk pooling to two generations seems very arbitrary, and that social security issues and government debt management issues should be analyzed as integrated parts of public policy.

3.5 The government is a safe provider of social security

A pension scheme is an insurance against the uncertainty with respect to an individual's life span. Almost by definition, the provider of such insurance must be reliable. While private insurance companies might default on their obligations, we have grown used to regarding the government as a safe provider.

Contracts entered by the government, however, are not always formulated in the same waterproof way as are contracts entered by private corporations; they are subject to a political risk. First, there might be small, technical changes in the contracts – changes that are not subject to a political discussion at all, but are just implemented by the executive branch. The Swedish ATP system, which was introduced in 1960, is an illustrative example. Until 1999, it had not yet been subject to any major reform – but over the years, the malfunctioning of the system had made minor, technical adjustments necessary. One can show that if exactly the same benefit rules that were decided in 1960 were still honored, pensions would be on the average 12–17 percent higher today than they actually are.[15] These changes have hardly been subject to political discussion, since each individual change has been too small to be bothered with. Still, these minor adjustments have accumulated over the years. If a private insurance company would have tried to reduce contracted payments by small successive amounts each year, such behavior is likely to have been observed – and challenged in court. Since those changes have been decided by the government, however, there is no legal way for the buyers of the insurance to legally enforce the original contract.

One might say that those changes were necessary, since changing circumstances had made the original contract unrealizable. This is true, but beside the point. The basic problem is that the government originally entered an unrealistic contract. A private provider, knowing that contracts are enforced by the law courts, would have had stronger incentives to study the demographic and macroeconomic trends (as in fact private insurance companies are, and are forced to do by the regulatory authorities), and never to enter an unrealistic contract.[16]

Second, there might be large changes in the system. Such reforms have usually been on the political agenda for several years, and they have a democratic legitimacy that the previously mentioned, gradual erosion of the social security systems are maybe lacking. Still, large reforms, too, create uncertainty for the individuals. In a recent paper, McHale (1999) has studied large changes of the benefit rules in a number of countries. It turned out that such reforms have deprived the average (45-year-old) worker of roughly 10 to 20 percent of his or her social security wealth.[17]

Third, there is the particular uncertainty associated with delays in the decision process. Sweden provides an illustrative example in this case, too. Two decades after the ATP system had been introduced in 1960, it was evident that it was unstable. The first government committee in charge of working out a reform proposal was appointed in 1984. The last committee was appointed in 1990 and presented its proposal in 1994. Although leading politicians successively expressed their support for "the basic ideas" in the proposal, discussions of technical details dragged on for five years. And "technical details" could of course be of great economic importance to individuals planning their professional careers and lifetime earnings profiles. The final decisions were thus not taken until the summer of 1999, which means that for almost twenty years, the Swedish people knew that the rules of the social security system were likely to change, but nobody knew what the new rules would look like.

These three forms of political uncertainty raise several questions. One could for example say that if the PAYG system is unstable, it would be pointless to force the government to honor the contract just like a private insurance company. If the system runs a deficit, and the rules cannot be changed, the deficit has to be covered by the government budget – and thus the uncertainty of the buyers of the pension scheme is just shifted to the taxpayers (who are roughly the same persons). This is true, and I guess this is an argument for privatization; a private provider would have an incentive to avoid entering unrealistic contracts, which would reduce uncertainty, both for buyers of pension schemes and for taxpayers.

Another argument is to regard political uncertainty just like any uncertainty in the capital market. In a portfolio context, such uncertainty might be just as desirable (or undesirable) as any other uncertainty. A government-run system (whether PAYG or fully funded) should thus not be ruled out *a priori*; its desirability is an empirical matter. The counterargument is that while normal uncertainty is relatively easy to assess (it is simple to estimate the covariance matrix used in the numerical example in Section 2 above) the probability distribution of the political changes is much harder to estimate.

Finally, one might say privatization does not protect social security against political risk; the government could still tax the savers. While this is true in principle, it seems like any government is less prone to levy explicit taxes on individual wealth than to change complicated (and to most people, obscure) benefit rules. As Peter Diamond (1996: 80) observes, this might also hold for a government-run PAYG system with notional accounts; it may be politically more difficult to reduce those accounts by a well-defined amount than to make subtle changes in benefit rules. It is thus not an argument for privatization *per se*, but rather for individual accounts, transparency and, perhaps, actuarial benefit rules.

3.6 Conclusion

The conclusion to be drawn from this is that the first step of a reform should be to make the benefit rules actuarial. After that, the gains from proceeding further, into a funded system, are not due to the fact that such a system has a higher yield. The gift to the first PAYG generation has already been given, and a funded system cannot remove that cost. What we can accomplish, by means of government debt management, is to shift it over the generations. The main reason for funding the system seems to be that it thus can be privatized. And the main reason for privatization is that of transparency and safety; competition will guarantee that the rules remain actuarial, and the political risk may thus be reduced.

Notes

1 I am indebted to Olivia S. Mitchell and Hiroshi Yoshida for valuable comments on an earlier version of this chapter.
2 There are two main changes in demography that affect social security: increased longevity and changing cohort sizes. In this section, we only discuss the longevity issue. The problem of changing (i.e. falling) cohort sizes is important in its own right; it means that the notional "yield" on the pay-as-you-go system falls, and is therefore equivalent to a falling yield on a fully funded system.
3 For unanticipated changes, however, things are different. Private pension funds would need a buffer fund to cope with such changes – but that is not the issue here, since the demographic changes that are rocking the public pension schemes are the results of long-term trends that have been known and anticipated for many years.
4 For the Swedish ATP pension, 75 percent of the contribution is a tax with no relation to later pension benefits. See Persson (1998) and the references cited therein.
5 This has for example been the case of Sweden; see Ståhlberg (1990).
6 In fact, this is the kind of reform that has just been decided in Sweden.

7   There is no reliable bond index for any long time period. The data refer to the bond portfolio of the Swedish national pension fund (the AP Fund) which could perhaps be regarded as a useful proxy. Since there was no well-functioning bond market before the early 1980s, the yield figures from the years before 1984 are very unreliable, and serve as a hypothetical illustration only.

8   In fact, the overlapping-generations framework used in Section 4, where each time period in the model is half a lifetime, is perhaps the most appropriate approach to pension fund management.

9   Of course, in a full general equilibrium, wages will be endogenous too. In this context, where we limit our analysis to the capital market, we disregard such a complication.

10 At this level of abstraction, we disregard the distinction between the growth rate of the labor force, the growth rate of the wage sum, and the growth rate of GDP. At the practical level of actual PAYG systems, the Golden Rule interpretation is not that straightforward.

11 In the portfolio approach there are several interest rates. It is therefore difficult to relate such a world to the concepts of neo-classical growth theory, since it is not obvious which interest rate should be compared to the growth rate of the economy. For simplicity we disregard such complications and just assume that dynamic efficiency, however defined, is not an issue.

12 See Shiller (1998) and Thøgersen (1998) and the references cited therein.

13 If income does not follow a stationary process, or if the parameters of that process are unknown, things get more complicated since we cannot assure that the government's solvency constraint is satisfied. This problem is however not limited to the case of using government debt to achieve intergenerational risk sharing; using only the social security system for that purpose will also be difficult in such a case.

14 Cf. Barro (1995).

15 Cf. Persson (1998) for references.

16 Of course, even very prudent projections of demographic trends and financial developments might *ex post* turn out to be incorrect, but a private provider would nevertheless have to honor a contract; that is the rationale for substantial capital adequacy requirements in the insurance industry.

17 Workers at retirement age have lost considerably less, which probably reflects the fact that younger persons could more easily adapt to a change in the rules.

References

Barro, R. J. (1995) "Optimal debt management," *NBER Working Paper* 5327.

Diamond, P. (1996) "Proposals to restructure social security," *The Journal of Economic Perspectives* 10(3): 67–88.

Feldstein, M. (1996) "The missing piece in policy analysis: social security reform," *American Economic Review* 86(2): 1–14.

McHale, J. (1999) "The risk of social security benefit rule changes: some international evidence," *NBER Working Paper* 7031.

Persson, M. (1980) "The distribution of abilities and the progressive income tax," *Journal of Public Economics* 22(1): 73–88.

Persson, M. (1998) "Reforming social security in Sweden," in H. Siebert (ed.), *Redesigning Social Security*, Mohr Siebeck Verlag: Tübingen, 169–85.

Shiller, R. J. (1998) "Social security and institutions for intergenerational, intragenerational and international risk sharing," forthcoming in the Carnegie-Rochester Conference Series on Public Policy.

Ståhlberg, A.-C. (1990) "Life cycle income redistribution of the public sector: inter- and intragenerational effects," in I. Persson (ed.), *Generating Inequality in the Welfare State: The Swedish Experience*, Oslo: Norwegian University Press.

Thøgersen, Ø. (1998) "A note on intergenerational risk sharing and the design of pay-as-you-go pension plans," *Journal of Population Economics* 1(3): 373–8.

Varian, H. R. (1980) "Redistributive taxation as social insurance," *Journal of Public Economics* 14(1): 49–68.

4 Social security privatization and financial market risk

Lessons from US financial history[1]

Gary Burtless

4.0 Introduction

All major industrial countries face problems connected with population aging. Depressed birth rates and rising longevity have increased the aged dependency ratio throughout the industrialized world. Demographic projections of the United Nations suggest that the percentage of people past age 65 in developed countries will double over the next five decades, and the ratio of aged dependents to working-age people will climb steeply.

As populations in the rich countries grow older, the cost of paying for pension and health benefits must rise, boosting tax burdens and threatening the government's ability to finance other obligations. Only one G7 country, the UK, has overhauled its public pensions in a way that is likely to hold down future spending to a level that is comparable to today's. The favorable outlook for British public pensions is the result of policies that tightly restrain growth in basic public benefits and strongly encourage active workers to abandon the second-tier, earnings-related public program in favor of private pensions. Future retirees are expected to derive much more of their retirement income from privately managed and invested pension accounts rather than the public pay-as-you-go system. Other leading industrial countries still face major challenges in paying for or fundamentally reforming their main public pension programs (Bosworth and Burtless 1998).

Policymakers in a few rich countries show interest in following the British example and replacing part or all of their public systems with private pensions organized around individual retirement accounts. Champions of this reform point to the experience of Chile, where a costly and failing public system was replaced by a less expensive private system in the early 1980s. So far, Chile's private pension system has received high marks for sound administration, good returns, and broad political acceptance. Some may wonder whether the experience of a country that scrapped its public pension system while under the sway of a military dictatorship is relevant to democratic states. Nonetheless, the expected surge in public retirement costs has made many voters and policymakers receptive to the idea of a private alternative to the existing public system.

This chapter surveys the relative advantages of public and private systems. More important, it assesses the financial market risks facing contributors in a private system based on individual retirement accounts. The first part of the chapter describes the differences between public and private systems and considers the main economic and political arguments for privatization. A principal claim is that private plans can provide better returns to contributors. If this were true, it seems appropriate to weigh possible risks associated with the improved returns. Some of the most important risks are those associated with financial market fluctuations.

The second part of the chapter provides evidence on these risks by considering the hypothetical pensions US workers would have obtained between 1911 and 1999 if they had accumulated retirement savings in individual accounts. The 89 hypothetical contributors are assumed to have identical careers and to contribute a fixed percentage of their wages to private investment accounts. When contributors reach retirement age, they convert their retirement savings into level annuities. To make the calculations comparable across time, all contributors are assumed to have an identical career path of earnings and to face the same mortality risks after retirement. Contributors differ only with respect to the stock market returns, bond interest rates, and price inflation they face over their careers. These differences occur because of the differing start and end dates of the workers' careers.

The analysis demonstrates that the financial market risks in a private retirement system are empirically quite large. Although some of these risks are also present in a public retirement system, a public system has one important advantage over private pensions. Because a public system is backed by the taxing and borrowing authority of the state, it can spread risks over a much larger population of potential contributors and beneficiaries. This makes the risks more manageable for active and retired workers, many of whom have little ability to insure themselves privately against financial market risk.

4.1 Public and private pensions

The main goal of a pension program is to provide replacement for labor earnings lost as a result of old age, premature death, or invalidity. The usual way rich countries have achieved this goal has been with mandatory, publicly financed pensions. The typical system offers a pension starting at a specified age that is calculated on the basis of the worker's years of coverage under the system and her average covered wages while contributing to the system (World Bank 1994: 102–9). Benefit payments are usually financed with current tax contributions from employers and workers, with contributions scaled according to each worker's wages (often up to a maximum taxable limit). Only a few public systems have built up large enough reserves to pay for a high percentage of future pension obligations. Almost all public defined-benefit systems are financed under the pay-as-you-go principle, that is, out of current contributions from workers, employers, and, in some cases, the state budget.

Because pay-as-you-go systems can provide generous benefits to early contributors at modest cost, they were both politically popular and hugely effective in reducing old-age poverty within a few decades of their introduction. Unfortunately, the pay-as-you-go financing method is encountering serious problems in most rich countries. These nations face a steep drop in labor force growth that limits the size of the workforce available to pay for public pensions. Declining mortality rates have boosted the relative size of aged populations. The increase in life expectancy in rich countries has been reflected almost exclusively in longer periods of retirement rather than longer active work careers. In fact, several Western European countries effectively reduced the early entitlement age for benefits in the 1970s and 1980s as a policy response to increases in structural unemployment (Gruber and Wise 1999). The slowdown in growth of labor productivity and real wages has also slowed the expansion of the tax base used to finance the system. In combination these factors have boosted the public cost of supporting an aging population.

4.1.1 The private alternative

Privatization is based on a simple idea. Instead of contributing to a collective, pay-as-you-go retirement program, workers would be required to build up retirement savings in individually owned and directed private accounts. Workers could withdraw their funds from the accounts when they became disabled or reached the retirement age, and their heirs could inherit any funds accumulated in the account if the worker died before becoming disabled or reaching the retirement age. At the time a worker chooses to start receiving a pension, some or all of the funds in the worker's account would be converted into an annuity that would last until the worker dies. In most privatization plans, workers would be free to decide how their contributions were invested, at least within broad limits.

Private defined-contribution pension plans differ from public systems in two important ways. First, the worker's ultimate retirement benefit depends solely on the worker's contributions and the success of the worker's investment plan. Workers who make larger contributions receive bigger pensions, other things equal. Workers whose investments earn high returns enjoy more comfortable retirements than workers who invest poorly. Second, in a private system workers' pensions are paid out of accumulations of their own previous savings. In contrast, public pensions are financed mainly by the payroll taxes of active workers and their employers. This difference between the two kinds of system implies that the savings accumulation in a private plan would be many times larger than the reserves needed in a pay-as-you-go public system.

Because the connection between individual contributions, investment returns, and pension benefits is very straightforward in a defined-contribution pension program, a private retirement system offers less scope for redistribution in favor of low-wage workers and other favored groups. Redistribution favoring low-wage and other kinds of workers must take place outside these accounts. Most public pension formulas explicitly favor low-wage workers and workers with short careers in order to minimize poverty among elderly workers who become eligible for public pensions. To duplicate public pension programs' success in keeping down poverty among the elderly, a private system must supplement the pensions from individual retirement accounts with a minimum, tax-financed pension or with public assistance payments.

No rich country can immediately scrap its public retirement system and replace it with a private system. In the US, for example, more than 44 million people – about one in six residents – collects benefits under the public Social Security system. About 1.6 million workers began to collect new retirement benefits during 1998 and another 600,000 were awarded new disability pensions. Even if the US replaced Social Security with a private system for young workers, Americans who are already retired or who will enter retirement within the next few years would continue to receive public pension checks for several decades. Public funds must be appropriated to pay for these pensions, regardless of the system established for workers who will retire in the distant future.

The need to pay for the pensions of people who are already retired or near retirement age poses a challenge to all plans for privatizing public pensions (except in the handful of countries that never established a large public system). Money must be found for existing pension liabilities at the same time workers will be asked to contribute to a new type of private pension account. Because young workers will be required to finance pensions for retired workers and active workers near retirement, they may resist being forced to pay for their own retirement pensions through contributions to new private accounts.

4.1.2 Claimed advantages of a private system

Privatization potentially offers both economic and political advantages over a pay-as-you-go public system. If workers are permitted to invest their retirement savings as they choose, many will obtain utility gains by investing in portfolios tailored to their individual taste for financial market risk. Workers enrolled in a single public system are obliged to accept the portfolio choices of that system.[2] Even more important, proponents of privatization claim workers will receive larger pensions and the economy will grow faster under a private rather than a public retirement system.

Almost all advocates of a private retirement system argue that pension contributions would be more affordable or benefits more generous if countries adopted a private system. Stated crassly, most workers could expect a better deal under a private system than they can obtain under existing public pension systems. This argument is based on a straightforward calculation. If workers invested 10 percent of their earnings in a private retirement account yielding a moderate rate of return (say, 3 percent a year after adjusting for inflation), most would collect bigger pensions than they can expect under a fully mature pay-as-you-go public pension system requiring the same level of contributions.

Samuelson (1958) and Aaron (1966) showed that contributors in a fully mature pay-as-you-go pension system can expect to earn an annual rate of return on their contributions equal to the sum of the annual growth rate in the work force plus the annual growth rate of real wages. In the 1950s and 1960s, for example, the US labor force was growing $1\frac{1}{2}$ percent to 2 percent a year and wages were rising $2\frac{1}{2}$ percent to 3 percent a year. The real rate of return on contributions was expected to be 4 percent to 5 percent a year when the US Social Security system became fully mature. That was a better rate of return than most workers then earned on other investments available to them. By the 1990s the expected return on contributions to a pay-as-you-go pension system was sharply lower for young workers in most industrialized countries. The labor force was growing much less rapidly than it did in the 1960s, and in some countries the workforce was actually declining. The productivity slowdown has meant that real wages are increasing much more slowly than they did in the early postwar period. The expected real rate of return for workers who will retire in the next century may be 1 percent or less in many industrialized countries. Workers can expect to earn better returns under a funded private pension system. Proponents of privatization suggest that workers in a funded system could reliably earn 4 percent or more a year on their contributions if pension savings were invested in a mix of stocks and bonds.

Privatization is not essential if future workers are to obtain a better return, however. Public pension systems could shift from pay-as-you-go financing toward advance funding of pension obligations. Public pension managers could invest the new pension reserves in high-expected-return assets, including equities, real estate, and corporate bonds. If the public system invested in the same mix of assets that workers collectively would have chosen for their own individual accounts, the rate of return on public reserves would be the same as on assets in the private account system. In fact, the rate of return on worker contributions would almost certainly be higher in the public system, because the lower administrative costs of a collective system would boost net returns.

In the short run, of course, the shift to more advance funding can only be achieved by reducing some workers' rate of return. Some workers or taxpayers must accept lower pensions or higher taxes and contributions if the public system is to accumulate more reserves that it would under pay-as-you-go financing. But the same sacrifice is required if a new private pension system is established to replace or supplement traditional public pensions. Some workers must contribute more to the public and private systems, or some retirees must accept smaller pensions, if reserves are to be accumulated in the newly established private system while pensions continue to be paid under the old public program. The higher rate of return promised by private systems depends on adopting a new retirement saving strategy and a more aggressive approach to investing pension reserves. Both of these changes can be accomplished by reforming the existing public pension system as well as by establishing a new system of private retirement accounts.

Many advocates of privatization believe that full or partial privatization will boost saving rates. If national saving could be increased, income growth might accelerate, making it easier for the nation to afford the extra burden of supporting a large retired population in the future. Unlike most public retirement systems, which are financed on a pay-as-you-go basis, a private retirement system requires huge accumulations of assets in individual retirement accounts. Because workers would be setting aside a percentage of their pay in private accounts for their own retirement instead of sending in contributions that are immediately spent on pension payments, the introduction of a privatized system could lead to a jump in saving.

Privatization is not really needed to achieve higher national saving, however. The same increase in saving would occur if the public retirement system moved away from pay-as-you-go financing toward advance funding. This could occur if the government increased the contribution rate to the public system or reduced benefits, increasing the annual surplus of the program. The public program would accumulate larger reserves than are anticipated under current law. Instead of accumulating assets in millions of individual retirement accounts, as in a private system, the saving would take place in a single public fund. The crucial policy change needed to boost national saving is the move to advance funding rather than a shift to private management or to individual retirement accounts.

4.1.3 Political feasibility

Even if long-run rates of return and national saving could be increased within existing public pension systems, critics of public retirement systems are skeptical that the funds accumulated within a public fund would actually be saved. They fear that governments would use the funds to finance deficits in other government accounts or to increase non-pension public spending. Privatization advocates therefore believe it is more realistic to think pension saving will actually take place in millions of privately owned accounts, outside the reach of a revenue-hungry government.

Privatization can also offer a politically acceptable method of managing the accumulation of huge reserves and company stocks. In a system where the accumulation takes place in a single public system, public officials are ultimately responsible for allocating the funds among investment alternatives and purchasing the stocks or bonds of individual companies. Opponents of a funded public system fear that politicians' investment decisions would be guided by political rather than economic considerations, reducing the yield of the investments, diverting investments into unproductive uses, and intruding on the business decisions of company managers. In a private system of individual accounts, decision making authority over the accumulation would rest with millions of workers. Through their choices among investment alternatives and specific investment funds, workers and private fund managers rather than public officials would exercise ultimate authority over the allocation of investments.

A private retirement system, with its broad dispersion of asset ownership, has another advantage over a public retirement fund when it comes to accumulating corporate stocks. If retirement asset accumulation took place within a single public fund and if the public fund owned shares in thousands of companies, national legislatures or public officials would have to decide how these shares should be voted. Voting decisions might be determined by political rather than economic criteria, possibly reducing the efficiency and profitability of the nation's business sector.

Many advocates of a private retirement system also believe that workers would be more willing to accept an increase in their contribution to the retirement system if their extra contribution took the form of deposits into individually owned and managed investment accounts. While workers would resist a hike in the payroll tax, they will tolerate – and may actually welcome – compulsory saving in individually owned accounts. This argument for privatization is essentially pragmatic. Voters or public officials are more likely to take needed steps to increase national saving and prepare for an older population if workers have direct ownership of their extra contributions to the retirement system.

4.1.4 Economic versus political advantages of privatization

This brief survey of the claimed advantages of privatization makes clear that private, individual account systems have only one inherent economic advantage over public systems. Private systems permit individual workers to fashion an investment strategy for their retirement saving that reflects their risk aversion. A single collective system forces at least some workers – those with no other savings to invest – to accept the portfolio allocation of the public pension system. This gain from privatization may be offset, in whole or in part, by the higher management cost of administering a system with millions of individual accounts, a feature of private pensions that reduces net rates of return.

As noted by Diamond (1997), the main issues dividing supporters and opponents of privatization hinge on political rather than economic considerations, since all but one of the claimed economic advantages of privatization can be achieved within a redesigned public system that is partially funded and that pursues a sound investment strategy. The crucial political questions are these. Will a nation's political institutions permit the accumulation of enormous reserves within a public retirement system? If reserve accumulation is actually achieved, will it be offset by lower taxes or increased non-pension spending elsewhere in the government sector, eliminating the effect of reserve accumulation on national saving? Even if the reserve accumulation is accomplished and is not offset by larger deficits in other parts of the government budget, will pension reserves be prudently invested? Or will political influence divert investments into uneconomic projects, producing sub-par returns? Assuming that the public pension reserves can be prudently invested, will public officials exercise their privileges as corporate shareholders to meddle in the internal affairs of private companies, reducing corporate efficiency and profitability? Observers who distrust the motives, discipline, and capacity of public officials believe that a funded pension system will be better managed and produce better results if it is under private rather than government control (see Diamond 1999: 67–110).

4.2 Riskiness of pensions

A public pension system enjoys one important advantage over a private system with individual accounts. Because its benefit promises are ultimately backed by the government's power to tax, the public system can spread risks across a broader population, including workers who have not yet entered the labor force. In a private individual account system, each worker's pension depends on the level and pattern of his contributions and the success of his investment strategy. Workers who claim pensions after a long period of low returns will receive small pensions; workers who retire after periods of exceptional returns will collect large pensions. Workers who make well-informed or lucky investment choices will obtain big pensions; workers who invest imprudently or unluckily will receive small benefits. The wide variation in outcomes is reduced under a common public system, where all contributors who make similar contributions can be assured of similar benefits.

A defined-contribution system allocates risks in a very different way than a collective, defined-benefit system. Under most public pension systems, workers born in the same year who have similar earnings records receive similar retirement benefits. Because of political constraints on democratically elected governments, the public pension formula changes very slowly and only after protracted political debate. Since this debate involves both contributors and beneficiaries, changes in contribution and benefit formulas tend to reflect a compromise between the interests of the two groups. The effects of unanticipated demographic, labor market, and financial market developments are rarely if ever borne by a single cohort. They are spread across a number of cohorts through gradual changes in contribution rates and benefit levels. In contrast, workers participating in a defined-contribution system bear many more of the risks associated with financial market fluctuations.

Workers enrolled in a defined-contribution pension plan face three kinds of financial market risk. They are exposed to the risk that the real return on their contributions may fall below the historical norm over the course of their working careers. If workers obtain unexpectedly low returns on their retirement savings, they may enter old age with too little savings to finance a comfortable retirement.

Second, at the point they retire workers may find it expensive to purchase annuities. Workers who want to ensure they will not outlive their assets will seek to convert their retirement savings into an annuity around the time they retire. The market price they pay for annuities depends on four factors: their expected life span when they purchase annuities, the amount of adverse selection among the population buying annuities, the profit requirements needed to induce insurance companies to offer annuities, and the market rate of interest at which insurance companies can invest their reserves. Even assuming that mortality risk among workers at the same age is identical, adverse selection among potential annuity buyers is negligible, and insurance companies would sell annuities at zero profit, workers will still pay wildly varying prices for annuities over time because of fluctuations in market interest rates.

Finally, workers who buy level nominal annuities are subject to inflation risk. The amount of inflation that occurs after a worker retires has a dramatic impact on the purchasing power of the worker's pension. If inflation turns out to be unexpectedly low, the worker's retirement consumption can be much higher than initially anticipated. If it turns out to be unexpectedly high, the worker may reach advanced old age with very little spendable income and face destitution. The risks just mentioned are substantial, even in an economy like that of the US, which has efficient and well regulated capital markets, a long tradition of respect for property rights, and has enjoyed more than two centuries of relative prosperity. The risks are so daunting, in fact, that they challenge the ability of a pension system based solely on individual accounts to deliver reliable income replacement in old age.

Indexed defined-benefit pensions in a pay-as-you-go program such as US Social Security are not directly affected by these risks. Benefits are mainly financed by the current contributions of active workers rather than the market returns earned on workers' past contributions. Benefits are legally prescribed in terms of each worker's past covered earnings and do not depend on the worker's investment skills. Inflation risks in this system are manageable. The contribution base is likely to rise in line with price inflation. In addition, benefit promises are ultimately backed by the government's power to borrow and tax, not by the assets held in an individual retirement account.

Public retirement systems are subject to political, economic, and demographic risks, of course. Slow wage growth and lengthy economic slumps deprive the system of needed taxes. A sharp decline in fertility or immigration slows the growth of contributions without changing the need for funds to pay for benefits in the short run. Future voters might resist paying higher taxes, and benefits would then have to be cut or the budget deficit would soar. This does not mean public pension benefits must cut to zero, as some workers may fear. But it does mean taxes will have to be increased or benefits trimmed if the system is to be kept solvent in the long run.

Future tax rates and benefit payments will be determined by legislators who have not yet been elected (and may not even have been born). This fact introduces substantial political uncertainty around future benefit levels and tax burdens. Future voters and elected officials might decide to fundamentally change the structure of the existing pay-as-you-go, defined-benefit system. Legislators might decide to scale back the system's benefit promises, including its promises to people who are already retired or on the threshold of retirement.

These political risks are easy to overstate, however. Elected officials are keenly aware of public opinion. Mature public pension systems are among the most popular programs run by democratic governments. Most voters recognize that the elderly and disabled rely on public pensions for a sizable portion of their income. Millions of people collect public pension benefits, and many of these recipients vote faithfully. Most contributors to public pension programs have relatives and friends who collect pensions, so even among contributors there would be resistance to big benefit cuts.

It should also be noted that political risk can affect pension contributions and benefits in a private, individual account system as well as in a public system. Legislatures can change the terms under which contributions to individual accounts are calculated, accumulated, redeemed, or taxed, affecting the net value of individual retirement annuities. The idea that private retirement pensions are somehow immune to political risk is a serious misconception.

4.3 Effects of financial market fluctuations

The remainder of the chapter focuses on financial market risks affecting the value of pensions under a private, defined-contribution plan. The size of these risks is relevant to considering whether an individual account pension system can deliver dependable income replacement in old age. To assess these risks I calculate the value of savings accumulation available to workers at retirement, the initial annuities that they can purchase given their accumulations and interest rates at the time they retire, and the real value of annuity flows after retirement given the actual pattern of inflation over the twentieth century. The calculations are based on historical stock market prices and dividends, bond market returns, and price inflation in the US for the period since 1871.[3]

To calculate real stock and bond returns during a worker's career and the purchasing power of an annuity during the worker's retirement, it is necessary to convert nominal returns and nominal pension flows into dollars that have constant purchasing power. I use Bureau of Labor Statistics (BLS) estimates of the January producer price index for finished goods for the period from 1871 to 1912. Starting in 1913, the BLS began estimating a consumer price index for urban workers. I have spliced these two series together to form a price level series for the entire 1871–1999 period. Calculations that require a projection of the price level after 1999 are performed under the assumption that annual price inflation will be 2.5 percent starting in 1999.

Figures 4.1 and 4.2 show real U.S. stock and bond returns over the past century. Because stock market prices fluctuate so much from year to year, the first figure shows the annual rate of return on a dollar invested in the stock market 15 years before the end of the indicated year. This method of calculation smooths out much of the annual variability in real returns, but it still reveals the wide variability of returns over different 15-year periods. The 15-year trailing return was negative in 1920 and 1980, but it exceeded 12 percent in the mid-1930s, 1960s, and late 1990s. The heavy line in Figure 4.22 shows the nominal rate of return on government and other low-risk bonds. For years after 1923 it is based on the average market yield on US government bonds with a maturity of at least 10 years. To convert this nominal yield into a real interest rate, I subtract the average annual inflation rate during the next five years. This seems an appropriate way to measure the real return on bonds, because their ultimate return depends on the value of the real income flows they generate for investors. This depends on actual inflation in years after the bond is issued rather than in the year of issue or in years before the issue.

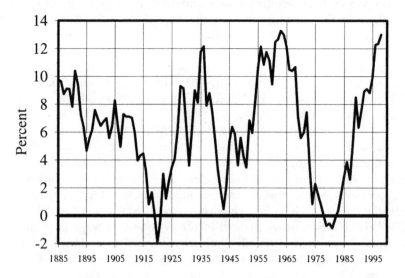

Figure 4.1 Real stock market returns, 1871–1998

Source: Standard and Poor's composite US Stock market data cited in Shiller (1989), updated through 1999, and US Bureau of Labor Statistics.

Note: Annual real rate of return on investment in US stocks for fifteen-year period ending on the last day of the indicated year.

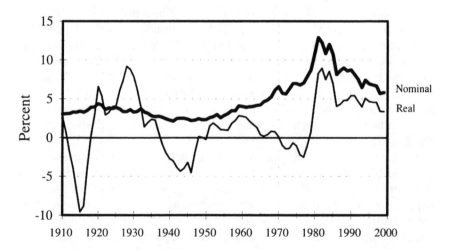

Figure 4.2 "Riskless" long-term interest rate, 1910–99

Source: Federal Reserve Bank of St. Louis and US Bureau of Labor Statistics.

Note: "Riskless" rate is assumed equal to nominal US Treasury long-bond rate from 1924–98 and equal to adjusted high-quality railroad bond rate 1910–23 (see text). Real rate is obtained by subtracting the annual inflation rate over the next five years from the nominal interest rate.

US stocks have produced substantially higher average returns than bonds over the past century. In the period since 1910 the geometric mean annual rate of return on stocks has been 6.9 percent. The mean real return on bonds was only 1.6 percent in the same period. In exchange for higher expected returns, owners of stocks have had to accept considerably greater short-term risk. The standard deviation of the annual returns was 18.8 percent for stocks but just 3.8 percent for bonds between 1910 and 1999.

In order to calculate the effects of stock and bond yields on workers' pensions, it is necessary to define a standard career path of earnings and pension contributions. All the calculations that follow are based on male earners who have a full, 40-year career. In the absence of economy-wide wage growth, these workers are assumed to have a lifetime path of real earnings that matches the age-earnings profile of employed US men in 1995.[4] In addition, wage growth in the economy at large is assumed to average 2 percent a year after adjusting for inflation. This is similar to the rate of wage growth in the past few years, but it is higher than average wage growth since 1973 and is somewhat slower than typical wage growth over the twentieth century.[5] Each worker is assumed to enter the work force on his twenty-second birthday and to work for 40 years until the day before his sixty-second birthday, which is assumed to occur on January 1st. Thus, a worker who begins to work at the beginning of 1871 is assumed to begin receiving his pension on the first day of 1911.

The worker saves 6 percent of his earnings and invests his retirement savings in some combination of bonds and common stocks. All stock dividends are reinvested in stocks, and all bond interest payments are reinvested in newly issued long- or short-term bonds.[6] The income flows from both kinds of assets are assumed to be free of individual income taxes at the time they are reinvested. Unlike ordinary investors, who must pay trading fees and commissions when buying and selling stocks and bonds, the worker is assumed to face no transaction costs in making his investments.

On his sixty-second birthday the worker converts his accumulation into a single-life annuity that is fixed in nominal terms. The insurance company selling the annuity bases its charge on the expected mortality experience of American males who reached age 65 in 1995, using mortality projections of the Social Security Actuary.[7] The Actuary's projections take account of gradual improvements in mortality experience that older males are expected to enjoy over the next several decades. Unlike annuities actually available in the US market, the insurance company does not charge a load factor to cover its profit requirements and possible adverse selection among people who wish to buy annuities. (Thus, the worker is assumed to purchase a "fair" annuity.) In determining the sales price of the annuity, the insurance company assumes it will be able to invest the worker's funds at the long-term riskless bond rate prevailing when the annuity is purchased (the nominal yield in Figure 4.2). The annual annuity payment is fixed in nominal terms. That is, unlike Social Security pensions the annuity is not adjusted from year to year to reflect changes in the price level.

Fluctuations in the value of defined-contribution pensions can be computed in a variety of ways. I emphasize two principal measures of pension value, the replacement rate and the real internal rate of return on workers' contributions. For a given worker, both the replacement rate and the internal rate of return may differ depending on the age at which they are measured. I estimate them at the age workers enter retirement (age 62) and also at the end of their life.

4.3.1 Alternative investment strategies

In light of the wide differences between stock and bond returns, workers' decisions about how to invest their pension savings can have large effects on their pension accumulations by the time they retire. To investigate the impact of portfolio choice, I calculate pensions under three contribution allocation strategies: 100 percent stocks, 50 percent stocks/50 percent bonds, and 100 percent bonds. Workers are assumed to steadily invest their new contributions in stocks or bonds following these investment proportions. Because stock returns are always higher than bond returns for investment periods of about 15 years or more, the worker who invests half of his contributions in stocks and half in bonds will reach retirement with a much larger portfolio of stocks than of bonds.

One way to measure the size of the worker's pension accumulation is to calculate the worker's stock accumulation on the day of his retirement and then divide this amount by his average annual earnings when he was between 54 and 58 years old. This "nest egg/pay" ratio is roughly equivalent to the worker's wealth/income ratio around the time of his retirement. When economy-wide real wages are growing 2 percent a year, as assumed in this exercise, a worker's annual earnings are likely to reach a peak sometime around age 55. Both the numerator (the worker's retirement nest egg) and the denominator (his peak career earnings) are measured in constant dollars. The ratio thus measures the worker's lifetime retirement savings as a multiple of his peak career earnings. Since each worker is assumed to have the same pattern of career earnings, the variability of the nest egg/pay ratio is due solely to variations in average investment returns during the 40-year accumulation phase when the worker is contributing to his retirement saving plan.

Workers who invest exclusively in US stocks accumulate more pension assets than workers who invest in bonds or in a combination of stocks and bonds. Workers retiring after 40-year careers in 1964 through 1999, for example, would have accumulated more than three times as many assets if they had invested their pension savings exclusively in stocks as they would have obtained if they invested exclusively in bonds. Stock market investments have delivered widely varying accumulations over time, however. The worker retiring in 1921, after a period of exceptionally poor stock market returns, managed to accumulate a retirement nest egg of only a little more than two years' peak earnings. In contrast, the worker retiring in 1966 accumulated more than 12 times his peak career earnings. The first column in Table 4.1 shows distributional statistics on the nest egg/pay ratio for workers retiring between 1911 and 1999, assuming all pension contributions were invested in stocks. The average nest egg ratio for the 89 forty-year careers is 6.1 with a median ratio of 5.1 and a standard deviation of 2.6.

4.3.2 Initial replacement rate

A common measure of the adequacy of pension income is the replacement rate, which measures pensions as a percentage of the worker's earnings before retirement. Figure 4.3 shows workers' initial replacement rate, where that rate is defined as the ratio of a worker's initial real annuity divided by his peak real earnings. The three lines in the figure correspond to replacement rates under the three alternative investment strategies described above. The top line in the figure shows replacement rates obtained by workers who invest all their pension contributions in US stocks. The lowest initial replacement rate under this strategy, about 20 percent, was obtained by the worker retiring in 1921; the highest replacement rate, slightly over 100 percent, was obtained by the worker retiring in 1966. Since both workers have identical expected life spans and career earnings patterns, the astonishing difference in their replacement rates is due solely to differences in stock market returns and in the interest rate

Table 4.1 Stock accumulation and initial replacement rates of male workers retiring after forty-year careers, 1911–99

	Nest egg/ Pay ratio	Initial replacement rate (% of career high earnings) Single life annuity	Joint survivor annuity
Average	6.08	52.2	40.6
Minimum	2.18	18.2	14.0
1st quartile	4.19	35.1	26.2
Median	5.09	47.4	35.9
3rd quartile	7.58	63.8	49.8
Maximum	12.17	100.2	78.1
Standard deviation	2.63	22.2	17.5

Note: Pension contributions are invested entirely in US stocks.

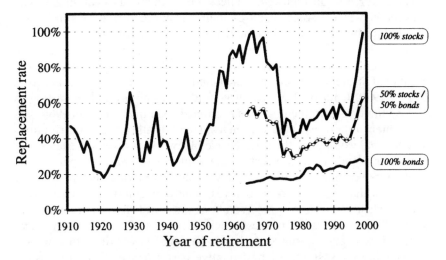

Figure 4.3 Male single-life annuity as a percent of career high annual earnings (measured at age 62)

Note: "Replacement rate" is the worker's initial annuity divided by his average real annual earnings when he was 54–58 years old.

used by the insurance company to determine annuity charges. The time series pattern of replacement rates is generally similar to the time series pattern of nest egg ratios. This suggests that stock market variability has historically been more important than interest rate variability in causing ups and downs in the real value of initial pensions for workers who invest their pension savings in equities.

The second column in Table 4.1 shows statistics describing the distribution of initial replacement rates for workers who invest their pension contributions in stocks. The mean and median initial replacement rates are 52 percent and 47 percent, respectively; the standard deviation is 22 percent. Similar calculations can be performed to determine the replacement rate available to a husband-wife couple purchasing a level, joint survivor annuity. The couple is assumed to accumulate the same retirement nest egg as the single male worker who retires in the same year. A married couple purchasing a joint survivor annuity would obtain a lower annual pension payment, however. Because a joint survivor annuity continues until the death of the longer-lived spouse, the insurance company can anticipate making annuity payments for substantially longer than it would if the annuity ended with the death of the male pensioner.[8] The median joint survivor annuity is thus about one-quarter lower than the median single life annuity (36 percent versus 47 percent of the male worker's career high earnings).

The lower lines in Figure 4.3 reflect replacement rates for single male workers who invest some or all of their pension contributions in bonds. The middle line shows replacement rates for men who invest half their contributions in US Treasury bonds; the lower line shows rates for men who invest all their contributions in bonds. Replacement rates under these investment strategies cannot be calculated for the full span of years from 1911 to 1999. Data on US Treasury yields are only available starting in 1924, so the first retirement we can examine is one that occurs in 1964. The replacement rate of workers who invest some or all of their contributions in bonds is always below the rate received by workers investing exclusively in equities. Workers who invest 50 per cent in stocks and 50 per cent in bonds, for example, receive an initial replacement rate that is typically about half that of workers who invest solely in equities. Workers who invest exclusively in bonds receive about one-third the replacement rate obtained by workers who invest solely in stocks, although the relative success of workers who invest in bonds has varied over time. In comparison with stock investors, the best relative performance of bond investors occurred for workers retiring in the early 1980s, when US stock market prices were very depressed. Even in that year, however, the pension based on bond investments was only about half the pension that was produced by investments in US equities.

The estimates in the figure overstate the typical pensions workers would obtain under the economic conditions prevailing between 1871 and 1999. As noted earlier, the calculations assume that stocks and bonds can be bought, sold, and held without any transactions costs. The typical US mutual fund charges customers a little more than 1 per cent of assets under management to handle customers' funds. Even efficient and exceptionally well-managed funds charge 0.20 percent a year for management and selling costs. Over a 40-year career, this charge would seriously erode the real value of the pension accumulation in comparison with the estimates shown in the figure. Also as noted earlier, the calculations also assume that 62-year-old retirees can purchase fair annuities, whereas in practice insurance companies, banks, and mutual fund companies impose a load charge amounting to about 10 percent–15 percent of the capital converted when the person buys an annuity.

Some of the variation in replacement rates in Figure 4.3 arises because of fluctuations in the long-term interest rate, which determines the sale price of annuities when workers convert their pension savings into an annuity. The nominal interest rate has varied widely over the twentieth century. Figure 4.2 shows the nominal rate on long-term riskless bonds between 1910 and 1999. From 1910 through the mid-1960s, the nominal long-term rate ranged between 2 percent and 4 percent, and it moved sluggishly. After 1965 the rate soared, permitting insurance companies to sell annuities at a substantially lower price. With the same retirement nest egg, a worker retiring after 1965 could purchase a larger annual annuity than a worker retiring before that year. The nest egg/pay ratio accumulated by a stock-investing worker who retired in 1982 was about the same as that accumulated by workers during the worst years of the Great Depression. Yet the replacement rate of the 1982 retiree was about two-thirds larger (45 percent versus 27 percent). The reason for the difference is straightforward. The nominal interest rate was almost 13 percent in the early 1980s but just $3\frac{1}{2}$ percent in the early 1930s. An insurance company selling annuities in 1982 could expect to receive far more interest income on its investments than a company selling annuities in 1932. The difference in the company's expected interest earnings is reflected in the sales price of annuities. Annuities are cheaper to buy when interest rates are high.

3.3 Internal rate of return

Another way to summarize a worker's success in saving for retirement is to calculate the real internal rate of return on his contributions. Figure 4.4 shows the time series pattern of internal rates of return for workers retiring between 1911 and 1999 under the three investment strategies. The average real return on contributions in a plan that is exclusively invested in US equities is 6.3 percent, measured at the point a worker's retirement nest egg is converted into an annuity (see column 1 in Table 4.2). Real stock market returns have been somewhat higher in recent years. If we exclude careers that began before 1924 (in other words, if we ignore retirements that occurred before 1964), the average real return on contributions is 6.7 percent.

Table 4.2 displays statistics on the distribution of internal rates of return when pension contributions are invested solely in equities. The first

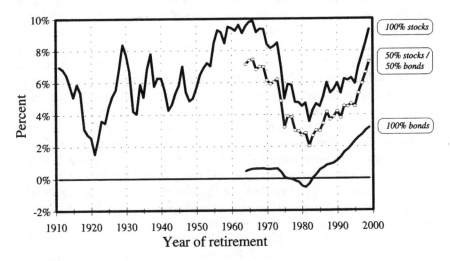

Figure 4.4 Real internal rate of return measured at age 62, 1911–99

Table 4.2 Internal rates of return on pension contributions of male workers retiring after forty-year careers, 1911–99

| | Real internal rate of return on contributions (%) | |
	Measured at age 62	Measured at end of life[a]
Average	6.30	5.10
Minimum	1.54	2.20
1st quartile	5.02	3.78
Median	5.96	5.19
3rd quartile	7.76	6.27
Maximum	9.87	7.89
Standard deviation	1.95	1.46

a The assumed inflation rate after 1998 is $2\frac{1}{2}$ percent a year.

Note: Pension contributions are invested entirely in US stocks.

column in the table shows the distribution of returns when the internal rate of return is calculated at age 62, in the month the worker's pension accumulation is converted to an annuity. The mean and median returns are 6.3 percent and 6.0 percent respectively, but the range of returns is surprisingly wide. The lowest return, attained by a worker retiring after the stock market collapse following World War I, was just 1.5 percent, more than $4\frac{1}{2}$ points below the long-term historical average. The highest return, almost 10 percent, was achieved by workers retiring in the mid-1960s. These workers had the happy experience of accumulating stocks during lengthy periods when stock market prices were depressed and converting their nest eggs into annuities when stock prices were exceptionally high. Workers retiring in the late 1990s enjoyed similar good fortune.

The fluctuations in realized returns, even over short periods, are often startling. Between 1921 and 1929 the internal rate of return on contributions rose from 1.5 percent to 8.4 percent, and the real return then plunged to 4.1 percent in 1933. The return fell from 8.5 percent in 1973 to 5.0 percent in 1975 and to 3.6 percent in 1982 before recovering to 9.3 percent in 1999. While it is certainly true that common stocks offer exceptionally good returns compared with alternative investments, it is also the case that no worker can be confident of achieving the historical average return over an investment career spanning 40 years. Figure 4.4 shows realized returns for 89 workers who invested their pension contributions exclusively in stocks. Among these workers, 57 percent achieved a real return that was below the historical average return, and more than 10 percent achieved a return that was less than two-thirds of the historical average. Workers with the worst investment experiences obtained returns no better than those obtainable in mature pay-as-you-go pension systems.

The two lower lines in Figure 4.4 show that workers who include US government bonds in their portfolios manage to reduce the variability of their returns, but they obtain returns significantly below those of workers who place all their contributions in US equities. For workers retiring between 1964 and 1999, those who invested exclusively in bonds achieved a real return of just 0.9 percent compared with the 6.4 percent average return obtained by workers who invested solely in stocks.

Figure 4.5 shows the tradeoff between expected real return and investment risk as workers vary the percentage of their pension contributions placed in stocks. The estimates are based on potential rates of return enjoyed by workers retiring between 1964 and 1999, which in turn are determined by stock and bond returns between 1924 and 1999. The expected real internal rate of return is measured on the vertical axis, and the standard deviation of returns is measured on the horizontal axis. Workers who invest exclusively in stocks can anticipate higher returns, but they must accept considerably more variability in outcomes. Workers who invest exclusively in bonds achieve very low average returns, but see comparatively little variability around those returns. The estimates imply that a portfolio consisting only of bonds throughout a worker's career can never be optimal. By investing a small fraction of his annual contributions in equities, the worker can increase his expected annual return by up to 0.5 percent without accepting any additional risk. A lifetime portfolio consisting exclusively of bonds has somewhat greater risk than a portfolio that also includes a small share of equities.

4.3.4 Inflation after retirement

The discussion so far has emphasized risks associated with stock and bond market fluctuations over the period workers contribute to a pension fund and at the point they convert pension accumulations to annuities. After

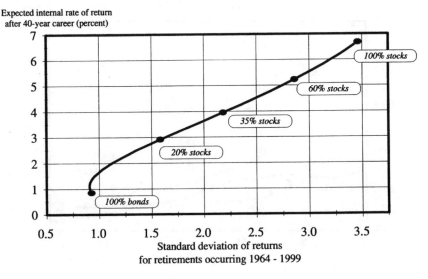

Figure 4.5 Risk-expected return trade off for stock and bond pension investments

workers retire they face another risk – price inflation. Public pensioners in most of the rich countries have been spared this risk as a result of indexing. For example, from 1950 through 1972 the US Congress informally adjusted Social Security benefits every two or three years to keep pensions current with prices. Since 1972, Social Security benefits have been annually adjusted to reflect changes in the consumer price index. Workers who purchase private annuities are rarely protected against inflation.[9] In some countries, the government issues bonds indexed to inflation. The US Treasury recently began issuing inflation-indexed bonds, for example, so it should eventually be possible for private companies to sell indexed annuities. Such annuities are not available in most industrialized countries today, however.

In a world where private markets fail to provide indexed annuities, retired workers face substantial risk from inflation. Figure 4.6 shows the real replacement rate of retired workers as they age. The figure shows replacement rates from age 62 through age 110 for US workers retiring in four selected years – 1921, 1929, 1933, and 1966.[10] As noted earlier, the worker retiring at the beginning of 1921 received the smallest initial pension of any worker considered here; the worker retiring at the beginning of 1966 received the largest initial pension (see Figure 4.3). The experiences of these two workers also differed after they retired. Prices were stable or falling during most of the 1920s and early 1930s. A worker retiring in 1921 therefore saw the purchasing power of his annuity increase over much of his retirement. In contrast, American workers who retired in 1966 saw prices climb without interruption after their retirement. (In years after 1999, I assume inflation is 2.5 percent a year.) The worker retiring in 1966 saw his real replacement rate fall steeply and continuously, shrinking

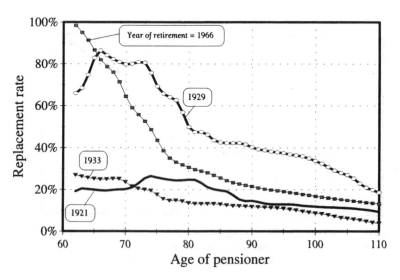

Figure 4.6 Real annuity as percent of career high annual earnings at selected ages

from almost 100 percent at age 62, to 65 percent at age 70, and to 31 percent at age 80. In contrast, the worker retiring in 1921 saw his replacement rate increase from 19 percent to 26 percent between ages 62 and 75.

The experience of the worker retiring in 1966 has been more typical of US experience since World War II. In fact, all workers retiring after the mid-1930s suffered significant losses in purchasing power during retirement. Figure 4.7 displays the time series pattern of real replacement rates at two different ages – 70 and 80. (These calculations are based on the experiences of workers who invest all their pension contributions in equities.) The solid line shows replacement rates at age 70 for workers retiring between 1911 and 1999; the lightly dotted line shows replacement rates at age 80 for workers who retire in the same years. On average, replacement rates fell somewhat more than a fifth (or 11 percentage points) between age 62 and age 70. They shrank by almost half (or 27 percentage points) between ages 62 and 80. The drop in the real purchasing power of pensions has been particularly severe for workers retiring after 1960. For recent retirees, replacement rates fell about 30 percent between ages 62 and 70 and by almost 60 percent between ages 62 and 80. If retired workers depended solely on their pensions to pay for consumption in old age, these losses in purchasing power would cause painful reductions in real spending as pensioners reach advanced old age.

Consumer price increases after retirement, if they are large enough, can substantially erode the real return that workers obtain on their pension contributions. I have calculated the real internal rate of return on worker contributions at age 110, the oldest age at which any pensioners are assumed to survive. This return is calculated for the 89 workers who retire

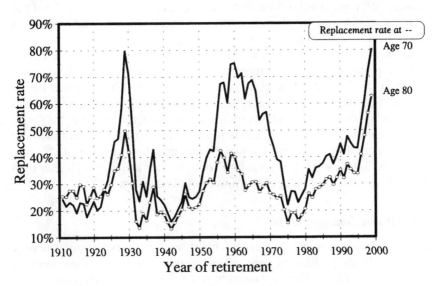

Figure 4.7 Real annuity as percent of career high annual earnings at 70 and 80

in successive years from 1911 through 1999 and who invest all their pension contributions in stocks. The annual real value of contributions to the pension fund is 6 percent of each worker's projected real earnings at every age between 22 and 61. The expected real value of the pension in any year after retirement is simply the worker's initial pension adjusted to reflect price changes that occurred after age 62, multiplied times the probability that the worker will survive to that year. (The probability of survival to age 111 is zero.) The internal real rate of return on the worker's tax contributions is the interest rate that is required so that the discounted value of real contributions before age 62 is exactly equal to the discounted value of real pension payments after age 61.

The second column in Table 4.2 provides a statistical description of the internal rate of return on contributions when that rate is measured at the end of workers' lives. Note that the peak rate of return is two percentage points lower when returns are measured at the end of life rather than at age 62. The average return is about one percentage point lower (compare the first and second columns in Table 4.2). The lower average value of returns when returns are measured at the end of life should not be surprising. When workers convert their pension savings into an annuity, they are essentially trading stock market investments for a long-term bond investment. Their lifetime return represents a weighted average of the return earned when their funds are invested in stocks and when they are invested in bonds. Since bonds have historically offered a lower real return than stocks, the weighted average of stock and bond returns is likely to fall short of the return earned when all funds are invested in common stocks.

This theory is confirmed in the data. In only 15 of the 89 retirement years between 1911 and 1999 did the lifetime return on contributions exceed the return earned by age 62. In the other 74 years the lifetime return was less than the return measured at age 62. The gap was greatest for workers retiring between 1932 and 1979, when a combination of low nominal interest rates and comparatively high (and often unanticipated) inflation produced poor bond returns. In contrast, workers retiring in the early 1980s enjoyed higher lifetime returns on their pension contributions than the returns they had obtained up through age 62. The high nominal interest rate on long-term bonds combined with a steep decline in inflation after 1981 meant that these workers were able to purchase annuities on terms that turned out to be very favorable. For these workers, real bond returns after age 61 were higher than the stock market returns they had enjoyed up through age 62.[11]

4.3.5 *Protections against risk*

As this exercise demonstrates, replacement rates can vary enormously over relatively short periods of time when workers invest all their pension savings in equities. The replacement rate was almost 100 percent for workers retiring in 1969, but just 42 percent for workers retiring only six years later in 1975. Pensions depend crucially on when workers buy stocks and when they convert their investment portfolios into annuities. The real value of a pension also depends critically on the course of inflation between the date an annuity is purchased and the time of death of the annuitant.

Workers can follow a couple strategies to reduce the uncertainty of private pensions. First, they can invest a portion of their retirement savings in bonds rather than stocks, diversifying their investment portfolio. This strategy reduces the volatility of the worker's replacement rate, but it significantly reduces the expected value of the annuity. Over nearly all 10-year periods in this century the real return on US bond investments has been lower than the real return on US equities. If workers invest all their pension savings in government bonds, the calculations in this chapter imply they will obtain lower returns than those available under a pay-as-you-go pension system, at least in the US.

Second, workers can convert their retirement nest eggs into annuities over several years rather than at a single point in time, as assumed in the calculations. For example, workers could convert their nest eggs into annuities in more or less equal annual installments beginning several years before they retire. Under one plan, each worker would purchase five annuities rather than only one. The annuities would differ in size depending on stock market prices and interest rates at the moment of conversion. Since the conversion occurs in five successive years rather than only once, workers would not convert all their retirement savings into an annuity at a time when stock market prices and interest rates make it particularly disadvantageous to do so.

Figure 4.8 shows replacement rates at age 62 under this annuitization

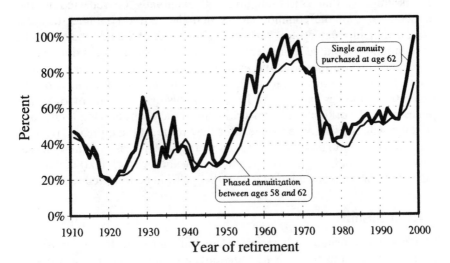

Figure 4.8 Replacement rates under one-time and phased annuitization, 1911–99

Note: "Replacement rate" is the worker's real annuity at age 62 divided by his average real earnings when he was 54–58 years old.

strategy. For purposes of comparison, I also show the replacement rates workers obtain when they convert their retirement savings to an annuity on their sixty-second birthdays. (Both sets of computations assume that 100 percent of pension contributions are invested in stocks.) The strategy of phased annuitization yields a distribution of replacement rates that has less variability, but the strategy also yields a lower average replacement rate. The standard deviation of replacement rates is 22 percent if the entire annuity conversion takes place at age 62, but it falls to 18 percent when annuitization is phased over five years. The average replacement rate also drops 5 percentage points, however, falling from 52 percent to 47 percent when workers adopt the phased annuitization strategy. This decline in average replacement rates is hard to avoid. As noted earlier, when workers purchase an annuity they are exchanging stock market investments for a bond market return. By converting his pension accumulation to an annuity approximately two years earlier than would be the case if a single annuity were purchased at retirement, the worker who follows a phased annuity strategy is exchanging two years of stock returns for two years of bond returns. This reduces both the variance and the expected return of his retirement savings.

To protect themselves against price inflation that occurs after they retire, workers can retain some of their retirement savings as a nest egg that continues to be invested in the stock market. Alternatively, they could purchase variable annuities based on a combined portfolio of stocks and bonds. Common stocks represent an ownership claim on real assets whose nominal value may eventually increase with the general price level. Under the assumption that price inflation will eventually be reflected in the nominal value of the common stocks that the retiree continues to hold, stock ownership may protect retirees against some of the adverse effects of price inflation. Holding retirement savings in the form of stocks during part of retirement also increases the expected return on the worker's savings. As we have seen, however, it substantially increases the investment risk to which the worker is exposed. In light of the historical variability of equity prices, retired workers will be uncertain how much consumption their stock holdings will buy five or ten years after they retire. If the ultimate goal of a mandatory pension system is to assure workers of at least a minimum real income during old age, a variable annuity backed by stock market assets is unlikely to provide any guarantee that the goal will be achieved.

4.4 Conclusions

The argument usually advanced for moving away from pay-as-you-go retirement pensions to a private individual account system is that workers could make smaller contributions and obtain higher benefits under the private system. Most workers would get a better deal under the private system than they can obtain under public retirement systems.

The argument has two problems. First, the contribution rates to existing public systems and to a new individual account are not comparable. Contributions to public programs include a large implicit tax to pay for the unfunded liabilities that were accumulated in the past. Virtually all of this tax will have to be paid, regardless of whether the present public system is maintained or is replaced with a new system of private accounts. To make a meaningful comparison between the contribution rates to public and individual-account systems, it is necessary to either subtract this implicit tax from the social security contribution rate or add it to the rate needed to fund the new private accounts.[12]

Second, a defined-contribution system allocates risks in a very different way from a collective, defined-benefit system. Under most public systems, workers born in the same year who have similar earnings records are provided similar retirement benefits. Pensions are financed with taxes imposed on current workers and their employers, and they are ultimately backed by voters' willingness to tax themselves in order to keep benefits flowing. They are usually indexed to price changes. In the rich democracies, real benefit cuts typically occur gradually and only after intense political debate.

In contrast, pensions under a private, individual account system are paid out of financial market assets held in individual retirement accounts. The real value of the payment flows is limited by the current market value of assets held in the accounts. Although proponents of individual accounts are confident that workers can purchase safe assets that will yield high rates of return, US experience over the past century suggests that neither the value of financial assets nor their real return is assured. Workers who follow an identical investment strategy but who retire a few years apart can receive pensions that are startlingly unequal. The investment strategy that produces the highest expected return and biggest pension is also the one that yields the widest swings in pension entitlement. The investment strategy that offers the most predictable pension yields an expected rate of return that in the US is lower than the return available in a pay-as-you-go retirement system. In addition, the real value of private pensions is subject to sizable inflation risk after workers retire.

Even though American workers on average can obtain good pensions under an individual account system, there is wide variability in outcomes. Assuming workers deposit 6 percent of their annual pay into a retirement account that is invested in common stocks, historical experience suggests their initial pensions can range from less than 20 percent of their peak career earnings to more than 100 percent of peak earnings. Averaged over their full retirements and taking account of the effects of inflation, workers' real pensions ranged between 15 percent and 70 percent of peak career earnings.

While all workers would welcome the opportunity to earn better returns on their contributions to the retirement system, defined-contribution accounts would expose workers to a substantial hazard that their pensions would be too small to finance a comfortable retirement. The most often cited benefit of private retirement systems is that they can provide better returns to covered workers. If public systems were reformed to include advance funding and prudent investment of reserves, they could provide the same expected return to workers with far less financial market risk. An interesting question is whether such a reform is feasible or politically sustainable.

4.5 Notes

1 This chapter was prepared for the internatinal conference on 'Social Security Reform in Advanced Countries,' University of Tokyo, Japan, September 6–7, 1999. Partial research support for this chapter was received under a grant from the US Social Security Administration to the Retirement Research Consortium at Boston College. The views are soleley those of the author and should not be ascribed to the Social Security Administration, the Retirement Research Consortium, or the Brookings Institution.

2 Of course, workers who wish to save more for retirement than the amount they save in the public system can choose to invest their private funds in a way that offsets the portfolio choices of the system. However, empirical studies of saving behavior suggest that for a large percentage of workers, the overwhelming share of household saving takes the form of a home purchase and contributions to the public pension system. Many worker households have few assets aside from their home and pensions and thus cannot offset the portfolio choices of the public pension program.

3 Stock market data are based on the Standard and Poor Composite Stock Price Index dating back to 1871. These stock data and some of the price and interest rate data are taken from Chapter 26 ("Data Appendix") of Shiller (1989), with most series updated through 1999. See http://www.econ.yale.edu/~shiller/chapt26.html. Estimates of the long-term government bond rate are published by the Federal Reserve Bank of St. Louis for years back through 1924. For the period from 1906 through 1923 I formed an estimate of the riskless long-term bond rate using Macaulay's estimates of the yield on high quality railroad bonds. Since even high quality private bonds are subject to default risk, I predicted the riskless (Treasury-equivalent) yield for 1906–23 by estimating the yield premium of railroad bonds over government bonds for the period 1924–36, when observations of both railroad bond rates and long-term Treasury bond rates are available. See http://www.stls.frb.org/fred/data/irates.html.

4 Estimates of annual earnings by age and gender can be found in US Census Bureau (1996).

5 The assumed rate of economy-wide wage growth has important effects on some of the calculations. With a slower assumed rate of growth, pension contributions and investment returns early in a worker's career become relatively more important in determining his pension, because earnings when the worker is young represent a larger percentage of the worker's lifetime wages. At the same time, with slower wage growth it is easier to attain a high pension replacement rate, where the replacement rate is defined as the real value of the pension divided by the worker's real average wages near the age of his retirement.

6 When a bond-investing worker reaches age 53 and is less than 10 years from retirement, he is assumed to invest in short-maturity rather than long-maturity bonds to avoid the risk of accepting capital losses when he converts his bonds

to an annuity at retirement. From age 53 through 61 his new retirement contributions as well as the interest earnings on the long-maturity bonds already in his portfolio are used to buy bonds which have a yield equal to the one-year US Treasury bond rate. Under this investment strategy, all bond holdings are redeemed at par when the worker retires.

7 The Social Security Actuary's mortality projections are reported in Mitchell, Poterba, and Warshawsky (1997). These were supplemented with estimates of actual mortality rates in US Census Bureau (1998), Table 130.

8 To calculate the fair annuity premium, I assume that both spouses are the same age. The wife's mortality experience is assumed to follow the Social Security Actuary's projections for a woman who attains age 65 in 1995. I assume the mortality experiences of husbands and wives are independent.

9 Some American insurance companies offer "graded annuities" that increase over time. This kind of pension does not offer retired workers complete protection against inflation, however, because the annual percentage increase in the annuity is not directly linked to changes in the price level. If a worker buys a graded pension that rises 3 percent a year, the real value of the pension would still decline in each year that annual inflation exceeds 3 percent.

10 The replacement rates are calculated for workers who invest all their pension contributions in equities. The initial replacement rates shown in Figure 4.6 differ slightly from those in Figure 4.3. The latter are calculated using the price level in the January when the worker attains age 62. The replacement rates in Figure 4.6 take account of changes in the price level that occur over the full calendar year when the worker is first retired. This change in price level is relevant unless the worker receives and spends all his annuity income in January.

11 The estimates of internal rates of return at the end of a worker's life depend for some workers on my predictions of inflation in 1999 and later years. If inflation turns out to be higher or lower than $2\frac{1}{2}$ percent a year, which seems quite likely, the estimated internal rate of return will be incorrect. The inflation prediction error obviously has little effect on estimates pertaining to retirements that occur before 1980, but it could have a big impact on estimates for retirements in the 1990s. The possibility of this kind of error does not affect any of my estimates of rates of return or replacement rates measured at age 62.

12 In the United States, approximately 90 percent of current Social Security contributions are used immediately to pay for benefits to retired pensioners and their dependents. The contributions needed to finance these benefits must be collected whether the public retirement system is maintained or is replaced by a new system of individual accounts. It is thus incorrect to treat as equivalent the contribution rate to Social Security and to an individual retirement account. See Geanokoplos, Mitchell, and Zeldes (1998).

4.6 References

Aaron, Henry J. (1966) "The social insurance paradox," *Canadian Journal of Economics* Vol. 32: 371–4.

Bosworth, Barry P., and Burtless, Gary (1998) "Population aging and economic performance," in Barry P. Bosworth and Gary Burtless (eds) *Aging Societies: The Global Dimension* Washington, DC: The Brookings Institution.

Diamond, Peter (1997) "Macroeconomic aspects of social security reform," *Brookings Papers on Economic Activity* 2.

—— (ed.) (1999) *Issues in Privatizing Social Security: Report of an Expert Panel of the National Academy of Social Insurance*, Cambridge, MA: MIT Press.

Geanakopolos, John, Mitchell, Olivia, and Zeldes, Stephen P. (1998) "Would a privatized social security system really pay a higher rate of return?" in R.D. Arnold, M.J. Graetz, and A.H. Munnell (eds) *Framing the Social Security Debate: Values, Politics, and Economics*, Washington, DC: National Academy of Social Insurance.

Gruber, Jonathan, and Wise, David A. (eds) (1999) "Introduction," *Social Security and Retirement Around the World*, Chicago: University of Chicago Press.

Mitchell, Olivia S., Poterba, James M., and Warshawsky, Mark J. (1997) "New evidence on the money's worth of individual annuities," *NBER Working Paper* No. 6002, Cambridge, MA: National Bureau of Economic Research.

Samuelson, Paul A. (1958) "An exact consumption-loan model of interest with or without the social contrivance of money," *Journal of Political Economy* Vol. 66(6): 467–82

Shiller, Robert J. (1989) *Market Volatility*, Cambridge, MA: MIT Press.

US Census Bureau (1996), *Money Income in the United States: 1995*, Series P60–193 Washington, DC: US Government Printing Office.

—— (1998) *Statistical Abstract of the United States 1998* Washington, DC: US Government Printing Office.

World Bank (1994) *Averting the Old Age Crisis* Oxford and New York: Oxford University Press.

5 Private mandatory retirement provision

Design and implementation challenges[1]

Hazel Bateman, Suzanne Doyle and John Piggott

5.1. Introduction

In 1992, Australia introduced the Superannuation Guarantee, the first private mandatory retirement saving policy in the English-speaking world. At that time, the only country to have adopted a policy of this type was Chile, in 1981.[2] Private mandatory policies require either employers and/or employees to invest some fraction of the employee's wages with a private sector organization, with the aim of eventually helping to finance the employee's retirement. Typically, these worker accumulations are defined contribution (DC), fully funded, and kept in individual accounts.

In the eight years since 1992, more than a dozen countries, mostly from Latin America and the transition economies of Central Europe, have either adopted mandated private retirement provision or have stated their intention to reform their pension policies along these lines.[3] Further, a number of developed countries have either reformed their pension systems in this direction (for example, the UK) or have debated doing so (the US). Rarely has a novel policy design spread so swiftly across disparate nations.

Private mandatory retirement provision stands in sharp contrast to public provision, which is typically defined benefit (DB) and unfunded. Two differences are immediately apparent. First, while public provision permits centralized administration, competitive private service providers do not enjoy these benefits of scale. Special attention must therefore be paid to administrative cost, and by implication administration (and investment) charges that will adversely affect the net rate of return on accumulations. Second, public provision covers both accumulation and payout phases of retirement provision, with the central authority playing the role of plan sponsor. With private mandated policies, no plan sponsor exists. All that is defined is the contribution, and regulations and employer obligations associated with the accumulation phase typically expire at retirement. Payout regulations must therefore be separately stipulated. However, very few countries that have adopted private mandatory retirement saving have actually stipulated payout regulation. Often retirees are left to make the best use of their saving via retirement products and alternative investments offered by the private market. Those left to participate in the private market for retirement products are more likely to face substantial 'transaction' costs due to issues such as adverse selection, thereby leading to lower retirement incomes.

In this chapter, we address these two questions – administrative charges and, payout design and market structure – in some detail. We draw on Australian and Chilean experience, but our analysis is designed to be relevant to a generic economy in which private mandatory retirement provision is being implemented or considered.

It is useful to begin by illustrating the importance of these design issues with a simple numerical example. In Table 5.1, we take the hypothetical case of a male who works for 35 years, saving 9 per cent of his earnings in a defined contribution pension plan. Real wage growth is assumed to be 1 per cent per annum, and the real rate of return is set at 5 per cent.

Illustrative results clearly indicate how administrative charges can combine with annuity market failure to dramatically reduce replacement rates. With administrative charges of 0.5 per cent of assets and actuarially fair annuity availability, the replacement rate, defined as first year annuity income divided by final year salary, is about 60 per cent. This is close to the range of two thirds to three quarters widely accepted as satisfactory by retirement planners. If the annuity is bought in the private market for individual annuities, however, replacement falls to 51 per cent. And if administrative charges rise to 2 per cent of assets, replacement is 38.3 per cent, well below the level generally considered to be satisfactory.[4]

This illustration suggests that administrative charges and the payout phase of retirement saving will be critical areas of policy design within the mandatory private paradigm, and this is borne out by Australian and inter-

Table 5.1 Illustrative replacement rates under alternative annuity and administrative charge assumptions[a]

| | Administrative charge[b] (percentage of assets under management) | | | |
	0.50%	1.0%	1.5%	2.0%
Voluntary market annuity	51.0%	46.3%	42.1%	38.3%
Actuarially fair annuity	59.9%	54.4%	49.5%	45.1%

a The analysis assumes a male working for 35 years, starting on A$40,000 pa with 1 per cent real wage growth, 9 per cent of earnings paid as pension contributions, a real rate of return of 5 per cent, and retiring at age 65. Voluntary annuity payments are based on Australian offers for a single non-graduated life annuity for a male aged 65 at June 1999: the median payout for a A$100,000 annuity was A$8,550 (Rice Kachor 1999a, Table F, page 28). In line with the literature and our own calculations, we assume a loading of 15 per cent on actuarially fair annuities. The replacement rate reported is the ratio of the first year annuity payout to the final year salary.
b The asset charge applies in the accumulation phase only.

national experience. It is these questions which have proved the most controversial in the policy debate, and which have been the most challenging in terms of policy design.

We first analyse the question of administrative charges, and then turn to the annuity market.

5.2 Analysing administrative costs and charges

Under private mandatory retirement provision net rates of return are crucial to the adequacy of retirement incomes and it is essential that they are not compromised by high administrative charges. As well, high administrative charges could reduce the credibility of reforms towards mandatory private retirement saving.

The economic analysis of administrative costs and charges for retirement provision is undeveloped.[5] While there is broad agreement that there are economies of scale in account administration and asset management, we have little understanding of the impact of policy design, institutional practices and regulatory requirements – such as the governance of the retirement saving organisation, employer (as opposed to employee) choice of retirement saving organisation or specific charge regulations – on administrative costs and charges. In Australia, data and analysis focus separately on account administration and/or investment charges for, a single year,[6] while it is the combined impact of these over a lifetime of retirement saving which is more relevant. The international debate is preoccupied with the privatisation of US social security.[7]

In this section we present a preliminary investigation of administrative costs and charges.[8] We consider both the quantum and type of administrative costs and charges, the economic impacts of alternative charging regimes and the role of policy design and institutional features. Due to the additional complexity associated with the pricing of private retirement income streams, we consider costs and charges in the accumulation phase only. However, in doing so, we attempt to take account of all costs and charges – including account administration, communications, investment and marketing.

Next we provide a formal analysis of charge regimes and outline the economic implications of alternatives. This is followed by a discussion of the nature of administrative costs and alternative charge regimes, and a review of the Australian and Chilean experience. Finally we identify issues for consideration in policy design.

5.2.1 A formal analysis of administrative charges

Administrative charges, like taxes, can be imposed on contributions, assets under management and/or benefits.[9] The charges may be flat rate or variable. For the moment we consider variable (percentage) charges imposed on contributions, assets, and benefits.[10]

Consider mandatory private retirement saving by an individual over a period of T years. A contribution C is made at the beginning of each year, which earns a real rate of return of $r\%$ per annum. Assuming a percentage charge on gross-of-charge contributions of βC, and a discount rate which is assumed to be equal to the real rate of return r, the present value of the administrative charges over the T years of retirement saving, PVC_C, is given by

$$PVC_c = \sum_{t=1}^{T} \frac{\beta cCt}{(1+r)^t} \tag{1}$$

Similarly, if instead we assume a percentage charge on assets under management of βA, the present value of administrative charges, PVC_A, is given by

$$PVC_A = \sum_{t=1}^{T} \beta A \left[\sum_{t=1}^{T} \frac{C_x(1+r)^{x-t}(1-\beta A)^{x-t}}{(1+r)^t} \right] \tag{2}$$

Finally, if we assume a percentage charge on benefits (the retirement accumulation) of βB, the present value of the administrative charges, PVC_B, is given by

$$PVC_B = \beta B \sum_{t=1}^{T} \frac{C_t(1+r)^{T-t}}{(1+r)^T} \tag{3}$$

A number of results follow. Firstly, if we set $PVC_A = PVC_B$

$$\sum_{t=1}^{T} \frac{\beta CC_t}{(1+r)^t} = \beta \sum_{B t=1}^{T} \frac{C_t(1+r)^{T-t}}{(1+r)^T} \tag{4}$$

and rearrange, we find that equation 4 reduces to $\beta C = \beta B$. This result implies that for a given present value of charges (and in the absence of taxes, or other withdrawals such as insurance premiums) a percentage charge on contributions of βC is equivalent to a percentage charge on benefits equal to βB and will lead to a decline in the retirement accumulation of βC per cent.[11]

Further, if we set $PVC_C = PVC_A$ and rearrange, we can specify a relationship between βC and βA (and consequently βB and βA) as follows:

$$\beta C = \beta A \left\{ \sum_{t=1}^{T} \left[\sum_{x=1}^{t} \frac{C_x(1+r)^{x-t}(1-\beta A^{x-t})}{(1+r)^t} \right] \middle/ \sum_{t=1}^{T} \frac{C_t}{(1+r)^t} \right\} \tag{5}$$

The relationship between βC and βA thus depends on the accumulation period T and the real rate of return r.

These results can be clarified with numerical simulations. Using the above methodology we can derive values of βC, βA and βB which give the same present value of administrative charges, or equivalently the same retirement accumulation, for a given accumulation period (T).

Table 5.2 illustrates the impact of alternative charge regimes of varying magnitudes over a working life of mandatory private retirement saving. Contribution periods of 20 and 40 years are considered. We make the simplifying assumption that charge regimes and amounts are maintained over the entire working life.

The essential message is that the impact of administrative charges on retirement accumulations varies by charge type, length of accumulation period, and rate of return. For 40 years of contributions (and an annual real rate of return of 5 per cent), a 2 per cent per annum charge on assets would reduce the retirement accumulation by 38.7 per cent. This is equivalent to a 38.7 per cent charge on contributions (or a 38.7 per cent charge on benefits).

The simulations also illustrate the differential impacts of front loaded (contribution) charges and back loaded (asset) charges. Consider a given asset charge of 2 per cent per annum. As the contribution period increases from 20 to 40 years, the consequent decline in the retirement accumulation rises from 20.7 per cent to 38.7 per cent. In other words, asset charges at a given rate have a greater impact, the longer the contributory period. However, a 10 per cent contribution charge would reduce the retirement

Table 5.2 Reduction in retirement accumulations due to administrative charges[a]

	Charge as proportion of assets under management (%)	Equivalent[b] contribution or benefit charge (%)	Decline in retirement accumulation (%)
20 years of contributions	0.5	5.7	5.7
	1.0	11.0	11.0
	2.0	20.7	20.7
	3.0	29.1	29.1
40 years of contributions	0.5	11.8	11.8
	1.0	22.1	22.1
	2.0	38.7	38.7
	3.0	51.2	51.2

a The analysis assumes a male on average weekly earnings who contributes 9 per cent of wages to a defined contribution superannuation/pension fund. Real wages are assumed to grow by 1 per cent per annum, the real rate of return is equal to 5 per cent per annum, taxes on contributions or fund earnings and insurance premiums are ignored and administrative charges are deducted from account balances.

b The present value of administrative charges is equivalent for each charge regime.

accumulation by 10 per cent – irrespective of the length of the contribution period.

While the three illustrative regimes considered here would yield the same aggregate charge in present value terms, they have different time profiles[12] and therefore different behavioural impacts. In any given year the different regimes would have a differential impact on account balances (where mandatory contributions are set gross of charges) and consumption patterns (where mandatory contributions are set net of charges). For 40 years of retirement saving, a 1 per cent asset charge is equivalent to a 22 per cent contributions charge. This contribution charge, equal to one fifth of each contribution, would have a much greater impact on the account balance in the early years (when assets are small) than a 1 per cent asset charge (and vice versa). Consequently, those with a short contribution period would be disadvantaged by contribution charges – while asset charges would have a greater impact the longer the contribution period (and therefore, the larger the asset base).[13] As result, contribution charges may deter labour force participation, while asset charges may bring forward the retirement decision.[14]

5.2.2 *Identifying administrative costs and charges*

Administrative costs fall into two main categories – account administration and funds management. The costs relate to the three main functions involved in the facilitation of private mandatory retirement saving – the collection of contributions and the administration of the individual accounts; the investment of assets; and the payment of benefits.[15] Within each of these there may be marketing costs. The importance of each will reflect policy design as well as institutional practices, regulatory requirements and industry structure.

Contributions may be collected directly from fund members, or through intermediaries such as employers, clearing houses, or government agencies. Account administration involves the setting up and ongoing administration of individual accounts. This includes creating accounts, updating balances, managing records, organising withdrawals and transfers, deducting administration charges, insurance premiums and taxes, as well as communicating with fund members, complying with government requirements (for example audits or actuarial assessments) and reporting to relevant government agencies. These costs will depend in part on scale economies and regulatory and compliance complexity.

Account administration marketing costs will arise where there is choice of retirement saving organisation and where the retirement saving organisation contracts out to specialist service providers. The amount of the marketing costs will depend on the target audience – individual employees, employers or trustees. Marketing costs could be minimised through limited choice or group choice, but this raises principal-agent issues.

The investment function involves the management of members' assets. Assets may be directly invested or placed in (active or passive) managed funds. As well, members may be offered some choice of investment strategy. Investment marketing costs will arise to the extent that investment managers seek the business of trustees and will be exacerbated where individuals are offered investment choice.

Finally, costs arise with the payment of benefits. For defined contributions arrangements a point of separation arises between the accumulation (retirement saving) phase and the payouts phase. Administrative charges will differ by the form of benefit allowed (and taken) and the organisation used to deliver these benefits. As noted earlier, this chapter does not consider administrative costs in the benefits phase.

The costs may be recouped by a variety of charge regimes – which, in the short run, need not mirror actual costs.

International practice varies. In Australia and Chile, the contributions are made directly to the superannuation or pension funds (known as AFPs in Chile).[16] In Australia, employers are required to choose a superannuation fund, while in Chile contributions are made to AFPs chosen by employees. In Australia specialist superannuation fund administrators are widely used, while in Chile these functions are generally performed in house. One of the proposals for privatisation of US social security involves the government undertaking the collection and administration functions (Diamond 1999b), while in the Mexican and Swedish arrangements a centralised agency collects and then distributes contributions to the pension funds (Mexico) or investment managers (Sweden).

Turning to investment charges. In Australia, many superannuation funds delegate asset management to external investment managers. Actual practice varies, and includes the use of pooled superannuation trusts, single or several specialist managers and additional specialists such as asset overlay consultants. Individual investment choice is not mandatory, but is widely offered. Chilean AFPs funds were initially not allowed to hire specialist managers, but this restriction has now been removed. However, Chilean AFPs do not offer investment choice.

In Australia, with the exception of 'member protection' of small amount accounts,[17] administrative charges are determined freely and are generally a combination of flat rate charges per account (and/or percentage contribution charges) and charges calculated as a percentage of assets under management. In Chile, however, only two charge regimes are allowed – charges on contributions (which may be flat rate and/or variable) and transfers. Asset management charges are banned.

Charge restrictions are increasingly used. When Bolivia introduced private mandatory retirement saving in 1997, the asset management rights were auctioned off to two investment companies, which were chosen partly on their ability to minimise fees. The UK government proposes to introduce a personal pension product, for which charges will be capped at

100 basis points (Murthi *et al.* 1999) and, under the new individual accounts system in Sweden, investment managers are required to negotiate their fees with a centralised administration agency.

In the remainder of this section we consider in detail administrative costs and charges in Australia and Chile – as the two countries with the most developed private mandatory retirement saving arrangements.

5.2.3 Alternative institutional arrangements: impact on charges

5.2.3.1 Estimating administrative charges in Australia

In Australia, the administrative charges associated with private mandatory retirement saving (the Superannuation Guarantee) are generally a combination of account administration charges (which may be flat rate or calculated as a percentage of contributions) and asset management charges calculated as a percentage of asset under management.[18] The administration charges are deducted from account balances and the asset management charges from asset returns.[19]

While there are five broad types of superannuation fund in Australia – corporate, public, industry, retail and self-managed-industry funds and master trusts (a form of retail fund) are the most common destinations of the mandatory contributions. The current charging schedules for representative industry funds and master trusts are summarised in Table 5.3.[20]

Table 5.3 Current charging schedule for illustrative superannuation funds[a]

Average industry fund[b]	*Representative master trust*[c]
Administration charge of A$47.84 per annum	Administration charge of up to 4.5% of each contribution
+	+
Investment management charge of 0.3 – 0.7% of assets	Member charge of A$42.36 to A$70.80 per annum
	+
	Asset administration charge of 0.8% assets (less rebates for large plans)
	+
	Investment management charge of 0.4–1.08% assets

a Data from Rice Kachor (1999b), Superfunds (various issues) and Super Review (various issues).
b Based on industry fund averages in 1998.
c Based on charges for a representative master trust in 1998.

5.3.2.2 Cost comparisons – industry funds and master trusts

As presented, the charges identified in Table 5.3 tell us little about relative administrative charges. However, if we assume that these charges apply over the working life of mandatory private retirement saving, we can use the formal analysis developed earlier to convert the disparate charging schedules to the three alternative metrics. The results are summarised in Tables 5.4 and 5.5, and show that under reasonable assumptions, over a

Table 5.4 Industry funds – charges under alternative assumptions[a]

Investment charges (% assets)	Decline in retirement accumulation (%)	Equivalent contribution charge (%)	Equivalent assets charge (%)
0.3	8.1	6.8	0.37
0.4	10.2	8.5	0.47
0.5	12.2	10.2	0.57
0.6	14.2	11.8	0.67
0.7	16.1	13.4	0.77

a Simulation assumptions – see Table 5. 2. We assume the average industry fund annual administration charge of A$47.84. Australian superannuation taxes are included in these simulations. We assume a contributions tax of 15 per cent, an effective earnings tax of 8 per cent and an annual charge for insurance premiums of A$67.60. Note that with the introduction of taxes and insurance premiums, the equivalence between, βC and βB no longer holds.

Table 5.5 Representative master trust – charges under alternative assumptions[a,b]

	Decline in retirement accumulation (%)	Equivalent contribution charge (%)	Equivalent assets charge (%)
Small – medium plans (assets < A$2 bill)			
< 100 members	33.4	27.7	1.81
> 1500 members	32.7	27.2	1.76
Large plans (assets A$2–5 bill)			
< 100 members	26.4	22.0	1.35
> 1500 members	25.7	21.4	1.30
Very large plans (assets > A$5 bill)			
< 100 members	20.4	7.0	1.01
> 1500 members	19.6	16.4	0.96

a Simulation assumptions – as for Table 5.4.
b Charges are also lower where contributions are electronically transferred. For the very large plans with more than 1500 members, this translates to a reduction in the final benefit of 19.5 per cent rather than 19.6 per cent, an equivalent contribution charge of 16.2 per cent and an equivalent assets charge of 0.95 per cent.

working life of mandatory retirement saving, master trusts are a more costly vehicle.

The analysis of industry funds in Table 5.4 shows that, over a lifetime of retirement saving (and assuming the current structure of charges is maintained), and for the representative range of investment charges (0.3–0.7 per cent of assets), the reduction of retirement accumulations range from 8.1 per cent to 16.1 per cent. Similarly, the equivalent contribution charges range from 6.8 per cent to 13.4 per cent of contributions and the equivalent assets charges range from 0.37 per cent to 0.77 per cent of assets under management.

The analysis of master trusts in Table 5.5 shows that lifetime administrative charges differ markedly by plan size. For the small to medium size plans, the lifetime impact of the current charge regime is to reduce the retirement accumulation by one third (or twice the impact of the upper range of the average industry fund). However, this impact reduces the larger the plan (in terms of both members and assets). For large plans, the lifetime impact is a reduction in the retirement accumulation of about one quarter. However, for very large plans the impact would be a reduction in the retirement accumulation of around one fifth. Under current assumptions this would be analogous to an industry fund with industry average account management charges and investment charges of 0.9 per cent.

The analysis raises a number of issues. First, how can we account for this difference in charges? Second, can this difference be sustained? And third, what do these results imply for policy design? To answer the first question one needs to consider some fundamental differences between industry funds and master trusts while the answer to the second will depend upon the evolution of retirement policy and industry practice. The third question can be answered more constructively following consideration of the administrative charges of Chilean AFPs.

5.2.3.3 Why are the lifetime charges so different?

In the absence of empirical analysis, we speculate that the large differential in the lifetime charges of Australian industry funds and master trusts can be explained by a combination of differences in governance, historical ethos, institutional practices and industry structure. The relevant differences between Australian industry funds and master trusts are summarised in Table 5.6, which also sets out the features of Chilean AFPs.

A particular difference relates to fund governance. In the current context governance refers to both the form and philosophy of the retirement saving organisation. Industry superannuation funds were set up with the sole objective of providing low cost superannuation to workers covered by industrial awards. The funds were (and many still are) governed by boards of trustees comprising equal representatives of participating members and employers who are sympathetic to low cost mandatory

Table 5.6 Retirement saving organisations in Australia and Chile

	Industry funds	Master trusts	AFPs
Characterisation Historical	Industry superannuation fund Industrial relations, associated with unions push for low cost superannuation	Retail superannuation fund Personal superannuation, sponsored by large financial conglomerates	'Open' pension fund Specifically introduced for private mandatory retirement saving
Nature of mandate	Employer choice of retirement saving organisation	Employer choice of retirement saving organisation	Employee choice of retirement saving organisation
Regulation of charges	No – except protection of small amount accounts Mandatory contribution set gross of charges	No – except protection of small amount accounts Mandatory contribution set gross of charges	Restrictions on charge type Mandatory contribution set net of charges
Governance	Mutual – stakeholders are fund members Trustees – participating employees and employers, equal representation	Embedded in a corporate structure, stakeholders include shareholders Independent trustees	Embedded in corporate structure, stakeholders include shareholders Independent trustees
Services provided	Life and disability insurance, increasing investment choice, group discounts on home and business loans and health insurance, retirement planning advice	Life and disability insurance (tailored), substantial investment choice, access to financial services provided by promoter of master trust	Life and disability insurance, phased withdrawals, agency for public (minimum) pension
Level of service	Moderate	High	Moderate
Market structure – member accounts – asset management	Captive (some becoming retail) Institutional	Retail Institutional	Retail Institutional
Marketing and distribution	Little marketing – captive membership No distribution network No commissions paid	Substantial marketing Wide distribution network Commissions paid	Substantial marketing Wide distribution network Commissions paid

private retirement saving. While many industry funds have a captive membership, they are not profit maximisers – but operate for the benefit of their members. This unique relationship between members, employers, and trustees helps to address the agency issues that arise from employer choice of superannuation fund in the Australian arrangements.

The governance of master trusts is quite different. Master trusts are set up as public offer arrangements with the promoter managing the fund as a business venture. In contrast to industry funds, master trusts are essentially 'for profit' organisations, with the trustees having no direct relationship with members. Historically, master trusts were involved in the provision of voluntary personal superannuation through retail markets. This market structure is less able to address the agency problems that arise with employer choice of superannuation fund.

Further, while both industry funds and master trusts operate in the institutional market for asset management, master trusts operate in the retail market for member accounts. They must attract small and large employers and therefore face higher marketing costs than industry funds that have historically had a captive membership. However, the market structure is changing. Industry funds are increasingly becoming public offer funds – so are increasingly operating in the retail market for member accounts. As well, the clientele of master trusts are gradually changing from small employers to large employers wishing to 'contract-out of' corporate superannuation plans.

While it may be argued that the higher costs associated with master trusts reflect different services provided – it is unclear what is required beyond account administration, asset management, and payment of benefits. Similar services are provided by both – although master trusts offer greater investment choice (through alternative managed funds), and are generally associated with financial conglomerates, which can offer employers a complete package of financial services. It may also be argued that the higher costs are associated with better performance, but little can be said in the absence of comparable risk adjusted rates of return.

It is possible that master trusts have thrived because they can utilise the distribution networks and marketing services of their promoters. By contrast industry funds have no distribution network, do not pay commissions and, with a historically captive clientele, spend little on marketing. This has made it difficult for industry funds to attract members outside the traditional 'award' workers. However, this too is changing as more industry funds become public offer funds.

These observations raise an important principal-agent issue. Under current legislation employers are responsible for fund choice, yet they have little incentive to choose the fund that will maximise net-of-charges returns. This issue is partly addressed in the case of industry funds which are characterised by participating trustees and an ethos of low cost retirement saving. For master trusts, however, the additional feature of no employee trustee representation and commercial management leaves employees without representation in the determination of their retirement income interests. But it is unclear whether the unique governance characteristics of Australian industry funds can be maintained over the long term.

5.2.3.4 Comparison with Chile

In Chile the private mandatory retirement saving takes place through AFPs. The essential features of AFPs are shown in Table 5.6. In summary AFPs were specifically introduced in 1981 for the management of private mandatory retirement savings. When the AFP system commenced, there were 12 AFPs. By the early 1990s this had increased to 21, but following a number of mergers, has since fallen to 8. The AFPs are limited liability corporations. Ownership and control is varied with some organised on an industry basis and others controlled by Chilean or international financial groups. All AFPs are 'open' to all employees.[21]

Administrative charges are highly regulated. Asset charges are specifically disallowed,[22] charges cannot be levied on inactive accounts and the same charge schedule must apply to all members. In fact only two charge regimes are allowed – charges on contributions and transfers (which may be flat rate and/or as a percentage of the contribution). Administrative charges are calculated in advance by the AFPs and apply in addition to the mandatory contribution of 10 per cent of earnings.[23] When the AFP system commenced in 1981, the average fee was over 20 per cent of contributions, but has gradually fallen since then.

In 1998 total 'official' administrative charges averaged 16.8 per cent of contributions[24] – of which 15.7 percentage points were made in addition to the mandatory contribution with the remainder being flat rate charges subtracted from accounts.[25] Under reasonable assumptions, the contribution charge corresponds to an annual asset charge of 0.78 per cent.[26]

Comparison with the Australian results reported in Tables 5.4 and 5.5, shows that the average AFP charge of 16.8 per cent of contributions lies between the analogous contribution charge for industry funds and master trusts – which range between 6.8 per cent and 27.7 per cent of contributions. Bateman and Valdes-Prieto (1999) report similar findings, using a different methodology.[27] An important implication of the Chilean practice of applying charges in addition to the mandatory contribution is that the charges reduce current consumption rather than retirement accumulations.

Some indication of the reasons for these charge differences can be found by considering the institutional and regulatory differences identified in Table 5.6. In Australia, the nature of the mandate requires employer choice of fund. This, combined with the existence of long standing employer superannuation practices, has meant little switching of accounts and, for industry funds – which have a captive membership (and therefore do not operate in the retail market for member accounts) – very low marketing costs. In Chile, the nature of the mandate is that employees choose AFPs and can switch freely between the eight AFPs. Salespeople working on commission have facilitated excess switching by sharing their commissions.[28] These practices have led to huge AFP marketing costs (which in 1998 accounted for around 45 per cent of total AFP costs) although regulations introduced in late 1997, which require requests for switching to be made in person, have significantly reduced switching. It is unclear how these differences will evolve as Australian policy moves towards greater employee choice of fund and industry funds increasingly seek members outside their traditional clientele.[29]

Administrative charge types are regulated in Chile but are considerably more transparent than in Australia. Most charges are calculated in advance and added to the mandatory contribution. With the exception of member protection of small amount accounts Australia does not regulate charges.[30] Nor does it require that fund charges be disclosed in a standard format.

Finally, governance differs. Australian industry funds are managed by boards of 'participating' trustees (with equal representation) with an emphasis on member benefits. Chilean AFPs (and Australian master trusts) operate 'for profit' for the benefit of shareholders, customers and staff and use independent trustees.

Other differences between Australia and Chile relate to set-up costs, coverage, access to economies of scale and the level of economic development. Set up costs were lower in Australia, which used existing institutions and regulatory framework. As well, the Australian arrangements exempt very low income earners from the mandatory contributions and facilitate greater use of specialist service providers. More generally, the Australian economy and financial system is more developed.

In the absence of any empirical analysis we suggest that differences in governance, transparency, and the nature of the mandate are probably the most important determinants of the charge differential between Chilean AFPs, Australian industry funds, and Australian master trusts. The unique governance characteristics of industry funds has led to an emphasis on low cost provision, employee choice of fund (and the subsequent switching) has led to high AFP marketing costs, while charge transparency may have held back AFP charges (relative to Australian master trusts). This suggests that Australian industry funds currently offer the best combination of characteristics. As well, the unique nature of their boards of trustees means that the principal–agent issues associated with group choice are minimised. However, this is changing. Master trust costs are being driven down by a change in focus away from personal superannuation and small employers towards large corporate plans and increasing competition between master trust products. Simultaneously, the unique governance characteristics of Australian industry funds are dissipating as they increasing opt to become public offer funds.

5.2.4 *Summary and policy implications*

The preceding discussion suggests that administrative charges associated with private mandatory retirement saving are determined, not only by policy design, but also by a complex combination of history, institutional practices, industry structure and regulatory arrangements. Important among these is fund governance. This analysis, in conjunction with other recent analytical and empirical research on administrative charges,[31] suggest a number of stylised facts which should be considered in policy reform towards mandatory private retirement saving:

- There are considerable economies of scale and scope in account administration and asset management.[32]
- Individual choice increases marketing costs and, as illustrated by the Chilean 'switching festival', facilitates abuse, but group choice introduces agency issues.
- Passive asset management is less costly than active management.
- Transparency, through full (and standardised) disclosure, may dampen excess charges.
- Charges may be moderated where governance emphasises member benefits.[33]

Reform towards private mandatory retirement saving should ensure that the institutional practices and regulatory arrangements provide the potential to maximise retirement benefits. This requires a sufficient contributory period combined with high net-of-charges returns.

At the very least policy should encourage or require fund governance that emphasises member benefits (while addressing the principal–agent issues that arise with group choice), an institutional framework that minimizes marketing costs, and full and standardised disclosure of lifetime charges. As well, policy design should acknowledge the differing behavioural impacts of alternative charge regimes.

5.3 Annuity design and market structure

We now turn to an exploration of the appropriate development of policy towards retirement income streams in a privatised retirement policy environment. Fundamental to the idea of private retirement provision is a DC accumulation structure. Under such a policy design, regulations and employer obligations associated with the accumulation phase typically expire at retirement, and any payout regulations must therefore be separately stipulated.

Just as with any publicly provided retirement income (i.e. social security), privately administered retirement provision will require a policy position on the nature of retirement benefits. The implications of interactions between annuity payouts and first pillar type social welfare, adverse selection in the voluntary annuities market, and prudential considerations, all suggest this. However, very few countries which have adopted privately mandatory retirement saving have directly regulated payouts. Instead, payouts have thus far been conditioned more by the pre-reform retirement policy status quo than by dispassionate consideration of sensible policy design. Yet it is the retirement phase where many of the financial risks associated with the elderly, which cannot be adequately insured against in an unregulated private market, are confronted. It is these, more than any other considerations that underpin the economic case for central intervention in retirement provision in the first place.

Insurance against retirement risks, however, whether provided by governments or privately, is expensive. Successful policy design must be sensitive to these costs, and responsive to the subtle trade-offs between insurance and expected income which they imply.

There are many sources of income uncertainty that a risk adverse individual confronting retirement would like to insure against. In the spirit of Bodie (1990a), we list the most important here:

- *Replacement rate risk* — the possibility that the retiree will not have enough income to maintain a reasonable standard of living after retiring, relative to that which he or she enjoyed during his/her pre-retirement years.
- *Annuity rate risk* — unanticipated variation in annuity price over time. If annuity purchase is mandated on retirement, then rest of lifetime income might be significantly affected by variations in the annuity rate.
- *Longevity risk* — the risk that the retiree will exhaust the amount saved for retirement before he or she dies. One way people insure against this risk is by investing in life annuities. In the absence of a policy compelling life annuity purchase, however, adverse selection can seriously limit retirees' effective access to this market.
- *Investment risk* — the possibility that retirement investment income flows will be uneven because the assets in which the accumulation is invested generate volatile returns.
- *Inflation risk* — the risk of price increases, which erode the purchasing power of lifetime savings.

Why should these risks be important to the retiree? The primitive assumption, broadly implied by empirical evidence, is that the typical individual likes to smooth their equivalent consumption, both between working and retirement, and within retirement. The retiree would like to have enough retirement income on average, and would like to insure against major variations in that flow.

Retirement income will be influenced by coverage, contribution levels, and investment performance (captured by replacement rate risk) during the accumulation phase, and by the annuity rate at retirement. This will depend on annuity type, and its going price (annuity rate risk). Variations in retirement income will be affected by longevity, investment volatility through retirement, and inflation (longevity, investment, and inflation risk).

Despite the importance of annuities for retirees, until recently they have been little researched by economists. Perhaps this is due to the prevalence of government funded social security support in developed economies.[34] Our analysis is therefore somewhat speculative. We consider what retirement income products offered in a private market might be best suited to the task of addressing the risks associated with retirement, and what restrictions should be placed upon annuity products.

5.3.1 Current benefit design in Australia and Chile[35]

To make discussion more concrete, it may be useful to briefly describe the current payout arrangements for mandatory DC retirement saving programmes in both Australia and Chile.

5.3.1.1 Australia

Prior to 1992, occupational retirement saving by the private sector was voluntary, and benefits were mostly drawn as a lump sum, rather than as an income stream.

While saving is now mandatory under the Superannuation Guarantee, the practice of taking lump sums has continued. About 85 per cent of the value of superannuation benefits are paid in this form. About 10 per cent is taken as an income stream and the remainder is taken as a death, temporary, or permanent disability benefit. Although income streams are not compulsory, they are encouraged through a variety of tax incentives and first pillar means test provisions.

Retirement income streams which attract preferential tax and/or means test provisions can be broadly classified into life annuities and pensions, term annuities that meet certain criteria, and allocated pensions and annuities (which are sometimes referred to as phased withdrawals).[36]

Recently, amendments to first pillar means testing arrangements have served to encourage life annuities and what might be termed life expectancy products.[37] A life expectancy annuity is a term annuity that must guarantee an income stream for the average life expectancy of the retiree at the time of purchase. Monies used to purchase these two types of annuities are exempt from the assets test and are given preferential income test treatment.[38] Allocated products are not exempt from the assets test, but they do enjoy the same income test treatment as the life and life expectancy annuity.

Allocated products are the most popular form of income stream in Australia. With an allocated product, an investment account is allocated to the annuitant, from which regular payments are withdrawn. The value of the account will depend on the earnings rate of the underlying funds, and the payments made. The annuity income can be varied within prescribed maximum and minimum levels. The maximum drawdown limit is set with the expectation that the account will be exhausted by the age of 80, while under the minimum limit the account will last indefinitely.

5.3.1.2 Chile

Chile's current second pillar retirement income policy was established in 1981, with the old social security system gradually being phased out. It is of the DC type, publicly mandated but privately administered. The government guarantees a minimum pension to workers with a record of 20 years of contributions whose accumulations fall short of set limits. The value of the minimum pension is indexed to inflation when the accumulated change in the CPI reaches 15 per cent. A subsistence pension is also available to those not eligible for the minimum pension.

At retirement, the retiree can make phased withdrawals from their individual account, regulated to guarantee income for their expected life-span; or buy an annuity to provide lifetime benefits; or choose a combination.[39] Phased withdrawals require reversion to a spouse, but life annuities do not. Lump sum withdrawals are also permitted, but only if the residual account value is sufficient to fund a benefit that is a 70 per cent replacement rate and equals 120 per cent or more of the guaranteed minimum pension. Only 25 per cent of the eligible retirees in Chile have taken lump sums.

The phased withdrawal is the most common income stream product in Chile. Accumulated funds are drawn according to an actuarially determined schedule. Any balance remaining after the beneficiary dies is inherited by heirs. Complete longevity risk is provided only in so far as the government will pay the minimum pension when the account is exhausted.

5.3.2 *Mandatory annuity purchase*

Around the world, voluntary annuity markets are thin. Various explanations have been put forward, none of them entirely convincing. They encompass: the desire to leave a bequest; a preference for frontloading retirement consumption; and the loadings on life annuities generated by administration costs and adverse selection.

One of the more intractable issues in annuity analysis is the extent and nature of adverse selection. The primary efficient market requirement which is violated is commonality of information, that is, the annuitant can be presumed to know more about his life expectancy than the annuity issuer. In a voluntary market, this presumption leads to higher quotes, or loadings, on annuities than are actuarially fair for the population at large.

For most retirees, load factors are one reason for avoiding voluntary life annuity purchase.[40] This is an especially important issue for the countries that have DC retirement schemes, where no retirement payout has been prescribed. Given that individual tailoring of annuity contracts is infeasible, there is a strong case for mandating life annuities. Adverse selection is very limited when everyone must buy an annuity, provided appropriate restrictions are placed on annuity offers. Compulsion may reduce commission costs, and in addition, mandatory annuities address the possibility of preference inconsistency in arranging finances through retirement.[41]

Annuity mandation immediately raises the question of what features such instruments should have. In what follows, we examine the implications of alternative annuity products, suggested by Australian experience, both from the perspective of the retiree and from the viewpoint of government outlays. For simplicity, we focus on a male with statistically average life expectancy, an assumption justified by mandatory annuity purchase. Reversion to a spouse is ignored. The analysis is conducted in a policy environment that guarantees participants a life pension set at 20 per cent of average earnings.

5.3.3 *Alternative annuity designs and retirement risk coverage*

To keep analysis tractable, we have chosen to examine five annuity designs. A life annuity, in which payouts are escalated at 3 per cent is used as a benchmark. Table 5.7 lists these annuities, and reports their salient features.

Variable, or with-profits annuities have been designed to provide insurance against longevity risk, while at the same time delivering higher expected returns by transferring investment risk to the annuitant. The annuity is written on the basis of an assumed investment return (the AIR). Payouts, however, are adjusted by the relationship between the performance of the underlying portfolio, which may be specified by the annuitant, and the AIR. Because investment risk is borne by the annuitant, the AIR may be significantly higher than the risk-free rate – in our calculations we have assumed an underlying portfolio of equities.

The allocated annuity appears at first sight to be more like a pure investment instrument than a retirement income stream product. Its essence is that a sum of money is invested at retirement, in a portfolio over whose composition the retiree has considerable control. Both income and capital can be drawn down to meet the retiree's needs, subject to upper and lower bounds. It does not provide complete longevity insurance.

Table 5.7 Alternative annuity products

Annuity type	Nature of annuity payout
Life annuity[a] (Escalated)	Provides an income stream until death, escalated annually at 3 per cent.
Variable life annuity (Variable)	Provides an income stream until death, with payments contingent on the market performance of some specified underlying portfolio. The AIR is set to generate an expected 3 per cent escalation.
Partial inflation indexed life annuity (CPI insured)	Provides a lifetime income stream escalated at 3 per cent with an inflation 'deductible' providing a real protection factor of 85 per cent – payments are indexed to inflation above this cumulative price level increase.
CPI indexed life annuity[a] (CPI indexed)	Provides a lifetime income stream indexed to the consumer price index.
'Life expectancy' annuity[a] (Term)	Provides a prespecified income stream, escalated at 3 per cent per annum, over life expectancy at time of purchase.
Allocated annuity with a deferred life annuity[b] (Allocated)	Income can be drawn down at the retiree's discretion within a range specified by regulation; typically, maximum drawdown limits are set to exhaust resources by life expectancy from time of purchase. Deferred standard life annuity payments then commence; the deferred annuity is valued at 10 per cent of the product purchase price.

a Annuities that are currently available in the Australian market.
b Allocated annuities are available in Australia, but attempts to market a deferred annuity have failed, mainly due to unfavourable taxation rates.

One way of providing more complete longevity insurance would be to market these products with a deferred life annuity starting at age 80.[42] This combination has considerable intuitive appeal, combining capital draw-down flexibility with partial longevity insurance. In the 15 years from purchase at age 65, the annuitant has considerable control over drawdowns. The deferred life annuity then cuts in, offering a rest-of-life annuity with an initial payout indexed to inflation, thereafter escalated at a pre-determined rate. The annuitant bears the investment risk of the allocated pension, but derives some inflation protection from the correlation between movements in the price of physical capital and the price level generally, and enjoys insurance against investment risk under the deferred annuity. In the event of death before age 80, a bequest results.

The deferred life annuity is not expensive – a 65 year old male needs to commit only about 10 per cent of his accumulation to the deferred annuity. This result occurs because of the combination of the probability of death before payouts begin, a lower initial payout, and the compounding of investment returns in the 15 years prior to the first payout. In addition, Australian male life expectancy at age 80 is only 7 years.

Even a modest inflation rate of 4 per cent will halve purchasing power of a constant nominal income stream in 18 years. Combined with 1 per cent wage productivity growth, purchasing power relative to community standards will halve in 14 years. For a retiree with a life expectancy of 15 or more years, as a male retiring at 65 would have in Australia, erosion of purchasing power through inflation is thus a significant risk. For women, the risk is even greater.

Escalated annuities partially address this problem, and escalation has been assumed in most of our numerical examples. However, this does not offer insurance against unanticipated inflation, which perhaps more than anticipated inflation 'creep', is the larger danger to annuitant welfare, precisely because of its unpredictability. Formica and Kingston (1991), developing analysis of Bodie (1990b), propose an annuity product offering inflation protection above some cumulative deductible. In periods of significant inflation and inflation volatility, this partial indexation allows significantly improved payouts relative to full inflation protection, while at the same time providing coverage against inflation surges. This product has been considered for commercial offer in Australia, but has not so far been marketed.

All these products offer partial insurance against one or more of the major risk types identified above. While private annuities can be designed to provide full insurance against longevity, investment, and inflation risk, such comprehensive insurance is very expensive. This quickly exposes retirees to replacement rate risk. For a given accumulation, the overall expected income stream would be lower, the more comprehensively these risks are covered. The partial insurance provided by some of the annuity designs considered here may therefore prove attractive, and in some cases will reduce the expected payout from publicly provided first pillar support.

5.3.4 Calculating the value of mandatory annuity payout streams

We calculate the income flows which different annuity types yield using variants of standard actuarial formulae. The general formula for the actuarially fair annuity payment for a standard life annuity is given by:

$$y = k / \sum_{t=1}^{\omega} {}_t p_x \frac{(1+s)^{(t-1)}}{(1+R)^t} \tag{6}$$

where K is the purchase price of the annuity ${}_t p_x$ is the annuitant's probability of survival t periods from age x, s is the escalation factor, R is the risk free rate of return, and ω is set at the maximum potential life span, measured from the annuitant's age, given by x, at $t=0$. Appendix 1 gives the formulae for each of the annuities we consider.

Investment returns for both the variable and allocated annuities are modelled using stochastic simulations, with each of the reported experiments based on 10,000 draws from a standard normal distribution. Similar procedures are used to simulate inflationary experience for all annuity types.

5.3.4.1 Annuity payout streams

Table 5.8 reports year one and year 15 annuity payouts using the procedures outlined above. For variable and allocated annuities, expected values are used. Estimated male average earnings are reported to provide a benchmark. First year payouts vary from A$16,409 to A$24,432, a very broad range.

Direct comparison of income streams generated by different annuity products, however, offers only a limited guide to their social merit. Of greater importance are individual preferences towards alternative income (or consumption) profiles.

5.3.4.2 Preference rankings

To gain some sense of how individuals might rank these alternative annuities, we adjust the income flows which different annuity types yield for assumed inflation. Income tested public sector first pillar payments are then added in. The resulting real income in each period is assumed to finance consumption in that period alone – there is no borrowing or lending in retirement, and no other source of income.

This gives an estimate of consumption for each period, and provides the basis for the utility score calculation.

Table 5.8 Annuity payouts by annuity type[a]

Annuity type	Annual payouts (A$ current)	
	Year 1	Year 15
Escalated	23,778	38,069
Variable	21,414	21,414
CPI Insured	16,409	24,934
CPI Indexed	19,333	28,800
Term	17,242	27,015
Allocated	16,415	28,643
Average wages	40,154	79,502

a See Table 5.7 for annuity description. Assumptions: annuity purchase price: A$166 970 (35 year accumulation at 9 per cent of average wages; historical investment returns); annuity return assumptions; real safe return: 4 per cent; real risky return: 8 per cent; expected inflation: 4 per cent; standard deviation on risky portfolio: 20 per cent; standard deviation on inflation: 2 per cent. Life expectancies: Average 65 year old Australian male. Deferred annuity: 9 per cent of purchase price, invested at risky rate for deferred period of 15 years.

We assume a standard iso-elastic (or power) utility function:

$$U_t(c_t) = \frac{1}{1-\gamma}(c_t^{1-\gamma} - 1) \qquad\qquad (\gamma \geq 0; \gamma \neq 1) \qquad\qquad (7a)$$

$$U_t(c_t) = \ln(c_t) \qquad\qquad (\gamma = 1) \qquad\qquad (7b)$$

and

$$c_t = \frac{y_t}{(1+\pi)^t} \qquad\qquad (8)$$

where c_t gives consumption in period t, y_t is the total retirement income, π is the inflation rate, and γ is a measure of risk aversion.[43] Utilities are discounted for survival probability and time, and period by period utilities are aggregated to give an overall rest-of-lifetime score:

$$V = \sum_{t=1}^{\omega} U_{t\,t} p_x / (1+\rho)^t \qquad\qquad (9)$$

where ρ is the discount rate, set at 3.5 per cent. The crucial parameter in the preference function specification is the coefficient of relative risk aversion, γ. The higher is the value of this parameter, the more risk averse the individual's preferences. Traditionally, quite high values of γ have been used, but over the last 10 years or so, estimates of γ have fallen.[44] We report a range of values from 0.5 to 2.5.

For given revenue outlays, policy efficacy will be indicated by the utility score. If alternative designs incur varying revenue outlays, then these must be factored into the policy ranking. The present value of revenue outlays are calculated in each case according to:

$$PV(T) = \sum_{t=1}^{\omega} \frac{T_t(1+\pi)^{(t-1)}}{(1+\rho)^t} \tag{10}$$

where T_t gives the value of first pillar transfers in period t.

Table 5.9 reports rankings for our menu of annuity products for values of γ ranging from 0.5 to 2.5, for a range of wage levels. (Wage level impacts upon the implied value of public pension outlays.) The present values of public pension outlays and, where applicable, expected bequests are also reported.

The variable annuity, however, delivers these same features, with a significantly higher expected payout. For those who are less risk averse,

Table 5.9 Utility rankings of mandatory annuities by annuity type and present values of pension and bequests by income level (A$)

	Annuity type	Utility ranking by risk aversion (γ)			Present value of	
		0.5	1.5	2.5	Pension (A$)	Bequests (A$)
50% of average earnings	Escalated	3	3	3	1,118	
	Variable	1	1	1	12,205	
	CPI Insured	4	4	4	4,125	
	CPI Indexed	5	5	5	1,868	
	Term	6	6	6	19,738	16,835
	Allocated	2	2	2	10,823	17,611
	Annuity type	**Utility ranking by risk aversion (γ)**			**Present value of**	
		0.5	1.5	2.5	Pension (A$)	Bequests (A$)
100% of average earnings	Escalated	5	5	5	749	
	Variable	1	1	2	3,417	
	CPI Insured	4	4	3	0	
	CPI Indexed	3	3	1	0	
	Term	6	6	6	16,191	33,670
	Allocated	2	2	4	2,208	35,223
	Annuity type	**Utility ranking by risk aversion (γ)**			**Present value of**	
		0.5	1.5	2.5	Pension (A$)	Bequests (A$)
200% of average earnings	Escalated	5	5	3	8	
	Variable	1	1	4	800	
	CPI Insured	4	4	2	0	
	CPI Indexed	3	2	1	0	
	Term	6	6	6	16,191	67,341
	Allocated	2	3	5	303	70,445

this is a preferred product. The first important message from Table 5.9 is that a CPI indexed life annuity scores well, across a range of risk aversion parameters, except for the poor. Longevity risk spreading is important here, as is the gradual reduction of purchasing power over time relative to community standards, a pattern consistent with the time discount rate used. Associated first pillar pension payouts are very low. For those who are very risk averse, this is the preferred product, unless they are poor and primarily reliant on first pillar support.

Expected public pension payouts are, however, higher. This is why the poor prefer the variable annuity – they can take more advantage of the safety net than higher income individuals. For the very risk averse, however, the variable annuity does not do so well.

At the other end of the ranking scale, the term annuity, a life expectancy product, scores very poorly. This is probably because there is no consistency of exposure to volatility over time. For the first 15 years, a safe, smooth return is offered; this appeals to the very risk averse, while those less averse to risk miss out on the higher expected returns generated by products associated with riskier portfolios. After that time, there is a considerable movement in consumption flows which the risk adverse dislike. No matter how preference toward risk is specified, this product has unattractive features. Furthermore, the public pension payout associated with term annuity purchase is very high. This product may of course score better if a bequest argument were incorporated into the preference function.

One of the more innovative products combines an allocated annuity with a deferred life annuity. Notwithstanding the fact that this product does not exploit longevity risk spreading for a duration equal to the life expectancy of the purchaser, it has considerable appeal. It is difficult, however, to capture its appeal in the preference framework used here. It generates a significant value of expected bequests, and also leaves considerable discretion over capital drawdown for the duration of life expectancy. Neither of these features is captured in our preference function, yet both are valued by individuals. Expected public pension outlays are about the same as for a variable annuity.

Time discounting may go some way to explaining why annuities offering partial inflation insurance score so poorly. An annuity offering inflation insurance with a deductible generates a payout profile whose real value reduces early in retirement, and is thereafter insured against. Yet the opposite pattern will score better in a preference function with time discounting. There is also some anecdotal evidence that individuals prefer to front load their retirement payouts, presumably on the basis that they will be less active in their later retirement (see Hurd 1990). Partial inflation insured annuities tend to score better with individuals who are highly risk averse.

In practice, load factors on CPI indexed annuities are higher than on standard life annuities. While the conventional explanation for this is couched in terms of inflation risk and the costs of building a matching asset base, it may be that adverse selection plays a further role here – only those with very long-life expectancies are concerned about purchasing power a long time into the future.

5.4 Concluding comments

This chapter has highlighted two design issues that are potentially crucial in implementing private mandatory retirement policies. Neither has received much research attention to date, and because of this our findings are speculative rather than definitive.

The first, administrative charges, arises because scale and externality effects which allow public administration of retirement provision to be delivered at low cost are not available to the private provider. Here we have fleshed out these questions, and argued for the importance of standardised charge disclosure, along the lines of regulations currently in force in Chile. Equivalence relations between contributions, benefits, and assets based charges, are derived.

While evidence is preliminary, it appears that in addition to scale effects and the complexity of regulatory compliance, governance, transparency and the nature of the mandate (who pays the contribution, and whether the contribution is specified gross or net of administrative charge), all seem to play a role in the level and pattern of costs and charges.

The second design issue revolves around the nature of retirement income streams. If retirement provision is publicly provided, the government acts as a sponsor for what is in almost all cases a defined benefit retirement income arrangement. Risk is therefore implicitly shared widely through the community, across age groupings, between workers and the retired, and even between generations. Generally speaking, annuity loadings are effectively lower for a government provided pension. With private mandatory policies, on the other hand, investment risk is borne by the individual, and other risks are covered only to the extent that annuities provide insurance. It follows that annuity market function and annuity design will be of critical importance in implementing a retirement provision policy of this kind.

Here we discuss and analyse the insurance attributes of a number of annuity designs that have been proposed or marketed in developed economies. Numerical simulation suggests that annuities, which leave the retiree with some degree of investment risk, may be preferred by at least some people. Full, rather than partial, coverage, against inflation risk seems to be preferred. In addition, some frontloading of annuity payments is preferred. This research is still preliminary, and a number of questions, such as the impact of incorporating a bequest motive, and the desirability of retaining a degree of control over payout profiles, have yet to be addressed. Nevertheless, research thus far does indicate that a fully indexed life annuity may not be the best specification for a retirement income stream under mandatory private provision, at least for a significant proportion of retirees.

Increasing electoral pressure for smaller government is leading to the replacement of public provision with mandatory private provision in many policy arenas. This trend is readily discernible in the area of retirement policy, because past extravagant promises to cohorts now retiring are combining with demographic transition to reveal large public authority liabilities in future decades.

As a result, debate over retirement policy is active throughout the developed world. Increased reliance on private retirement provision, however, brings with it challenges of its own. Private sector coverage against financial risks associated with old age, and traditionally insures against by the government authorities, raise issues of guarantee, moral hazard, and adverse selection which have not been fully analysed in the retirement context.

This chapter has explored two such challenges. It draws on the limited evidence available, and numerical analysis, to show the importance of keeping administrative cost low and of ensuring that the private annuity market functions efficiently. Its thrust is that if private mandating considerably replaces public provision as the major channel for retirement policy, great care must be taken in specifying how these aspects of the policy will operate. Its success or failure may well hinge on provisions which have a compounding impact on accumulations, or on the money worth of retirement income streams.

Many more issues, however, remain to be comprehensively researched. Pension tax design, the impacts of minimum guarantees, the role of intra-family transfers in retirement provision, and the limitations which privatised social security might have on the efficient allocation of risk, are all questions on which further research is needed.

Appendix

Annuity formulae

- A *term annuity* income flow is calculated using equation (6), but setting $_t p_x = 1$ for all t, and ω equal to the term of the annuity.
- A *variable annuity* is written on the basis of an assumed investment return (the AIR). Payouts, however, are adjusted by the relationship between the performance of the underlying portfolio given by R^m and the AIR. The formula is:

$$y_t = y_{t-1}\left(\frac{1+R^m}{1+AIR}\right) \tag{11}$$

where y_0 (not actually paid) is determined according to equation (6).

- The payout stream specification for an *allocated annuity* can be formalised by specifying the account accumulation at time t:

$$K_t = k_{t-1}(1+R^m) - y_t. \tag{12a}$$

The payout at time t of a phased withdrawal may be written:

$$\frac{K_{t-1}}{F^1_{t-1}} \geq y_t \geq \frac{K_{t-1}}{F^2_{t-1}} \tag{12b}$$

where F^1_t is the minimum drawdown factor, and F^2_t is the maximum.

The initial deferred annuity payout is given by

$$y = \lambda K / \left\{ \left[{}_dP_x \frac{(1_t+s)^d}{(1+R^s)^d} \right] \sum_{t=1}^{\omega-x} {}_tP_x \frac{(1_t+s)^{t-1}}{(1+R)^t} \right\} \tag{13}$$

where λ is the proportion of the retirement accumulation dedicated to deferred annuity purchase, d is the term of the deferral, and R^s is the observed historical return on a balanced Australia superannuation investment portfolio (6.3 per cent real).[45]

- Specification of the income flows for inflation indexed annuities is more complicated. Formica and Kingston (1991) discuss this in detail, and provide the following formula for the payout in year t:

$$y_t = K / \left\{ \sum_{t=1}^{\omega} {}_tP_x \left[\frac{(1-s)^{(t-1)}}{(1+R^s)^t} + c(t) \right] \right\} \tag{14}$$

where $c(t)$ represents the cost of the (usually partial) inflation insurance. (In the case of full indexation, s is set at unity.)

Notes

1 This chapter was presented at the conference: 'Social Security Reform in Advanced Countries', Centre for International Research on the Japanese Economy, University of Tokyo, September 6–7 1999. Many thanks to Yasushi Iwamoto, Olivia Mitchell and Salvador Valdes-Prieto for their useful comments.

2 Other developed countries that have similar, but less developed, policies of this type include Switzerland, Denmark, the Netherlands and Sweden.

3 See Palacios and Pallares-Miralles (1998), Table 12.

4 Although first pillar payments will raise total retirement income.

5 There is a disparate mix of research including comparisons between Chile and Australia (see Bateman and Valdes-Prieto 1999), costs issues in Mexico (Mitchell 1999) and the costs implications of alternative proposals for the privatization of US Social Security (see Mitchell 1998, James *et al.* 1998, Diamond 1999a and b, James *et al.* 1999) – but no generic economic analysis.

6 For example, Clare and Connor (1999).
7 For example, James *et al.* (1999) consider the administrative costs associated with privatization in the form of individual accounts invested in the retail market with relatively open choice or individual accounts invested in the retail market with constrained choice among investment companies.
8 The analysis in this chapter relates to charges faced by the individual, rather than the costs faced by the providers. In the long run we would expect these to be the same, but period by period charges may not reflect actual costs.
9 See Kingston and Piggott (1993) for an analogous treatment of the taxation of retirement saving.
10 And, as a further point of clarification, we consider contributions gross of administrative charges (as in the case of Australia), rather than net of charges (as in the case of Chile).
11 As compared to the no administrative charge case.
12 Which suggests that cost comparisons must be made over a working life of retirement saving, rather than at a point in time.
13 For more discussion of these impacts, see James *et al.* (1999: 5–7).
14 An analogy can be drawn with the impact of contribution and earning taxes (see Kingston and Piggott 1993).
15 A comprehensive listing of the tasks involved in private retirement provision can be found in Diamond (1999b).
16 AFP is an acronym for Administratoras de Fondes de Pensiones.
17 Member protection requires that administrative charges cannot reduce accounts below A$1000 – although amounts for taxes, losses and insurance can be deducted.
18 Although some superannuation funds do charge on the basis of a percent of contributions.
19 This differs from the Latin American experience where the administrative charges are added to the mandatory contribution.
20 A detailed discussion of the estimation of Australian charges is set out in Bateman and Valdes-Prieto (1999). Note that marketing costs are not explicitly identified. For industry funds there have been almost no direct marketing costs due to their 'captive' membership. For master trusts marketing costs are not disclosed.
21 Further details on mandatory private retirement provision in Chile can be found in Bateman and Valdes-Prieto (1999).
22 Asset charges have been prohibited since 1988.
23 Insurance premiums also apply in addition to the 10 per cent mandatory contributions.
24 Calculated as an asset weighted average of all AFPs.
25 These figures are further complicated by the practice of commission sharing by AFP salespeople, which reduce the 'effective' contribution rate. For example, 30 per cent commission sharing would reduce the effective contribution rate to 14 per cent. Commission sharing is ignored in this analysis.
26 Assuming 40 years of contributions, a real rate of return falling from 7 per cent per annum in the first 20 years to 5 per cent per annum in the final 20 years to reflect the transition from a developing economy and real wages growth of 2 per cent per annum.
27 They consider a representative worker rather than a full working life worker – where representative workers are assumed to face varying periods of unemployment and in Australia hold more than one mandatory retirement saving account. As well, they estimate single year and lifetime charges and present their results in PPP US dollars.

28 Or providing gifts such as bicycles or mobile phones.

29 The government supports employee choice of fund but cannot get the legislation passed by both Houses of Parliament. The proposed legislation requires employers to elect one of three models: limited choice of 4 funds, unlimited choice, a fund negotiated as part of a Workplace Agreement.

30 Except in relation to member protection which requires that administrative charges cannot reduce accounts below A$1000 although amounts for taxes, losses and insurance can be deducted.

31 Including Mitchell 1998, James *et al.* 1998, Diamond 1999a and b and James *et al.* 1999.

32 Mitchell (1998) reports that in the US, products aimed at the retail market are around three times as expensive as wholesale products.

33 Some countries – such as Bolivia and Sweden – have taken the approach of regulating charges.

34 In recent times interest in private market annuities has intensified, in particular, the issue of adverse selection, see Mitchell *et al.* (1999); Finkelstein and Poterba (1999), Walliser (1997).

35 Sources for the material presented in this section include Bateman (1998), Bateman and Piggott (1997), Davis (1995), Edwards (1998), and Stanton and Whiteford (1998).

36 An annuity can be purchased with savings from DC occupational retirement scheme, or other non-retirement savings money. However, an allocated annuity can only be purchased with occupational retirement savings. On the other hand, a pension is provided via a DB occupational retirement scheme.

37 Statistical life expectancy of an Australian male retiring at 65 is currently 15.49 years.

38 As part of the first pillar means test, both income and assets are assessed against set benchmarks.

39 This choice, however, is prescribed. Annuities must be purchased when withdrawals are taken early, and a phased withdrawal must be taken if the accumulation is not sufficient to fund an annuity equal in value to the minimum pension.

40 For recent research into annuity selection effects, see Mitchell *et al.* (1999), Walliser (1999) and Finkelstein and Poterba (1999).

41 An alternative approach to limiting adverse selection has been put forward by Brugiavini (1993). She suggests incremental deferred annuity purchase throughout the accumulation phase, to exploit the observed feature of annuity markets, that adverse selection increases with age. A similar idea has been suggested by Boskin *et al.* (1988). Incremental deferred annuity purchase would also serve to spread annuity rate risk, since the terms of annuity purchase would vary with each increment purchased (Bateman and Piggott 1999).

42 The age at which resources are exhausted under the maximum drawdown.

43 Technically, the coefficient of relative risk aversion.

44 In an influential study, Stock and Wise (1990) report values of γ from an econometric study of the retirement decision of 1500 salesmen. Values varied between about 0.2 and 0.4. Gourinchas and Parker (1997) estimate γ at about 0.5, and Shea (1995) reports estimates for high income individuals that vary from 0.2 to 0.4. On the whole, therefore, we attach more importance to rankings where γ is set below unity.

45 Where a deferred annuity is specified, the sum available for the phased withdrawal is correspondingly reduced.

References

Bateman, H. (1998) 'Three essays on the economics of mandatory private retirement saving', unpublished PhD thesis, University of New South Wales, Australia.

Bateman, H. and Piggott, J. (1997) 'Private pensions in OECD countries – Australia', *Labour Market and Social Policy Occasional Papers*, No. 23, OECD, Paris.

Bateman, H. and Piggott, J. (1999) 'Mandating retirement provision: the Australian experience', *Geneva Papers on Risk and Insurance* 24(1): 93–113.

Bateman, H. and Valdes-Prieto, S. (1999), 'The mandatory private old age income schemes of Australia and Chile: a comparison, mimeo.

Bodie, Z. (1990a) 'Pensions as retirement income insurance', *Journal of Economic Literature* 38: 28–49.

Bodie, Z. (1990b) 'Inflation Insurance', *Journal of Risk and Insurance*, 634–5.

Boskin, M., Kotlikoff L. and Shoven, J. (1988) 'Personal security accounts: a proposal for fundamental social security reform', in Wachter, S. (ed.) *Social Security and Private Pensions: Providing for Retirement in the Twenty-First Century*, Lexington: 179–206.

Brugiavini, A. (1993) 'Uncertainty resolution and the timing of individual annuity purchases', *Journal of Public Economics* 50: 31–62.

Clare, R. and Connor D. (1999) 'Cheaper admin is good news for members', *Superfunds*, November 1999, 22–5.

Davis, P. E. (1995) *Pension Funds: Retirement–Income Security and Capital Markets, An International Perspective*, Oxford:Clarendon Press.

Diamond, P. (1999a) 'Administrative costs and equilibrium charges with individual accounts', *National Bureau of Economic Research, Working Paper* 7050.

Diamond, P. (1999b) 'Issues in privatizing social security', *Report of the Expert Panel of the National Academy of Social Insurance*, Cambridge, MA: MIT Press.

Doyle, S. and Piggott, J. (2000) 'Mandatory annuity designs: a preliminary study'. Society of Actuaries, *Retirement Needs Framework*, SOA Monograph M–R500–1, Society of Actuaries, Illinois, 43–54.

Edwards, S. (1998) 'The Chilean pension reform: a pioneering program' in Feldstein, M. (ed.), *Privatizing Social Security*, National Bureau of Economic Research, Chicago and London: University of Chicago Press.

Finkelstein, A. and Poterba, J. (1999) 'Selection effects in the market for individual annuities: new evidence from the United Kingdom, mimeo.

Formica, A. and Kingston, G. (1991) 'Inflation insurance for Australian annuitants', *Australian Journal of Management* 16(2): 145–64.

Gourinchas, P. and Parker, J. A. (1997) 'Consumption over the lifecycle'. unpublished paper. Massachusetts Institute of Technology.

Hurd, M. (1990) 'Research on the elderly: economic status, retirement, and consumption and saving', *Journal of Economic Literature* XXVIII (2): 565–637.

James, E. Ferrier, G., Smalhout, J. and Vittas, D. (1998) 'Mutual funds and institutional investments – what is the most efficient way to set up individual accounts in a social security system?', paper presented to the NBER Conference on Social Security, December 1998.

James, E., Smalhout, J. and Vittas, D. (1999) 'Administrative costs and the organization of individual account systems: a comparative perspective', paper presented to the World Bank conference 'New Ideas About Old Age Security', September 1999.

Kingston, G. and Piggott, J. (1993) 'A ricardian equivalence theorem for the taxation of pension funds', *Economic Letters* Vol. 42: 399–403.

Mitchell, O. S. (1998) 'Administrative costs in public and private retirement systems', in Feldstein, M (ed.) *Privatising Social Security*, Chicago: University of Chicago Press.

Mitchell, O. S. (1999) 'Evaluating administrative costs in Mexico's AFORES pension system', *Pension Research Council Working Paper* 99–1.

Mitchell O. S., Poterba, J. M., Warshawsky, M. J. and Brown, J. R. (1999) 'New evidence on the money's worth of individual annuities', *American Economic Review,* forthcoming.

Murthi, M., Orszag, J. M. and Orszag P. R. (1999) 'Administrative costs under a decentralised approach to individual accounts: lessons from the United Kingdom', paper presented to the World Bank Conference 'New Ideas About Old Age Security', September 1999.

Palacios, R. and Montserrat, P. (1998) 'International Patterns of Pension Provision', mimeo.

Piggott, J. and Doyle, S. (1998), 'Annuitising mandated retirement accumulations: a primer', paper prepared for the Social Protection Department, World Bank.

Rice Kachor (1999a) *Annuity and Pension League Table*, July, Rice Kachor Research.

Rice, Kachor (1999b) *Master Trust Analysis*, Rice Kachor Research.

Shea, J. (1995) 'Union contracts and the life-cycle/permanent-income hypothesis', *American Economic Review* 85(1): 186–200.

Siegel, J. (1992) 'The equity premium: stock and bond returns since 1802', *Financial Analysts Journal*, January-February: 28–38.

Stanton, D. and Whiteford, P. (1998) *Pension Systems and Policy in the APEC Economies,* Pension Systems and Policy, Discussion Papers, Vol. 2, APEC.

Stock, J. and Wise, D. (1990) 'Pensions, the option value of work, and retirement', *Econometrica*, 58, 5, September, 1151–80.

Superfunds (various issues).

Super Review (various issues).

Walliser, J. (1997) 'Understanding adverse selection in the annuities market and the impact of privatizing social security', *Congressional Budget Office,* Washington DC.

World Bank (1994) *Averting the Old Age Crisis – Policies to Protect the Old and Promote Growth* Oxford: Oxford University Press.

6 Switching the Japanese social system from pay-as-you-go to actuarially fair

A simulation analysis

Tatsuo Hatta and Noriyoshi Oguchi

6.1 Introduction

Under the current Japanese pension system, the lifetime pension benefit of an average salaried man born in 1935 is greater than his lifetime pension contributions by $500,000. If he were faced with the contribution and benefit schedules that a person born in 2000 faces, his lifetime benefit would be less than his lifetime contribution by $250,000. This means that the net pension benefit is different between the two cohorts by $750,000 even under the assumption that their lifetime incomes are equal.[1]

Such extreme inequity between different cohorts is caused by the fact that Japan's public pension system is essentially a pay-as-you-go system.

Recently Hatta and Oguchi (1999) made various reform proposals that would switch the Japanese pension system to an actuarially fair one. They analyzed the future effects of these reform proposals using the Osaka University and Senshu University Public Pension Simulation Model (the OSU model).[2] Among their proposals is the "23 percent Reform Plan" of the Private Sector Employee Pension system.

In this chapter, we will outline the "23 percent Reform Plan" and show its effects both on public fund accumulation and on the net benefits of different cohorts.

Section 1 briefly outlines the current structure of Japan's public pension system, and Section 2 examines its redistributional effects. The pay-as-you-go scheme and the actuarially fair scheme will be compared in Section 3. In Section 4, the 23 percent Reform Plan is analyzed. Privatization is discussed in Section 5.

6.2 The Japanese public pension system[3]

There are three public pension systems in Japan: the National Pension (NP), the Private Sector Employee Pension (PEP), and the Government and Education Sector Employee Pension (GEP).[4] The NP covers all adults from 20 to 60 years old. The PEP covers employees in the private sector, and the GEP covers employees in the public sector and private schools.

The NP benefit is independent of the earnings of the insured, and is dependent only on the length of the participation period. The NP benefit is common to all three systems. The PEP and GEP benefits are proportional to the lifetime earnings of the insured. Those insured by PEP or GEP receive the corresponding benefits on top of the NP benefit. This is called a "two-tier scheme."

Those insured under the NP system are categorized into three groups. Group 2 consists of those also insured by the PEP or the GEP. They are automatically covered by NP without paying additional contributions. Group 3 consists of the dependent spouses of those insured by PEP and GEP, i.e. the spouses of members of Group 2. Group 1 consists of all other adults. Thus, full-time students, farmers, the self-employed, and their dependent spouses belong to this group.

In this chapter, we will call the insured of Group 1 the "self-employed," those of Group 2 the "employees," and those of Group 3 the "full-time housewives." Thus, a full-time housewife is a person whose husband is an employee, and whose own income is less than ¥1.3 million a year.

Self-employed people only join the NP. Each insured person makes the same contribution in this scheme until he or she reaches 60, and starts to receive the NP benefit from 65. The NP benefit is proportional to the period of participation. The spouses of the self-employed are treated the same as the self-employed. Hence, there is no redistribution of income through the NP within the same generation of self-employed people. The NP benefit is officially called the Old Age Basic Pension Benefit.

Employees are insured by either the PEP or GEP. At the same time, they are automatically insured by the NP without additional premium payments. Thus, their pension benefits are the sum of the NP benefit and the PEP (or the GEP) benefit. The contribution rate depends on lifetime "average standard monthly earnings" (hereafter we call it simply "monthly earnings"). The contribution rate does not depend on the marital status of the insured.

Figure 6.1 shows the relationship between monthly earnings and the income transfer through the PEP of a single salaried man born in 1961. Incidentally, such a person belongs to the first of the generations whose entire life span is covered by the post-1986 reform schedule. The vertical axis of Figure 6.1 measures the discounted present value of his lifetime pension benefits and contributions.[5] Since his contribution is proportional to his monthly earnings, it is represented by a straight line from the origin.

Figure 6.2 shows that income transfer is positive for those with monthly earnings below ¥170,000, and negative for those with monthly earnings above ¥170,000. Thus, there is an income transfer from an employee with a higher income to one with a lower income. In other words, there is a progressive income transfer within this cohort.

The pension contribution rate of the PEP is scheduled to grow under the current system as the thick solid line in Figure 6.2 shows. The pension

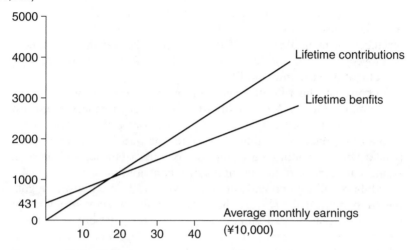

Figure 6.1 Average monthly pay and pension wealth for a single person born in 1961 in private sector employee pension system

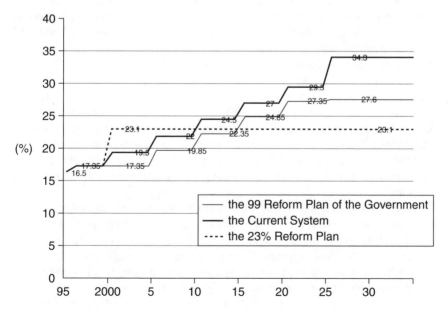

Figure 6.2 Scheduled contribution rates

benefit is scheduled to grow in proportion to the wage rate of the contemporary workers.

Full-time housewives, whose husbands are covered by PEP or GEP, are entitled to the same NP benefit as a self-employed person or his or her spouse. They do not make a contribution, unlike a self-employed person or their spouses. As Figure 6.1 shows, there is a progressive income transfer mechanism in PEP. In PEP, a full-time housewife is treated as an employee with no monthly earnings. Thus, full-time housewives get the most favorable treatment in PEP.

In contrast, the wife of a self-employed person is required to pay the contribution for her NP benefits just like other members of Group 1 of NP. Indeed, if a self-employed woman without a job marries a salaried man and becomes a full-time housewife, she becomes eligible for the NP benefit without continuing to pay the NP contribution, and there are no additional charges to the husband's PEP contribution.

While both husband and wife are alive, a full-time housewife gets only the NP benefit. If she survives her husband, she receives survivor's benefit from her husband's PEP in addition to her own NP benefit. The survivor benefit is three quarters of the husband's PEP benefit. Thus, the two-tier scheme works not only for employees but also for their spouses.

6.3 Intergenerational redistributional effects

The Japanese public pension system redistributes income between different cohorts. The upward-sloping solid line in Figure 6.3 depicts the lifetime contribution rate (i.e. the ratio of the lifetime pension contribution to the lifetime wage income) of an average employee in the PEP system.[6] The downward-sloping solid line shows the lifetime benefit rate (i.e. the ratio of the lifetime benefit to the lifetime wage income).[7]

The figure shows that the cohort born in 1935, which is now 65 years old receive a net benefit equal to 26.2 percent of its lifetime wage income. On the other hand, those born after 2005 will receive a net benefit equal to minus 13.9 percent of their lifetime wage, making a net excess payment to the system. These lines show that the lifetime contribution and the lifetime benefit are equal for the cohort born in 1962. The older cohorts receive positive net benefits, while the younger cohorts receive negative net benefits.

Figure 6.4 shows the net lifetime contribution and benefit of each generation in monetary terms. It shows how much an average person born in 1935 would have contributed and received if he had been faced with the lifetime contribution and benefit rate schedule that each younger cohort faces. According to this figure, an average person born in 1935 receives a net pension benefit of approximately ¥50 million ($500,000). However, the person would have paid ¥25 million ($250,000) more than the benefits received if faced with the contribution and benefit schedule of the cohort

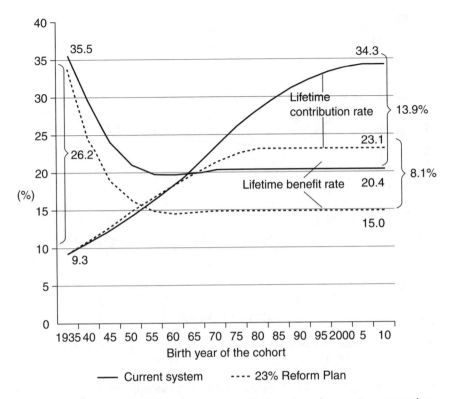

Figure 6.3 Lifetime contribution rate and lifetime benefit rate: a comparison between the current system and the 23 percent Reform Plan

born in 2005. The net receipt of ¥50 million by one cohort and the net payment of ¥25 million by another, makes the lifetime net receipt difference between the two cohorts ¥75 million.

This extreme inequity produced by the pension system is the heart of the pension problem in Japan.

6.4 Actuarially fair schemes

6.4.1 Switching to an actuarially fair scheme

The main cause of the generational conflict over public pensions is that the Japanese pension system is financed basically by the pay-as-you-go scheme, where the benefits for the retired at any given time are financed by contributions from the contemporary workers. In the pay-as-you-go scheme, therefore, the revenue from the pension contributions is not accumulated.

Under this scheme, increases in the size of the retiree population

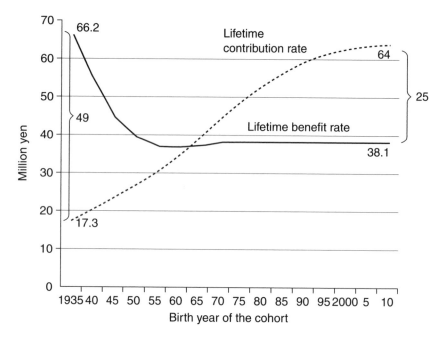

Figure 6.4 Lifetime contribution and lifetime benefit of the lifetime wage of the 1935 cohort

relative to the size of the working population push up the pension burden borne by each worker. As the population ages, therefore, the burden that each worker must pay to finance pensions increases. This means that the shape of the population pyramid, an incidental external factor, draws a line between generations that gain advantages, and generations that suffer losses. We can expect that Japanese pension finances will be put under a severe strain, precisely because Japan has opted for this pay-as-you-go approach when the population is declining in the long run.

The way to reduce the burden on future workers, then, is to switch to an actuarially fair scheme, under which each retiree receives a benefit that is actuarially fair in relation to the contributions made while working.[8] Under this scheme, there is no redistribution of income across generations. In other words, the net benefit each cohort receives is zero, regardless of demographic changes.

Apart from recovering fairness in the intergenerational pension burden, a switch to an actuarially fair system has another important advantage: it changes the nature of pension contributions from taxes to savings. In the existing pay-as-you-go system, the benefit eventually received is not directly linked to pension contributions. Contributions are thus perceived as taxes and the system distorts the labor supply. Under an actuarially fair system, on the other hand, payments into the system will be received as benefits, in amounts linked to market rates of returns. Hence, contributions will be perceived as a saving, and as a part of disposable income. The pension system would then be neutral to the labor supply.

6.4.2 *Rationale for the pay-as-you-go scheme*

Proponents of the pay-as-you-go scheme oppose a shift to an actuarially fair scheme on a number of grounds. For instance, they say that pensions should be seen as a means by which one generation supports another. Arguing that there is much merit in the spirit of looking after the generation of one's parents, they counsel against comparing pension burdens and benefits for each generation. Indeed, they support the pay-as-you-go scheme based on the virtue of "intergenerational help," rather than the actuarially fair method, which can be justified on the grounds of "self-help."

A generation that has lost its assets in war, or has been affected by an unanticipated lengthening of life spans, deserves help from younger people when it goes into retirement. Public support for such a generation is justifiable. However, it does not follow that everything should be left to intergenerational transfers. It should be sufficient to resort to intergenerational aid on a case-by-case basis as a supplement for unexpected circumstances,[9] while making the main financing scheme actuarially fair. Actuarially fair schemes should be the rule, intergenerational transfer the exception.

In tomorrow's aged society, the pay-as-you-go scheme will impose a heavy pension burden on workers' households. The advocates of the pay-as-you-go scheme would then be consistent only if they claimed that the imposition of a heavy load on the working generation is not a problem. Such a claim would stick faithfully to an ethical principle of intergenerational help. Trying to avoid the financial woes of the graying process while advocating the pay-as-you-go scheme, however, is rather like yawning and sneezing at the same time.

6.5 Financing the net pension debt

6.5.1 *Depletion of pension fund*

The solid line of Figure 6.5 shows our estimate of the pension fund based on the OSU model. The fund will be depleted in 2070.

Switching the system to an actuarially fair one does not solve this insolvency problem. If the pension system had started as an actuarially fair one, the system would be fully funded now, and the fund would not be depleted in the future. But if the existing system is more or less pay-as-you-go, the level of the fund will be far short of a full fund. Then switching it to an actuarially fair one does not prevent the system from becoming insolvent

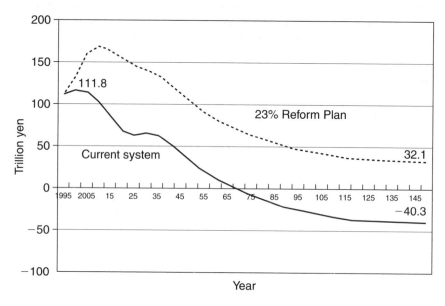

Figure 6.5 The balance of PEP pension fund (present value in 1995)

sooner or later, unless additional pension tax is imposed on top of the actuarially fair rate.

In order to figure out the level of additional tax required, one needs to know the net pension debt of the government, i.e. the shortage of the level of the actual fund relative to the full fund.

6.5.2 Pension debt

When the government collects pension contribution, it commits to pay a specified pension benefit in the future. The accumulated amount of the commitment is the pension debt of the government. If a pension system has enough funds to pay out the pension debt (= all the promised pension benefits), then the system is fully funded. Thus the amount of the pension debt is called the full fund. If the actual balance of the pension fund is short of the full fund, the difference is the net pension debt. Thus we have

(1) Net pension debt = Full fund (or Pension debt) – Actual pension fund

If the net pension debt keeps growing, then the pension system will eventually become bankrupt. However, even if the balance of the pension fund becomes negative temporarily, the pension system is financially healthy as long as expansion of the net pension debt is prevented. Thus the direction of the change in the net pension debt is crucial in determining the financial position of the pension system.

The chain line of Figure 6.6 duplicates the solid line of Figure 6.5, which shows the fund will be depleted in 1970. The solid line in Figure 6.6 shows the forecast of the pension debt (full fund) of the PEP system. From these two lines, the net pension debt is computed in terms of (1), and is depicted as the dotted line in Figure 6.6. It is clear from this figure that the net pension debt continues to grow in the future. Thus the pension system becomes insolvent under the present plan in the year 2070.

These lines show that the pension debt is ¥700 trillion at the end of 1995.[10] Against this debt, the balance of the fund was ¥110 trillion, resulting in the net pension debt of ¥590 trillion, that is, approximately 120 percent of the Japanese GDP.

6.5.3 Excess fiscal burden

From (1) the increase in net pension debt is equal to the increase in pension debt minus the increase in actual pension fund. The increase in each term can be further decomposed as follows:

Δ pension debt = increase in promised amount of the future benefit payment − actual pension benefit payment

Δ actual pension fund = actual contribution + interest on the fund + subsidy from general account − actual pension benefit payment

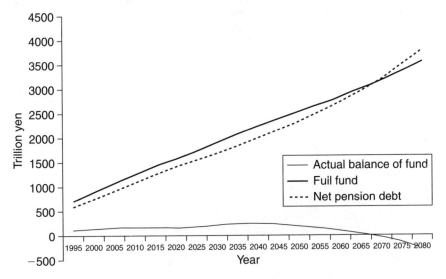

Figure 6.6 Net pension debt, full fund, and actual balance of fund of PEP

Thus from (1) we have

(2) Δ net pension debt = increase in promised amount of the future
benefit payment − (actual contribution + interest on the
fund + subsidy from general account)

If the pension contribution rate were set at the actuarially fair rate, then
the increase in the promised amount of the future benefit payment should
be exactly equal to the actual contribution during the period. Since they
are not equal in practice, we will call the difference (i.e. the actual contribution minus the actuarially fair lend level) the "excess contribution."
Then the following holds.

(3) Δ net pension debt = −(excess contribution + interest on the
fund + subsidy from general account)

The dotted line of Figure 6.7 depicts the future movement of excess contribution.

Finally, the excess fiscal burden is defined as the sum of the excess contribution and the subsidy from general account. Then we have

(4) Δ net pension debt = −(excess fiscal burden + interest on the
fund).

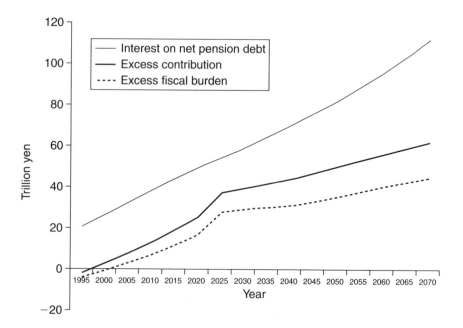

Figure 6.7 Interest on net pension debt and excess fiscal burden

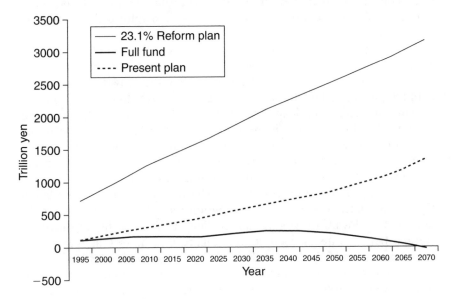

Figure 6.8 Projected balance of fund

The excess contribution grows rapidly since the contribution rate is raised. Also the subsidy from the general account proportional to the Basic Pension benefit payments grows steadily resulting in a rapid growth in the excess fiscal burden. The solid line of Figure 6.7 depicts the predicated level of excess fiscal burden. In Figure 6.6 the increase of the net pension debt is projected despite the planned increase of the excess contribution shown in Figure 6.7.

6.6 A reform plan

Coming up with countermeasures for Japan's graying society boils down to finding ways to narrow the intergenerational gap.

If the contribution rate can be varied for each cohort after the reform, setting the contribution rate of each cohort at the level of the downward sloping solid line in Figure 6.3 would make the system actuarially fair.

Such a reform would cause two problems, however. First, the new actuarially fair contribution rates for older working generations would exceed 30 percent. Second, in order to make the system solvent in the long run, additional pension taxes would be required on top of the actuarially fair rates to repay the net pension debt.

This will make the total burden on the older working cohorts exceedingly high, and their political resistance will be insurmountable. A politically feasible approximation of an actuarially fair reform would be to set a fixed contribution rate and maintain it until a full fund is accumulated.

Each cohort will then face a common contribution rate. Thus such a reform would face less political resistance than a reform that makes the system genuinely actuarially fair.

An example of such a reform is "the 23 percent Reform Plan" proposed in Hatta and Oguchi (1999), which fixes the contribution rate to 23.1 percent from now on till 2150, while curtailing the growth of the benefit until the per capita benefit becomes 20 percent lower than the level under the current system. Hatta and Oguchi (1999) show that this plan will accumulate a full fund in 2150 if the government continues to subsidize one third of the basic pension from the general account as it does now.

As Figure 6.1 shows, the contribution rate under this plan is higher than the current rate (17.35 percent), but it is much lower than the planned rate during the aged period (34.3 percent). The upward sloping dotted line in Figure 6.3 depicts the lifetime contribution rate of each cohort after this reform. The downward sloping dotted line of the same figure shows the lifetime benefit rate of each cohort. Figure 6.3 shows that the lifetime excess payments of the cohorts born after 1980 are around 8.1 percent of the lifetime wage income. Since this rate is 13.9 percent under the current system, the reform will substantially reduce the scale of the excess payment. The two dotted lines in Figure 6.3 show that the excess payment rates of the future generations fall from the current 13.9 percent to the new 8.1 percent.

This reform does not make the system actuarially fair, but makes the system much closer to an actuarially fair one than the current system. In other words, the 23 percent Reform Plan evens out the differentials among

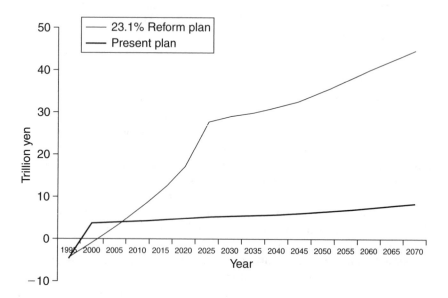

Figure 6.9 Excess contribution

generations by hiking premium payments now and cutting them later. It increases the load carried by those now 35 or over and lightens the load on the generations following them.

Because of today's sharp increases in premium payments, this plan will accumulate pension fund in the early twenty-first century, as Figure 6.5 shows. This implies that a system that accumulates pension fund now provides the kind of reform that equalizes the pension burden among generations. Reforms that make the system closer to an actuarially fair one can finance benefits for a record number of pensioners in the 2020s even if premium rates are then reduced.

6.7 Privatization

Privatization of the public pension system has been proposed as a means of reducing the fiscal burden of the pension system in the future. The privatized part of the pension will automatically become actuarially fair. It should be noted, however, that privatization by itself does not reduce the fiscal burden of future generations.

6.7.1 Privatization and redemption of the net pension debt

After privatization of the public pension takes place, the currently working cohorts will pay their pension premiums to pension companies. The pension companies will finance the benefits corresponding to these new premiums.

In addition, the benefits corresponding to contributions already paid before privatization, that is, the net pension debt must also be paid and financed by someone. (Beneficiaries of these benefits include both the current retirees and the current workers.) Even this part could be privatized by giving pension firms the entire public pension fund existing at the time of privatization, while obliging them to pay the corresponding benefits in the future on an actuarially fair basis. If the full fund were already accumulated, the expected value of the benefit of such a privatized pension would be equal to the benefit under the current system. Hence, privatization of this part of the benefit is likely to be accepted by the voters.

When a full fund is not accumulated, i.e. when there is net pension debt, full privatization of this part of the benefits is not possible. The public pension system must continue to pay at least part of the benefits to those who have already paid contributions.

As it was mentioned earlier, in Japan at present, the net pension debt is about ¥590 trillion. This must be financed by the government in the future. In other words, the public pension system must continue to exist for some 80 years even after privatization.

This implies that the current working generations must bear a double burden in order to finance the net pension debt: one through private pension companies for their own future benefits; and the other through the public pension system for the excess benefits that the older generations receive. The second burden, however, should be borne by the nation as a whole rather than by the private sector employee pension system, because this burden is caused by people who have nothing to do with the current participants of the private sector employee pension system.

It is often said that privatization of the public pension system will free future generations from the burden of the pension system. However, this is not correct. The burden to redeem the net pension debt of the government must be borne by future generations either through public pension contributions or through tax. It can be said, however, that privatization makes the net pension debt of the government explicit, and helps to make the burden more even among generations.

6.7.2 An example of privatization

As an example of privatization, let us suppose that the portion of the public pension system that corresponds to the "23 percent Reform Plan" is privatized. In other words, this portion is moved to define contribution pension plans provided by private pension companies. After privatization, a person in each cohort will pay premiums equal to the lifetime benefit rate depicted by the downward sloping dotted line in Figure 6.3.

The government gives the private pension companies the entire public pension fund, while obliging them to pay the benefits of the 23 percent Reform Plan, which is eventually 20 percent less than what the current system promises. But the actuarially fair contribution to this system is not sufficient to support benefits corresponding to past contributions. The funds given to the pension companies are not sufficient. Thus, the government must continue to subsidize the private pension companies' taxes or through contributions to the public pension for the partial contributors.

The two dotted lines in Figure 6.3 show that the lifetime excess payment rate of the cohorts born after 1985 is 8.1 percent under the 23 percent Reform Plan. This implies that even after this privatization, they must pay 8.1 percent of wages either in the form of tax or public pension contributions until 2150. This apparently excessive payment to the public pension system is necessary to redeem the government pension debt that exists at present.[11]

6.7.3 Patterns of privatization

Japan has a three-tier pension system. The first tier is the basic pension. The second tier is the income-proportional part of employee pension systems. The third tier is the private pension including individual pensions and corporate pension pensions.

There is wide national agreement that the basic pension should be provided publicly. This means that the National Pension (NP) and the Basic Pension portion of the PEP and GEP should continue to be publicly managed. There is also wide agreement that the third tier should be expanded through introduction of a defined-benefit corporate pension scheme.

As for the second tier or the income proportional part of PEP and GEP, proposals have been made to privatize it in one way or another, but there is hardly agreement on how it can be privatized. One extreme position is the "full privatization proposal," which advocates an abolition of the second tier and substituting the third tier for the abolished tier. Another is the "management privatization proposal," which advocates compulsory participation in the second tier whose funds are managed by the private sector.

In order to choose a concrete form of privatization, we need to examine the advantages of privatization. There are three:

First, privatization will force the pension system to become a defined benefit, i.e. actuarially fair. This will make the intergenerational transfer payments that are implicit in the current pension system explicit, making it possible to spread the burden more fairly among different cohorts.

Second, the private sector can manage the fund more efficiently than the government.

Third, participants can choose the level of pension benefits in the private pension program.

The first two advantages are self-evident, but the key issue is the third point. If the new private sector pension system allows for complete freedom of participation level, then it could allow the people the right of not participating in the pension scheme at all, making it a full-scale privatization.

A full-scale privatization, however, would eliminate the pension market for some people through adverse selection. Requiring a minimum participation would limit the freedom of choice regarding the amount of benefit. The benefit derived from the elimination of adverse selection by making the minimum pension participation compulsory, however, is likely to exceed the loss caused by limiting the freedom of choice regarding the amount of benefit.

The form of privatization that takes advantage of only the first two advantages will be the one that combines compulsory participation and private sector management of the funds. There are three possible institutional arrangements for such a system:

a Employers will collect compulsory contributions as they do now. However, the pension firms that the government designates then manage the fund.

b   Employers will collect compulsory contributions as they do now. Each participant chooses a pension firm to manage their fund.
c   A pension firm chosen by the employee directly collects the compulsory pension premium. This is like compulsory motor insurance.

It is sometimes said that in the US, (a) will cost less than (c) because of the transaction cost involved in (c). In Japan, (b) is likely to be the most efficient method. This is more or less like the Zaikei saving (government sponsored wealth forming saving), and its management know-hows are already accumulated.

6.7.4 Prospects for privatization

The portion of the benefits not backed up by the pension fund, but already promised by the public pension system, i.e. the net pension debt, must be financed either by tax or by public pension contributions, even after privatization. Setting up plans for the redemption of the net public pension debt of the government is the integral part of making the pension system actuarially fair. Since the public pension system will be forced into an actuarially fair form as preparation for privatization, privatization makes the net government debt explicit and forces the government to spread its burden fairly among different cohorts as our 23 percent reform plan does. This contributes to making the pension financing system healthy. In that sense, privatization can prepare the way for the reconstruction of pension financing.

6.8 Conclusion

Switching to an actuarially fair scheme has two practical advantages: (1) equalization of burdens across cohorts; and (2) the transformation of pension contributions into savings. As an example of such a reform, we analyzed the "23 percent Reform Plan" of the PEP in the present chapter. We showed that it attains a full fund in 2150, while reducing the net excess payment of the future generation from the current 14 percent to 8 percent.

In the present chapter, we proposed privatization of the management of pension funds, while keeping participation in the employee pension compulsory. If the full fund is already accumulated, the pension system can be completely privatized. If a full fund is not accumulated and there exists net pension debt, however, a complete privatization of the system cannot be attained; the government's financial contribution has to be made to repay the net pension debt even after privatization. Privatization of public pensions implies making the privatized part of the pension system actuarially fair. But simply making the system actuarially fair will not yield enough revenue to sustain the system. The system needs the revenue corresponding to the interest on the net pension debt. If we privatize the system now, therefore, the government still must continue to financially support pensions for an extended period. Privatization does not reduce the financial burden of the government alone.

Whether the system is privatized or not, it is necessary to make the pension system actuarially fair, and spread the net burden of pensions evenly among generations.

Appendix

The intra-generational redistributional effects

The present public pension system is run on a pay-as-you-go basis, in which an individual's pension contribution is not directly related to benefit. As a result, the system redistributes income in many different ways:

1   PEP and GEP redistribute income regressively for employees born before 1955. For those who were born after 1955, however, these pensions redistribute income progressively, as Figure 6.2 shows for those born in 1961.
2   PEP and GEP treat full-time housewives (non-working wives of employees) favorably. They receive NP benefits and widow's pension without paying contributions. Moreover, additional pension is paid to wives under 65.
3   Women are treated favorably in all the public pension systems. In setting contribution and benefit rates, the difference in the average life expectancies of the two sexes are ignored. Until 1995, the contribution rate and the starting age of benefit were lower for women, despite the fact that they live longer than men on average.
4   Poorer families are exempted from contribution payments in the NP system. They receive the reduced pension.
5   Net-transfer payments were given to the first generation of the public pension system.
6   The public pension system has expanded rapidly in the last 30 years. This was effective in reducing non-working elderly people. Thus, 246 out of 1000 aged families were on welfare programs in 1960, while the number declined to 165 in 1975, and to 70 in 1987. The public pension gave important income subsidies to retired people during this period.

Notes

1   The estimates in this chapter are based on the system as of 1999. In 1998, the Welfare Ministry of the Japanese Government presented five alternative reform plans. In this chapter, we call the Plan C among five alternatives 'the government reform plan of 1999'. In 2000, the Japanese congress passed a reform plan based on the Plan C of the five alternatives with some modifications. Thus the present system is slightly different from what we call 'the government reform plan of 1999' in this chapter.

2   For the detail of the OSU Model, see Hatta and Oguchi (1999) and http://www.ics.senshu-u.ac.jp/~thc0475 The model's assumptions on future economic and demographic variables are the same as those of the Welfare Ministry of the Japanese government, to make comparisons between the forecasts of the two models feasible.

3   For more detailed explanation of the system, see the references at the end of this chapter.

4   NP, PEP, and GEP are Kokumin Nenkin, Kosei Nenkin, and Kyosai Nenkin, respectively. Kyosai Nenkin is literally translated as Mutual Aid Pension.

5   Figure 6.2 simplifies reality slightly. In the actual scheme, there is a lower limit for low-income earners on both contribution and benefit. Also, there is an upper limit for high-income earners. For simplicity, we disregard these limits in the discussion below.

6   The total sum of the present values of the contribution paid at throughout one's life is called lifetime pension contribution. The sum of the present value of wage incomes throughout a person's lifespan is called the lifetime wage. The lifetime contribution rate is the lifetime ratio of lifetime contribution to lifetime wage. The upward-sloping solid line shows the lifetime contribution ratio of a male of average wage income who participated for the full 40 years. The benefit includes the pension benefit of his wife and basic pension benefit and a widow's benefit of his wife.

7   The lifetime benefit is the sum of the present value of the benefits one receives throughout one's life.

8   If a pension system has been actuarially fair throughout its existence, it will also be fully funded. If a pay-as-you-go system is switched to an actuarially fair one, however, it will not have a full fund.

9   Even when a generation is deserving of exceptional assistance, the burden can be spread across several succeeding generations rather than imposing it entirely on the children's generation.

10 The details of the method of calculation is explained in Hatta and Oguchi (1997).

11 We made two seemingly conflicting statements. First, the public pension system must continue to pay benefits for about 80 years after privatization. Second, it takes 150 years to redeem the net pension debt of the government. These statements are not conflicting. Indeed, if the public pension system issues new government bonds before the year 2080 in order to keep the balance of the pension fund position the system can completely redeem the newly insured band in 2150, by applying all of the 8.1 percent contribution to its redemption.

References

Hatta, Tatsuo and Kimura, Yoko (1993) "Kôteki nenkin wa sengyô shufu wo yûgû shiteiru" (The Japanese public pension system favors households with non-working wives), *Kikan Shakai Hoshô Kenkyû* (*Quarterly of Social Security Research*) 29(3): 210–21.

Hatta, Tatsuo and Oguchi, Noriyoshi (1997) "The net pension debt of the Japanese government," in Michael D. Hurd and Naohiro Yashiro (eds), *The Economic Effects of Aging in the United States and Japan* (National Bureau of Economic Research Conference Report), Chicago: University of Chicago Press, 333–51.

Hatta, Tatsuo and Oguchi, Noriyoshi (1999) *Nenkin Kaikaku-ron: Tsumitate*

Hoshiki e Iko Seyo (The theory of pension reform: switch to a funded system), Tokyo: Nihon Keizai Shinbunsha.

Horioka, Charles Yuji (1999) "Japan's public pension system: what's wrong with it and how to fix it," *Japan and the World Economy* 11(2): 293–303.

Horioka, Charles Yuji (1999) "Japan's public pension system in the twenty-first century," *ISER Discussion Paper* 482.

Pauly, Michael V. (1974) "Overinsurance and public provision of insurance: the role of moral hazard and adverse selection," *Quarterly Journal of Economics* 88: 44–62.

Wilson, C. (1977) "A model of insurance market with asymmetric information," *Journal of Economic Theory* 16: 167–207.

7 Integration of tax and social security systems

On the financing methods of a public pension scheme in a pay-as-you-go system

Akira Okamoto and Toshiaki Tachibanaki

Abstract

This chapter explores whether or not the contributions to public pension scheme in the pay-as-you-go system should be substituted by general taxes, e.g. a progressive labor income tax or a consumption tax. The chapter also investigates whether or not such possible integration of tax and social security systems is desirable from the aspects of both efficiency and equity. To analyze the problem, we adopt an extended lifecycle general equilibrium model of overlapping generations with heterogeneity in the ability of labor supply, using the household expenditure survey data. The simulation results indicate that a progressive expenditure tax with full integration is the most desirable policy.

7.1 Introduction

One of the most serious social and economic problems in Japan is the aging population. Drastic reform in both the tax and social security systems accommodating this drastic structural change is an urgent policy issue. This study proposes the guidelines of such reforms for Japan. The purpose of this chapter is the following. First, we investigate whether or not the integration of tax and social security (in particular, pay-as-you-go public pension) systems is desirable as regards efficiency and equity. Second, we evaluate what tax base (e.g. a progressive labor income tax, a proportional or progressive expenditure tax, and their combination) is preferable in the integration case.

Here, we will explain the implication of "integration" used in this chapter. The chapter does not address a problem with integration itself, such as a cost reduction by making two organizations one. We focus on the fact that the general government tax revenue currently covers one-third of the flat part (i.e. the basic pension) of public pension benefit in Japan, instead of the contributions to public pension scheme. We explore whether or not the ratio of one-third should be raised, for the purpose of getting the guidelines of structural reforms in the short term. We also investigate whether or not general taxes should cover not only the flat part but also the part proportional to remuneration for each individual, with the aim of obtaining the guidelines in the long term. Moreover, we evaluate what tax base is the best in terms of efficiency and equity, if it is desirable that the general tax covers a greater part of public pension benefit.

The crucial point is that the contributions to public pension scheme in the pay-as-you-go system in Japan essentially mean a proportional labor income tax. Hence, even if a proportional labor income tax replaces the contributions, this alternation would not affect economic variables such as the capital stock or the redistribution of income. Other taxes, for instance, a progressive labor income tax, a proportional or progressive expenditure tax, and their combination, have an influence on efficiency or equity. Thus, the term "integration" is employed, because we consider that general taxes replace the contributions along the lines of the current tax and social security systems in Japan.

There are three themes in this chapter.

First, in order to analyze the above problem, we adopt a lifecycle general equilibrium model of overlapping generations, the model being suitable as a basic theoretical framework to examine the problems related to the aging population.[1] There have been many papers which analyze the problems of an aging society by applying this kind of model. Nearly all, however, ignore the problem of intragenerational equity, namely the redistribution of resources among households who belong to the same cohort. For example, Auerbach *et al.* (1989) analyzes the effects of demographic transitions using this sort of model. The model, however, specifies only the behavior of a single representative individual, and thus it is impossible to deal with intragenerational income redistribution. It is vital to evaluate not only efficiency but also equity when handling tax reforms. Therefore, heterogeneous households with unequal incomes should be taken into account. We incorporate 275 households with heterogeneity in the ability of labor supply,[2] which enables us to treat the problem of intragenerational equity as well. Hence, our study will show some useful guidelines for tax and social security reforms in a comprehensive way.

Second, the public pension system in this chapter is more realistic than the earlier studies such as Homma *et al.* (1987a) or Kato (1998). In those papers, the public pension system consists of only the part proportional to remuneration of each household, and the public pension sector is financed independently and separately from the narrower government sector. By contrast, this chapter incorporates the basic pension into the public pension system, and one-third of the basic pension is covered or transferred from general tax revenues.

Third, this chapter lays a special emphasis on the empirical aspect. The parameter values assigned in the simulation are estimated using the data, "The Household Expenditure Survey 1995" by the Japan Cooperative Association. This permits us to conduct analysis in a model with a greater similarity to the real world.

This chapter is organized as follows. Section 2 identifies the basic model employed in simulation analysis. Section 3 explains the method of simulation analysis and the assumptions adopted. Section 4 evaluates the simulation findings. Section 5 summarizes and concludes the chapter, and discusses the policy implications.

7.2 Theoretical model

The lifecycle growth model employed in this chapter has several features. First, aggregate assets of the economy in each period consist of the assets of different generations who maximize their lifetime utility. This allows us to rigorously analyze changes in the supply of assets caused by demographic changes. Second, assets in the capital market, where aggregate assets appear as real capital, affect the level of production. Third, uncertainty over the length of life and unintended bequests are incorporated into the model, which enables us to estimate realistic age-profiles of consumption and savings for the elderly.[3] We calibrate the simulation to the Japanese economy by employing the population data estimated by the Institute of Population Problems of the Ministry of Health and Welfare in 1992.

The model has 75 different overlapping generations. Three types of agents are considered: households, firms, and the government. The basic structure of households is first explained.

7.2.1 Household behavior

Households are divided into 275 income classes: from the lowest to the highest income class. A single household type represents each income class. Each household has the same mortality rate and the same utility function. Unequal labor endowments, however, create different income levels. Each household appears in the economy as a decision-making unit at the age of 21 and lives to a maximum of 95. There is the risk of death in every period. Let $q_{j+1|j}$ be the conditional probability that a household of age $j + 20$ lives to $j + 21$. Then the probability of a household of age 21 surviving until $s + 20$ can be expressed by

$$p_s = \prod_{j=1}^{s-1} q_{j+1|j} \tag{1}$$

The probability $q_{j+1|j}$ is calculated from data estimated in 1992 by the Institute of Population Problems of the Ministry of Health and Welfare.

The utility of each household depends only on the level of consumption. There is no choice between leisure and labor supply. Each household works from age 21 to $RE + 20$ (retirement age). The labor supply is inelastic and after retirement is zero.[4] Each household makes lifetime decisions at age 21 concerning the allocation of wealth between consumption and savings, in order to maximize expected lifetime utility. The utility function of a representative household of income class i, whose form is assumed to be time-separable, is

$$U^i = \frac{1}{1 - \frac{1}{\gamma}} \sum_{s=1}^{75} p_s (1 + \delta)^{-(s-1)} \{C_s^i\}^{1 - \frac{1}{\gamma}}, \tag{2}$$

where C_s^i represents consumption (or expenditure) at age $s + 20$, δ the adjustment coefficient for discounting the future,[5] and γ the elasticity of intertemporal substitution on consumption. The superscript i ($= 1, 2, \ldots, 275$) denotes from the lowest to the highest income class in numerical order. The flow budget constraint equation for each household at age $s + 20$ is

$$A_{s+1}^i = \{1 + r(1 - \tau_r)\}A_s^i + \{1 - \tau_w(wx^i e_s) - \tau_p\}wx^i e_s + b_s^i + a_s^i - \{1 + \tau_c(C_s^i)\}C_s^i, \tag{3}$$

where A_s^i represents the amount of assets held by the household at the beginning of age $s + 20$, r the interest rate, w the wage rate per labor efficiency unit, and e_s the age-profile of earnings ability. x^i is the weight coefficient corresponding to the different levels of labor endowments among the income classes. b_s^i is the amount of public pension benefit, and a_s^i is the amount of bequest to be inherited at age $s + 20$. $\tau_w(wx^i e_s)$ is the tax rate on labor income, τ_c (C_s^i) that on consumption, and τ_r that on interest income. τ_p is the contribution rate to a public pension scheme in a pay-as-you-go system.

The tax system consists of labor income, interest income, and consumption taxes. Labor income or consumption (i.e. expenditure) is taxed progressively. The progressive tax schedule is incorporated in the same manner as in Auerbach and Kotlikoff (1983a, 1987). If the tax base is z, we choose two parameters labeled α and β, and set the average tax rate (τ_w and τ_c) equal to $\alpha + \frac{1}{2}\beta z$ for all values of z. The corresponding marginal tax rate ($\overline{\tau_w}$ and $\overline{\tau_c}$) is $\alpha + \beta z$. Setting $\beta = 0$ amounts to proportional taxation. One may make the tax system more progressive, holding the revenue constant, by increasing β and decreasing α simultaneously. If a progressive taxation is applied for labor income, the tax base z is equal to the gross wage rate, $wx^i e_s$. In the case of progressive expenditure taxation, z is equal to the annual level of consumption (or expenditure), C_s^i. In other words, a progressive taxation is applied to the gross wage rate or the level of consumption on an annual basis for each household. The symbols $\tau_w(wx^i e_s)$ and $\tau_c(C_s^i)$ in equation (3) denote that τ_w and τ_c are functions of $wx^i e_s$ and

C_3^i, respectively. The tax system for interest income is based on proportional taxation.[6]

The public pension system is assumed to be a pay-as-you-go system, which is close to the Japan's current system. The system consists of the basic pension (i.e. the flat part) and a part proportional to the average annual remuneration for each household. Variables related to the system are represented by

$$\begin{cases} b_s^i = f + \theta H^i & (s \geq ST) \\ b_s^i = 0 & (s < ST) \end{cases}$$
(4)

where the age at which each household starts to receive public pension-benefit is $ST + 20$, the average annual remuneration is H^i

$$\left(H^i = \frac{1}{RE} \sum_{s=1}^{RE} w x^i e_s \right),$$

the basic pension benefit is f, and the weight coefficient of the part proportional to H^i is θ. Thus, b_s^i reflects differences in the ability of labor supply among the 275 income classes.

There are unintended bequests caused by uncertainty over the length of life. The bequests, which were held as assets by deceased households, are handed over to surviving 50-year-old households.[7] Therefore a_s^i is positive if and only if $s = 30$, and otherwise zero. Inheritance is transferred within each income class. When BQ_t^i is the sum of bequests inherited by 50-year-old households at period t, a_{30}^i is defined by

$$a_{30}^i = \frac{BQ_t^i}{N_t P_{30}(1+n)^{-29}},$$
(5)

where

$$BQ_t^i = N_t \sum_{s=1}^{75} (p_s - p_{s+1})(1+n)^{-(s-1)} A_{s+1}^i,$$

N_t is the number of new households entering the economy as decision-making units at period t, and n is the common growth rate of the successive cohorts.[8]

Let us consider the case in which each household maximizes its lifetime utility under a constraint. Each household maximizes equation (2) subject to equation (3) (see Appendix A). From the utility maximization problem, the equation expressing evolution of consumption over time for each household is characterized by

$$C_{s+1}^i = \left[\left(\frac{p_{s+1}}{p_s} \right) \left\{ \frac{1+r(1-\tau_r)}{1+\delta} \right\} \left(\frac{1+\bar{\tau}_c(C_s^i)}{1+\bar{\tau}_c(C_{s+1}^i)} \right) \right]^\gamma C_s^i.$$
(6)

If the level of initial consumption, C_1^i, is specified, optimal consumption behavior of all ages can be derived from equation (6). The amount of assets held by each household for all ages can be obtained from equation (3). The expected lifetime utility of each household is derived from equation (2).

The social welfare function, which takes account of heterogeneity in the ability of labor forces and thus resulting distribution of consumption, is given by

$$SW = \sum_{i=1}^{275} U^i. \tag{7}$$

This function is obtained by a simple summation of the expected lifetime utilities of the 275 income groups. When comparing simulation cases in a steady state, it is not necessary to take account of the utilities of all overlapping generations existing at a period. An estimation of lifetime utility of a single cohort is sufficient, because our purpose is to compare the welfare level among cases. The function is of a "Benthamite type," but it depends largely on the utility of the low-income class, as does the "Rawlsian type." The function is maximized if after-tax income is equal for all income classes.[9]

As for the basic structure of firms, a single production sector is assumed to behave competitively using capital and labor, subject to a constant-returns-to-scale production function. See Appendix B for the details of the basic structure of firms and the government, and market equilibrium conditions.

7.3 Simulation analysis

7.3.1 Method of simulation

We will explain the method of simulation. The model is solved under the hypothesis of perfect foresight by households. The interest, wage, and tax rates are assumed to be correctly anticipated by households. The simulation model in the previous section can be solved using the Gauss-Seidel method, if tax and public pension systems are determined (see Appendix C for the computation process).

Five cases in the steady state in 1995 are considered under balanced budget policies. The assumption of tax revenue neutrality is normally imposed for a tax model to get the pure effects of tax reforms. Our study, however, intends to substitute general taxes for the contributions to public pension scheme. Hence, it is impossible to hold the total tax revenue, namely, $T_t(\tau)$, constant across cases. We decided to keep the general government spending except for a transfer to public pension sector, namely, $G_t(g)$, constant among all cases (see Appendix B for the definition of $T_t(\tau)$ and $G_t(g)$).

The size of population is the same in all cases, and general government expenditure per capita, g, is exogenously given as a constant. Thus, the general government spending, G_t, is exogenous and unchanged across all cases. Since the total tax revenue, $T_t(\tau)$, consists G_t and a transfer to the public pension scheme as indicated by equation (10), $T_t(\tau)$ in each case depends on the degree of the transfer. For the tax system, the tax rates on labor income, $\tau_w(wx^ie_s)$, and on consumption, $\tau_c(C_s^i)$, are exogenously given, resulting in the endogenous tax rate on interest income, τ_r. For the public pension system, the amount of the basic pension per capita, f, and the weight coefficient of the part proportional to remuneration for each individual, θ, are exogenously given. Hence, the contribution rate to public pension scheme, τ_p, is made endogenous.

7.3.2 *Five cases for simulations*

The following five cases are considered for our simulation. Case A is the benchmark in 1995, where there is the realistic progressive tax system on labor income, and the tax rate on consumption is 5 percent and that on interest income 20 percent. Cases B and C carry out partial integration, which will give us the reform guidelines in the short term. Cases D and E execute perfect integration, which will indicate the reform guidelines in the long term.

1   *Case A (benchmark case):*
    The case reflects the fact in 1995 that the general tax revenue covers one-third of the basic pension in the public pension system.
2   *Case B (partial integration and a progressive labor income tax):*
    The rate of tax transfer is raised from one-third to a half (i.e. a rise of one-sixth of the basic pension),[10] and the extra tax burden accompanied is covered by a progressive labor income tax. In other words, public pension contributions, which mean a *proportional* labor income tax, are substituted by a *progressive* labor income tax. Under the tax revenue neutrality, the adjustment in tax parameters on labor income is made only by the part proportional to labor income, β, holding the constant term, α, unchanged.
3   *Case C (partial integration and a proportional consumption tax):*
    The rate of tax transfer is raised from one-third to a half (i.e. a rise of one-sixth of the basic pension), and the additional tax burden accompanied is covered by a proportional consumption tax. In other words, public pension contributions, which signify a proportional *labor income* tax, are substituted by a proportional *consumption* tax.
4   *Case D (perfect integration and a proportional expenditure tax):*
    The tax revenue covers the total public pension payment which consists of the basic pension and the part proportional to remuneration for each individual. The source of overall tax revenue is only a

proportional expenditure tax. Labor income and interest income taxes
are eliminated.
5   *Case E (perfect integration and a progressive expenditure tax):*
In Case D, a *progressive* expenditure tax replaces a proportional one.
The degree of tax progressivity on expenditure is assigned in the
following way: the constant term, α, is half of that in Case D, and the
parameter of a part proportional to expenditure, β, is adjusted under
the tax revenue neutrality.

Empirical evaluation of each simulation from Case B to E in comparison
with the benchmark case A is made by the following formulation of *RWC*
(relative welfare changes by percentage figures):

$$RWC = \frac{-100 \times (U_j - U_A)}{U_A}, \tag{23}$$

where U_A signifies each household's utility in Case A, and U_j ($j = $ B, C, D,
E) means that in each simulation. The minus sign was added so that
improvements in *RWC* show positive numerical changes in welfare.

7.3.3 Data and parameter values

The household expenditure survey in 1995, which was collected and classified by the Japan Cooperative Association, is used as a data source. This
survey reports each household's income, consumption, tax, social security
benefit and contributions, etc. The number of observations is 275, which
enables us to evaluate changes in welfare of each household caused by tax
and public pension reforms. A rigorous quantitative examination on the
changes is feasible, provided that we can get the realistic figures concerning the various parameter values such as each household's labor endowments or taxes. The process for estimation of parameter values employed
in simulation analysis is presented and discussed (see Table 7.1 for the
assignment of parameter values).

7.3.3.1 Weight on labor endowments for each income class

The original survey included 363 households. Some of them are retired
households who do not work, and thus their consumption is based on their
pension benefits and spending from their accumulated wealth. Since the
starting age of receiving public pension benefits is currently 60, *RE* (i.e.
the parameter of retirement age) can be specified as 39. The retired household whose head is older than 59 is removed, resulting in the 276 working
households. However, one particular household's annual revenue is
¥678,350, which is below the subsistence level, while this household gets a
high amount of rent income, ¥5,803,760. This sample was excluded,

Table 7.1 Parameter values employed in simulation analysis

	Parameter values
Elasticity of intertemporal substitution in utility	$\gamma = 0.2$
Elasticity of substitution in production	$\sigma = 0.6$
Weight parameter in production	$\varepsilon = 0.2$
Scale parameter in production	$Q = 1.0127$
Retirement age	$RE = 39$
Starting age for receiving public pension benefit	$ST = 40$
Amount of basic pension benefit per capita	$f = 0.19815$
Weight coefficient of proportional part in public pension benefit	$\theta = 0.32224$
Parameter for discounting the future	$\delta = -0.0231$
Growth rate of the successive cohorts	$n = 0.01462$
New entrants at period t	$N_t = 1.5$

because it is not appropriate to include it for the purpose of estimating labor endowments for each income class. As a result, the total number is 275, which enables us to estimate the labor endowments.

Figure 7.1 shows the distribution of households' annual labor income, which is defined by the following formulation:

Labor income of a household = husband's wage + wife's wage + husband's bonus + wife's bonus + self-employed income + in-house revenue + other family members' revenue. (A)

The average labor income is ¥7,928,220 with its minimum ¥2,521,740 and maximum ¥17,193,603. By dividing each labor income by its average

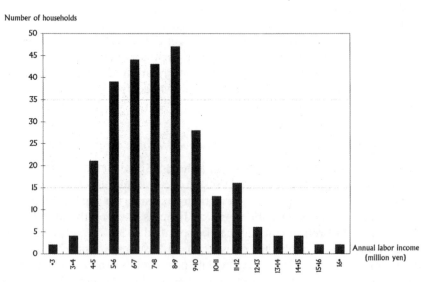

Figure 7.1 Distribution of households' annual labor income

and thus normalizing each labor income, each weight on labor endowments,

$$x^1, x^2, \ldots, x^{275} \text{ with } \sum_{i=1}^{275} x^i = 275, \text{ can be estimated.}$$

7.3.3.2 Estimation of the age-profile of labor efficiency, e_s

Figure 7.2 indicates the distribution of households' age-annual labor income. By regressing on x^i with the independent variables being each household's age and its squared form, it is possible to estimate the age-profile of labor efficiency, e_s. The results estimated by the OLS method are presented in Table 7.2.

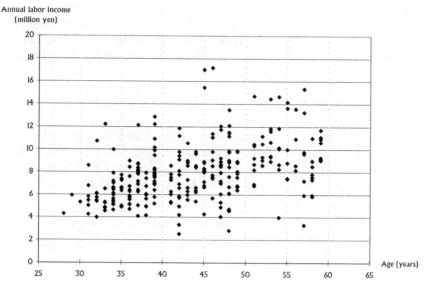

Figure 7.2 Distribution of age-annual labor income

Table 7.2 Estimation of the age-profile of labor efficiency

To estimate the age-profile of labor efficiency, e_s, the following equation is used:

$$X = a + bN + cN^2$$

where X denotes normalized annual labor income, i.e. x^i ($i = 1, 2, \cdots, 275$), and N age of the head of each household.

Variable	Estimated coefficient	Standard error	t-statistic
a	−0.455200	0.546139	−0.83349
b	0.049149	0.025009	1.96525
c	−0.0003498	0.000280	−1.25106

7.3.3.3 Estimation of the parameters of tax progressivity on labor income, α and β

The average tax rate on labor income is $\tau_w = \alpha + \frac{1}{2}\beta(wx^i e_s)$, as shown in Section 7.2. The estimation of parameters, α and β, in the benchmark case A was made in the following way. First, the tax burden on labor income of each household is calculated by the following formulation:

> Labor income tax burden of a household = husband's national income tax + wife's national income tax + husband's local income tax + wife's local income tax. (B)

By dividing (B) by (A), it is possible to get the tax rate on labor income for each household. The parameters, α and β, are estimated by the OLS method for the following regression equation: The dependent variable is the tax rate on labor income, and the independent variable is half of x^i, as indicated in Table 7.3. Table 7.4 shows the assignment of parameter values, α and β, in each simulation case.

Two notes are added. First, the regression equation ignores the weighting factors, w and e_s, but we_s is, of course, not always equal to unity. The value of a scale parameter in production, Q, is chosen so that the ratio of labor income tax revenue to labor income at macro level equals the realistic value of 6.678 percent. Second, a negative value of α includes the possibility of negative tax rates for some poor households. When negative tax rates were obtained for some households, we took the zero rates.

7.3.3.4 Estimation of the parameters for the public pension scheme

In the model, public pension benefit consists of the flat part, namely, the basic pension, and a part proportional to remuneration for each household. Under the current Japan's system, the general tax revenue covers

Table 7.3 Estimation of the parameters of tax progressivity on labor income

To estimate the parameters of tax progressivity on labor income, α and β, in the benchmark case A, the following equation is employed:

$$T = a + b\frac{1}{2}X$$

where T denotes the average tax rate on labor income and X normalized annual labor income, namely, x^i ($i = 1, 2, \cdots, 275$).

Variable	Estimated coefficient	Standard error	t-statistic
a	−0.018767	0.004704	−3.9896
b	0.155266	0.008962	17.3246

Table 7.4 Empirical results caused by different tax and public pension systems

Case	A (Benchmark)	B (Partial integration; Progressive labor income tax)	C (Partial integration; Proportional consumption tax)	D (Perfect integration; Proportional expenditure tax)	E (Perfect integration; Progressive expenditure tax)
Tax revenue per capita (τ)	*0.0954	*0.1038	*0.1038	*0.2163	*0.2168
Tax rate on labor income (τ_w)	Progressive $*\begin{cases}\alpha=-0.0188\\\beta=0.15527\end{cases}$	Progressive $*\begin{cases}\alpha=-0.0188\\\beta=0.17701\end{cases}$	Progressive $*\begin{cases}\alpha=-0.0188\\\beta=0.15527\end{cases}$	$*\begin{cases}\alpha=0\\\beta=0\end{cases}$	$*\begin{cases}\alpha=0\\\beta=0\end{cases}$
Tax rate on consumption (τ_c)	Proportional $*\begin{cases}\alpha=0.05\\\beta=0\end{cases}$	Proportional $*\begin{cases}\alpha=0.05\\\beta=0\end{cases}$	Proportional $*\begin{cases}\alpha=0.06201\\\beta=0\end{cases}$	Proportional $*\begin{cases}\alpha=0.31822\\\beta=0\end{cases}$	Progressive $*\begin{cases}\alpha=0.15911\\\beta=0.43283\end{cases}$
Tax rate on interest income (τ_r)	0.2000	0.2000	0.2000	0.0000	0.0000
Contribution rate (τ_p)	0.1650	0.1527	0.1525	0.0000	0.0000
K/L	3.094	3.130	3.206	5.570	5.800
Y/L	1.198	1.199	1.202	1.262	1.265
K/Y	2.584	2.610	2.667	4.415	4.583
Interest rate (r)	0.0408	0.0401	0.0387	0.0167	0.0157
Wage rate (w)	1.0715	1.0737	1.0782	1.1688	1.1745
U1	−8127.22	−7771.36	−7920.46	−8424.53	−6039.86
U50	−474.58	−463.45	−467.46	−481.04	−415.64
U100	−248.83	−244.69	−245.41	−243.90	−223.83
U150	−140.79	−139.49	−138.97	−132.50	−129.20
U200	−90.88	−90.65	−89.74	−82.20	−84.43
U250	−39.85	−40.41	−39.37	−32.65	−37.54
U275	−10.68	−11.30	−10.55	−6.75	−9.81
Social welfare	−93350.91	−90976.88	−91773.24	−94117.74	−79595.29

Note: Asterisks(*) before numerical values indicate that the variables are exogenous.

one-third of the flat part, and the public pension contributions cover both the remaining two-thirds and the overall proportional part. Hence, μ in equations (10) and (11) in Appendix B is assigned to $\frac{1}{3}$ in the benchmark case A. This rate for other simulations is changed to show desirable policy reforms. In the cases of partial integration, B and C, μ is assigned to $\frac{1}{2}$. In the cases of full integration, D and E, the following equation (10)' replaces equations (10), (11), (13), (14), and (15) in Appendix B:

$$T_t = G_t + B_t \qquad \text{where } B_t = N_t \sum_{s=ST}^{75} \left\{ p_s(1+n)^{-(s-1)} \sum_{i=1}^{275} b_s^i \right\}. \tag{10}'$$

The *White Paper on Welfare 1996* published by the Ministry of Welfare suggests that the monthly amount of basic pension for an individual is ¥65,458, and thus the annual benefit for a couple is ¥1,570,992. Since ¥7,928,220 is assumed to be standard in our simulation model, the value of a normalized parameter, f (the amount of basic pension per capita), is derived. The weight coefficient of the part proportional to remuneration, θ, is chosen so that the contribution rate in the benchmark case A equals the actual value of 16.5 percent in an employee's pension plan (Kosei Nenkin) in 1995.

7.3.3.5 Adjustment coefficient for discounting the future, δ

The parameter value of δ is adjusted so that individual consumption-savings behavior in the simulation is consistent with the actual relative scale of capital stock at macro level. The value, δ, is determined such that the capital–income ratio (K/Y) in the simulation equals 2.58, which is suggested by the *Annual Report on National Accounts 1996* published by the Economic Planning Agency.

7.3.3.6 Growth rate of the successive cohorts, n

According to the *Population Projections for Japan 1991–2090*, a 1992 publication by the Institute of Population Problems of the Ministry of Health and Welfare, the ratio of population of 65 and over to the population of 21 and over is estimated to be 19.2 percent in 1995. The parameter value of n is chosen under the given survival probabilities, p_s, in 1995, so that the ratio in the simulation equals the estimated value of 19.2 percent.

7.3.3.7 Number of overlapping generations

In the case of an overlapping generations model with 80-period life cycles, where households can live to a maximum of 100, households borrow money after 90. The reason is that at the final stage of old age, the weight on consumption in the utility function is much reduced because of a drastic decrease in expected survival probabilities (see Note 3). Hence, it leads to the low level of consumption, which is lower than the amount of public pension benefit. It is possible to rule out such borrowing behavior at the final stage, by assuming a 75-period model with a maximum survival age of 95, as in this chapter.

7.4 Simulation results

7.4.1 Simulation results and their interpretation

Before presenting the simulation results, the indexes of efficiency and equity adopted in this chapter are explained. The influence on capital accumulation is used as an indicator of efficiency. This is because under the assumption of inelastic labor supply, the level of total output depends only on the level of capital stock, as indicated by equation (8) in Appendix B. The social welfare function represented by equation (7) in Section 2 is mainly used as an indicator of equity (see Note 8). However, we should keep in mind that the function depends on not only the aspect of equity but also that of efficiency. Table 7.4 shows the numerical results of each simulation. Figures 7.3 and 7.4 are the graphical representations of Cases B and C, and of Cases D and E, respectively.

The overall result suggests that Case E achieves the best performance, where perfect integration of tax and public pension systems is implemented and a progressive expenditure tax is introduced. This conclusion is

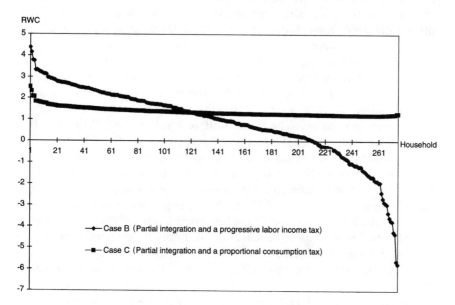

Figure 7.3 Changes in welfare of 275 income class households

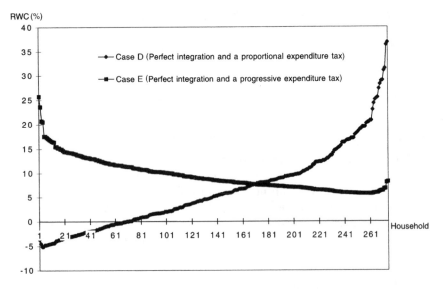

Figure 7.4 Changes in welfare of 275 income class households

derived from the following two observations. One is that, the highest value of 5.80 is attained for the capital–labor ratio (K/L) among all simulation cases. The other is that, the highest improvement of −79595 is achieved for the level of social welfare among all simulations. Moreover, the individual change in welfare is positive for all households. We will explain in detail the reasons why Case E is chosen as the most desirable policy reform.

First, we will examine policy reforms in the short-term view along the lines of the current Japan's system, through comparing Cases B and C. The transition from Case A to B means that a proportional labor income tax is substituted by a progressive labor income tax, because the contributions to public pension scheme have the same implication as a proportional labor income tax. The social welfare level of −90977 in Case B is higher than that of −93351 in Case A, which shows that the transition from proportionality to progressivity brings forth better outcomes in terms of equity. The transition from Case A to C signifies that a proportional labor income tax is substituted by a proportional consumption tax. The capital–labor ratio (K/L) of 3.21 in Case C is greater than that of 3.09 in Case A, which indicates that the substitution leads to better outcomes as regards efficiency. This is because a consumption tax burden continues to exist even after retirement, and thus it requires individuals to have a larger amount of savings than a labor income tax under the tax revenue neutrality.

According to the simulation results of Cases B and C, the move from public pension contributions to taxation, whether it is a progressive labor income tax or a proportional consumption tax, improves the overall welfare of the economy: the social welfare is −90977 and −91773, respectively. The capital–labor ratio (K/L) of 3.21 in Case C is larger than that of 3.13 in Case B, which shows that Case C is better than Case B from the resource allocation perspective, namely, efficiency. By contrast, Case B is superior to Case C in terms of equity perspective: the welfare level for lower-income households in Case B ameliorates by from 3 to 4.5 percent increase, but deteriorates for higher-income households by from 3 to 6 percent decrease. If the society has a consensus on a further redistribution from higher-income households to lower-income ones, Case B may be preferable.

We cannot, nevertheless, ignore the fact that Case C increases the individual welfare for all households by approximately 1.5 percent. A subjective judgement is required to select either Case B, which indicates a further redistribution, or Case C, which shows more capital accumulation and an increase in welfare for each household. Under an aging trend in the population structure, the aggregate household saving rate will decline, resulting in a less capital accumulation. This is because the trend will diminish the ratio of younger households in their accumulation phase to older households in their spending phase, based on the lifecycle motive. The choice of a consumption tax instead of a labor income tax may avoid such a decrease in capital accumulation. Unless the society has a high preference for a further redistribution, the policy reform represented by Case C should be adopted in the short term, especially in an aging society.

Second, we will investigate policy reforms in the long-term view, through comparing Cases D and E. In both of the cases, the whole public pension payment in addition to the general government expenditure is covered only by an expenditure (or consumption) tax. The simulation results of Cases D and E indicate a large increase in the capital–labor ratio (K/L) (5.57 and 5.80, respectively), which means significant contribution to capital accumulation. Thus, both of the cases are desirable in terms of efficiency. Case D, where a proportional expenditure tax covers the overall payment, however, poses an important problem; According to Figure 7.4, the welfare for higher-income households is greatly improved (i.e. 20~40 percent increase), while the welfare for lower-income households is lowered by an approximately 5 percent decrease. The reason is that there is no tax progressivity in Case D.

On the other hand, Case E, where a progressive expenditure tax covers the total payment, shows that the individual welfare for all households improves by an about 10 percent increase. Hence, Case E, which assumes progressivity instead of proportionality, should be regarded as a more desirable policy reform than Case D in terms of equity. Of course, it is possible to change freely the degree of redistribution in Case E, by changing the degree of tax progressivity on expenditure, namely, two parameter values of α and β.

Households' behavior is likely to be more distorted under the taxation on labor income than under the taxation on expenditure (or consumption), especially in the case of progressive taxation. This fact may be supported with the following two reasons.

First, when an expenditure tax is progressive and tax rates rise with age as in our analysis, it distorts the intertemporal consumption choice as shown in equation (6); rising marginal expenditure (or consumption) tax rates, like an interest income tax, raise the price of future consumption relative to current consumption. In this way, progressive expenditure taxation distorts individual age profiles of consumption. Hence, we might expect this distortion to lead to a substantial reduction in savings and thus in the long run capital stock. Progressive expenditure taxation, however, brings about more capital accumulation than progressive labor income taxation (see Okamoto forthcoming for the details). Moreover, according to Auerbach and Kotlikoff (1987), where labor supply is assumed to be elastic, the capital stock declines less with the move from proportionality to progressivity under the consumption tax than under the labor income tax, which continues to leave the intertemporal consumption decision undistorted.

Second, Auerbach and Kotlikoff (1987) also suggests that labor supply decreases more with the transfer from proportionality to progressivity under the labor income tax than under the consumption tax. This fault for progressive labor income taxation does not come out in our model with inelastic labor supply. In this sense, the taxation relatively has an advantage over progressive expenditure taxation in our analysis. The simulation analysis in Okamoto (forthcoming), which employs the same model as this chapter, nevertheless, reports that progressive expenditure taxation is superior to progressive labor income taxation in terms of both efficiency and equity. If labor supply were assumed to be elastic in our model, progressive expenditure taxation would bring forth even more favorable results than progressive labor income taxation. This fact should be stressed when we recommend progressive expenditure taxation as the most desirable tax structure.

7.4.2 Comments

The following five comments should be noted in interpreting the simulation results.

First, the simulation results show that progressive taxation promotes capital accumulation. However, this may depend on inelastic labor supply, which is one of the assumptions in our model. As labor supply is exogenous, the only effect of progressive taxation on income comes from the effect on savings. Given the age-profiles of labor income or consumption with an upward slope as in our analysis, progressive taxation increases savings and thus income. If the relationship between tax progressivity and labor supply incentive were explicitly taken into account, progressive taxation would not always give favorable outcomes. Since we address the Japan's economy, nevertheless, our simulation has some significant policy implications, keeping this assumption in mind (see Note 4).

Second, the social welfare function represented by equation (7) evaluates the utility of the low-income class with great significance (see Note 8). The function can be regarded as a measure of the degree of equity, because the effects of the efficiency aspect on social welfare are relatively low. If we take pre-tax income as given, then it is obvious from the social welfare function used that progressive taxation leads to higher welfare, because it is maximized when after-tax income is equal for all income classes. For instance, when comparing Cases C (partial integration and a proportional consumption tax) and D (perfect integration and a proportional expenditure tax), the capital–labor ratio (K/L) of 3.21 in Case C is much lower than that of 5.57 in Case D. But, the level of social welfare of -91773 in Case C is higher than that of -94118 in Case D. This is simply because there exists tax progressivity on labor income in Case C, while there is no progressivity in Case D, where a proportional expenditure tax covers the overall revenue.

Third, we employ cross-section data in the estimation of the difference in labor endowments among the 275 income classes within a cohort. The household expenditure survey in 1995 by the Japan Cooperative Association includes all age groups: young, middle, and old. Therefore, the estimated value concerns income distribution not of people who belong to the same cohort, but of all people who exist in the economy at a point in time (1995). So-called panel data, which traces people who belong to the same cohort for a long period, should have been used for the purpose of our analysis. This kind of data is at present, however, not available in Japan, and thus the cross-section data is employed as the second best source.

The difference based on educational background may also account for heterogeneity in the ability of labor supply. It is vital to understand how the simulation results would be revised, if such an alternative indicator were adopted as the difference in labor endowments. We have also estimated the difference based on educational background as another indicator. Then, the difference in labor endowments is smaller than that adopted in this chapter.

Fourth, all income classes are identical in our model, including the utility function, except for labor endowments. Empirical evidence such as Hausman (1979) and Lawrence (1986), however, suggests that the rate of time preference may be substantially higher for low-income individuals. If such a difference in the rate of time preference among households within a cohort were introduced, the simulation results would be modified. Similarly, the difference in elasticity of intertemporal substitution, γ, among them would also revise the results.

Finally, since the simulation results depend on given parameters, we must be careful about the effects of any changes in parameters. In particular, a slight change in the parameter of elasticity of intertemporal substitution, γ, greatly affects capital accumulation.

7.5 Conclusion

This chapter has investigated whether or not the contributions to public pension scheme in the pay-as-you-go system, which means a proportional labor income tax, should be substituted by (other) taxes such as a progressive labor income tax and a (progressive or proportional) consumption tax. The chapter has also examined what tax base is preferable as regards both efficiency and equity in such an integration case. To analyze the problem, we have adopted a simulation approach for an extended lifecycle general equilibrium model of overlapping generations with heterogeneity in earnings ability, using the household expenditure survey data in Japan.

Our main proposal based on the simulation results includes the following two items. First, the integration of tax and public pension systems is desirable. In other words, the contributions to public pension scheme should be replaced by general taxes such as a progressive labor income tax or a consumption tax. Second, the introduction of a progressive expenditure tax is recommended as a tax base in the integration case. Hence, our proposal is to introduce a progressive expenditure tax with full integration in terms of both efficiency and equity. As for structural reforms in the short term along the lines of the current Japan's system, we should promote the partial integration of tax and public pension systems as a transition process, substitute a consumption tax for the contributions, and implement a gradual shift towards perfect integration.

Three reservations are described here. First, there is only a partial impact of progressive taxation and no excess burden, because labor supply is assumed to be inelastic in our model. Elastic labor supply should be introduced in order to analyze comprehensively the effects of progressive taxation. Second, our model deals only with unintended bequests. Intended bequests should be included in the model. Strategic bequest motives are also likely to prevail in Japan. Finally, tax and social security reforms have different effects on different generations. Specifically, current and future generations receive different impacts of the reforms. Therefore, it is necessary to take account of the transition process to an aging society.

7.5.1 *The current state in Japan and policy implications*

When discussing policy implications based on the simulation results, it would be useful to show the fact that Japan has already partly introduced the integration of tax and social security systems. In other words, Japan is now in a transition process from a perfectly separate system to a completely integrated system. Let us take the example of the public pension system. The public pension system was drastically modified in 1985. The most significant reform was the introduction of a two-tier system on the benefit side: (1) a flat part (i.e. the basic pension) and (2) a proportional part (i.e. the part proportional to remuneration for each individual). The flat part currently pays about ¥65,000 per month to retired people. The amount is insufficient for each retired individual to survive, and thus lower than a level of national minimum. The notion of the basic pension, however, comes certainly from and is consistent with the idea of a national minimum.

More importantly, general government tax revenue currently covers one-third of the flat part of public pension benefit in Japan. In other words, a part of tax revenue is already transferred to the social security system. It is possible to conclude that the social security system in Japan has been partly integrated with the tax system, because the share of one-third is considerable. Hence, our proposal is to take it further and to have a perfectly integrated system of tax and social security. This optimum system is consolidated by the introduction of a progressive expenditure tax (see Hatta (1996) for a discussion about the introduction of an expenditure tax in Japan).

7.5.2 Justification for our proposals

We point out four reasons why integration of the tax and social security systems is desirable.

First, the integration facilitates the introduction of the notion of a civil minimum (or national minimum) for all people, because the general government tax can cover a universal minimum level more efficiently and equitably. Several countries, such as Australia and New Zealand, adopt general taxes instead of contributions in order to cover social insurance payments. General taxes can cover such a minimum level with simplicity and at a lower cost.

Second, related to the first point, the integration can eliminate a typical argument of "who gained and who lost from the intergenerational or intragenerational aspect" under the social security system where contributions cover the cost. The argument has been one of the central popular issues and has been excessively gaining momentum in Japan. If general taxes were used to pay for both public pension and medical care, it would be excluded that each individual contribution and benefit by social security can be calculated and compared in detail.

Third, a minimum subsistence guarantee by general taxes is consistent with the principle of social security, which intends to produce no desperately poor individuals. Such a goal can be achieved by the system which pays a minimum amount over the poverty level to all individuals. An individual, who desires a higher living standard or more sufficient security than a minimum level guaranteed by the government, can participate in such as enterprise pension, private pension, or private health insurance.

Fourth, the integration of tax and social security systems reduces considerably administration costs, because only one institution, namely, a tax bureau, collects revenue from the private sector. Coexistence of a tax bureau and a social insurance agency is costly regarding the administration cost of public revenues. A decrease in the administration cost would increase the total amount of payment for public pension and medical care.

7.5.3 *How can a progressive expenditure tax be implemented?*

Conceptually, it is easy to introduce a progressive expenditure tax. There are, however, potentially difficult problems in its implementation in the real world: that is to measure and grasp the figures of each individual expenditure. How can we measure a tax base which is defined by expenditure? We propose that it is feasible to measure it in the following method.

There is an equation that income is equal to consumption (or expenditure) plus savings. If the amount of both income and savings is available for each individual or household, the balance is equal to the amount of expenditure. The income figure is efficiently obtained using the current Japan's system of withholding taxes at the income source. The savings figure can be obtained through the self-assessment system. It should be emphasized that the self-assessment of savings is the exact opposite to that of income in terms of an individual incentive: the more an individual declares savings, the lower tax rates on expenditure applied become, which is contrastive to the case of self-assessment of income.

The savings figure can be consolidated using an electronic financial system. All financial institutions are requested to report the whole amount of financial assets held by each individual with the individual tax number (or the social security number) to a tax office. Thus, the tax office is able to grasp the overall wealth of each individual. Of course, it depends on the development of a computer-based financial system. The introduction of a progressive expenditure tax is our recommendation in the long-term perspective.

Acknowledgements

An early version of this chapter was presented to the 53rd Congress of the International Institute of Public Finance (IIPF) at Ritsumeikan University, the 1997 Annual Meeting of the Japan Association of Economics and Econometrics at Waseda University, the International Conference on Social Security Reform in Advanced Countries at the University of Tokyo in 1999, and the 2000 Annual Meeting of the Japan Fiscal Science

Association (Nihon Zaisei Gakkai) at Meikai University. We are grateful for insightful comments and suggestions by Professors Naosumi Atoda, Bev Dahlby, Yoshibumi Aso, Yukinobu Kitamura, Shigeki Kunieda, Masahiro Hidaka, Kyoji Hashimoto, Takao Fujimoto, and Shoji Haruna. We acknowledge the financial support from The Zengin Foundation for Studies on Economics and Finance, and the first author also acknowledges the financial support from the Ministry of Education, Culture, Sports, Science and Technology (the Grant-in-Aid for Encouragement of Young Scientists No. 13730064).

Appendix A

To consider the utility maximization problem over time for the representative household of income class $i\,(=1, 2, \ldots, 275)$, namely the maximization of equation (2) subject to equation (3) in Section 7.2, let the Lagrange function be

$$L^i = U^i + \sum_{s=1}^{75} \lambda_s^i [-A_{s+1}^i + \{1 + r(1 - \tau_r)\}A_s^i + \{1 - \tau_w(wx^i e_s) - \tau_p\}wx^i e_s + b_s^i$$

$$+ a_s^i - \{1 + \tau_c(C_s^i)\}C_s^i]$$

where λ_s^i represents the Lagrange multiplier for equation (3). The first-order conditions for $i = 1, 2, \ldots, 275$ can be expressed by

$$\frac{\partial L^i}{\partial C_s^i} = p_s(1 + \delta)^{-(s-1)}\{C_s^i\}^{-\frac{1}{\gamma}} - \lambda_s^i\{1 + \tau_c(C_s^i)\} = 0, \tag{a}$$

$$\frac{\partial L^i}{\partial A_{s+1}^i} = -\lambda_s^i + \lambda_{s+1}^i\{1 + r(1 - \tau_r)\} = 0. \tag{b}$$

The combination of equations (a) and (b) yields the equation which determines the slope of the age-consumption profile over the lifecycle:

$$C_{s+1}^i = \left[\left(\frac{p_{s+1}}{p_s}\right)\left\{\frac{1 + r(1 - \tau_r)}{1 + \delta}\right\}\left(\frac{1 + \bar{\tau}_c(C_s^i)}{1 + \bar{\tau}_c(C_{s+1}^i)}\right)\right]^\gamma C_s^i. \tag{6}$$

For a given C_1^i, equation (6) solves the consumption path. The transformation of equation (6) leads to the following expression:

$$C_s^i = \left[\left(\frac{p_s}{p_1}\right)\left\{\frac{1 + \bar{\tau}_c(C_1^i)}{1 + \bar{\tau}_c(C_s^i)}\right\}\right]^\gamma \left\{\frac{1 + r(1 - \tau_r)}{1 + \delta}\right\}^{\gamma(s-1)} C_1^i. \tag{6'}$$

Integrating equation (3) and using the initial and terminal conditions $A_1^i = A_{76}^i = 0$, caused by no intended bequests, yield the following equation:

$$\sum_{s=1}^{75}\{1+r(1-\tau_r)\}^{-(s-1)}[1+\tau_c(C_s^i)]C_s^i = \sum_{s=1}^{RE}\{1+r(1-\tau_r)\}^{-(s-1)}[1-\tau_w(wx^ie_s)$$

$$-\tau_p]wx^ie_s + \sum_{s=ST}^{75}\{1+r(1-\tau_r)\}^{-(s-1)}b_s^i + \{1+r(1-\tau_r)\}^{-29}a_{30}^i$$

To derive C_1^i, equation (6)′ is substituted into this lifetime budget constraint. Thus, the optimum solution for C_1^i can be obtained.

Appendix B

Concerning the simulation model, the basic structure of households is explained in Section 7.2. Those of firms and the government, and market equilibrium conditions are explained as follows.

Firm behavior

The model has a single production sector that is assumed to behave competitively using capital and labor, subject to a constant-returns-to-scale production function. Capital is homogeneous and non-depreciating, while labor differs only in its efficiency. That is, all forms of labor are perfect substitutes, but households in different income classes or of different ages supply different amounts of some standard measure per unit of labor input.

The production function is assumed to be of the constant elasticity of substitution (CES) form:

$$Y_t = Q[\epsilon K_t^{1-\frac{1}{\sigma}} + (1-\epsilon)L_t^{1-\frac{1}{\sigma}}]^{\frac{1}{1-\frac{1}{\sigma}}}, \tag{8}$$

where Y_t represents the total output, K_t the total capital, L_t the total labor supply measured by the efficiency units, Q a scaling constant, ϵ a parameter measuring the intensity of use of capital in production, and σ the elasticity of substitution between K_t and L_t. Using the property subject to a constant-returns-to-scale production function, the following equation can be obtained:

$$Y_t = rK_t + wL_t. \tag{9}$$

Government behavior

The government sector consists of a narrower government sector and a public pension sector. The narrower government sector collects taxes, and spends them on general government expenditure and a transfer to the pension sector. There is a transfer between the sectors. In the benchmark case A in 1995, the general tax revenue covers one-third of the basic pension (i.e. the flat part); and public pension contributions cover the rest of public pension payment, namely, remaining two-thirds of the basic pension in addition to all parts proportional to remuneration for each individual.

The budget constraint of narrower government sector at time t is given by

$$T_t = G_t + \mu F_t, \tag{10}$$

where T_t is total revenue from labor income, interest income, and consumption taxes (τ: the tax revenue per capita); G_t is the general government spending on goods and services, except for a transfer to public pension sector (g: the general government expenditure per capita); F_t is the total amount of basic pension benefits (f: the amount of basic pension per capita); and μ is the ratio of the part covered by general tax revenues to F_t.

The budget constraint of public pension sector at time t is given by

$$R_t = (1 - \mu)F_t + P_t, \tag{11}$$

where R_t is the total contributions to public pension scheme, and P_t is the total benefits of the part proportional to remuneration. T_t, R_t, F_t, and P_t are defined respectively by

$$T_t = LX_t + \tau_r r A S_t + C X_t \tag{12}$$

$$R_t = \tau_p w L_t, \tag{13}$$

$$F_t = N_t \sum_{s=ST}^{75} \{p_s(1 + n)^{-(s-1)} 275 f\}, \tag{14}$$

$$P_t = N_t \sum_{s=ST}^{75} \left\{ p_s(1 + n)^{-(s-1)} \sum_{i=1}^{275} \theta H^i \right\}, \tag{15}$$

where

$$T_t = N_t \sum_{s=1}^{75} p_s(1 + n)^{-(s-1)} 275 \tau,$$

LX_t and CX_t are tax revenues from labor income and consumption, respectively. The revenues can be obtained by a simple summation of the 275 income classes with a same weight, because each income group accounts for the same proportion of population:

$$LX_t = N_t \sum_{s=1}^{RE} \left[p_s(1 + n)^{-(s-1)} \sum_{i=1}^{275} \{\alpha w x^i e_s + \tfrac{1}{2}\beta(w x^i e_s)^2\} \right], \tag{16}$$

$$CX_t = N_t \sum_{s=1}^{75} \left[p_s(1+n)^{-(s-1)} \sum_{i=1}^{275} \{\alpha C_s^i + \tfrac{1}{2}\beta(C_s^i)^2\} \right]. \tag{17}$$

Similarly, aggregate assets supplied by households, AS_t, and aggregate consumption, AC_t, are derived from a simple summation of the 275 income classes, respectively:

$$AS_t = N_t \sum_{s=1}^{75} \left\{ p_s(1+n)^{-(s-1)} \sum_{i=1}^{275} A_s^i \right\}, \tag{18}$$

$$AC_t = N_t \sum_{s=1}^{75} \left\{ p_s(1+n)^{-(s-1)} \sum_{i=1}^{275} C_s^i \right\}. \tag{19}$$

Market equilibrium

Finally, equilibrium conditions for the capital, labor, and goods markets are described.

1   *Equilibrium condition for the capital market*
    Since aggregate assets supplied by households are equal to real capital, we get

$$AS_t = K_t. \tag{20}$$

2   *Equilibrium condition for the labor market*
    Measured in efficiency units, since aggregate labor demand by firms is equal to aggregate labor supply by households, we get

$$L_t = N_t \sum_{s=1}^{RE} \left\{ p_s(1+n)^{-(s-1)} \sum_{i=1}^{275} x^i e_s \right\}. \tag{21}$$

3   *Equilibrium condition for the goods market*
    As aggregate production is equal to the sum of consumption, investment, and government expenditures, we get

$$Y_t = AC_t + (K_{t+1} - K_t) + G_t. \tag{22}$$

An iterative program is performed in order to obtain the equilibrium values of these equations.

Appendix C

The simulation model presented in Section 7.2 can be solved using the Gauss-Seidel method, if tax and public pension systems are determined. The outline of the computation process is the following.

Step 1

The interest rate r^0, the wage rate w^0, the bequest amount for each income class $(a^i)^0$, the tax rate on interest income τ_r^0, and the contribution rate to public pension scheme τ_p^0 are chosen as initial values.

Step 2

Each household, who maximizes the lifetime utility, determines the time path of consumption $(C^i)^1$ and of savings $(S^i)^1$ for the entire lifecycle, by taking the previous values and the tax rate on labor income $\tau_w(wx^ie_s)$ and on consumption $\tau_c(C_s^i)$ as given.

Step 3

Aggregate capital K^1 is obtained by summing up the assets of each income class across cohorts, and by adding up them $(A^i)^1$ with a same weight within cohort. Then, the production equilibrium conditions which are led by equation (8) bring about a new interest rate r^1 and a new wage rate w^1. The sum of bequests for each income class $(BQ^i)^1$ is derived from the class's assets $(A^i)^1$, which generates a new amount of bequest $(a^i)^1$.

To balance the narrower government sector account, the tax rate on interest income changes to τ_r^1. Similarly, to balance the public pension sector account, the contribution rate changes to τ_p^1.

Step 4

Using r^1, w^1, $(a^i)^1$, τ_r^1, and τ_p^1 as new initial values, we return to Step 1. This method is iterated until we get equilibrium, or stable variables.

Notes

1 We employ a lifecycle general equilibrium model with overlapping genera-tions, but our simulations in this chapter are limited only in the current steady state. The transition process to an aging society should be investigated as the next step, in order to display even more the advantages of the model, because it is appropriate as a basic theoretical framework to examine the problems with demographic changes.

2 Auerbach and Kotlikoff (1983a) evaluates intragenerational income redistribu-tion by considering a model in which each cohort has three representative indi-viduals, corresponding to three income classes: poor, median, and wealthy. Fullerton and Rogers (1993) introduces heterogeneity in the ability of labor supply, based on twelve lifetime–income groups with a lifecycle model. The framework in that study is, however, different from our model in many respects.

3 In a model without uncertainty over the length of life, the age profile of con-sumption is linear and has an upward slope. With the introduction of life-length uncertainty, as in our model, the profile is no longer linear. The level of

consumption at the final stage of old age is low, because the weight on consumption is low. Since such consumption–savings behavior is realistic, economic values such as aggregate consumption or the capital stock can be also realistic in our study.

4 The labor supply can be assumed to be elastic by incorporating leisure into the utility function in addition to consumption, such as in Auerbach and Kotlikoff (1987). Several recent investigations, however, show that labor supply is fairly inelastic for the after-tax wage rate in Japan. For instance, Asano and Fukushima (1994) reports that the estimated value of compensated elasticity of labor supply is 0.27. It should be noted that their study estimates only the size of the substitution effect. If the income effect were also estimated, a still smaller elasticity of labor supply for the after-tax wage rate would be obtained in Japan.

5 The subjective discount rates can be obtained by considering both survival probabilities p_s and the adjustment coefficient δ. It is verified that the subjective discount rates take positive values.

6 The tax rate on interest income in our simulation is assigned to the actual constant rate in Japan, namely, 20 percent. Hence, a progressive tax system is not applied for interest income in this chapter.

7 The rate of n in our model is a gross size rate. It signifies the ratio between the size of a cohort and that of the next cohort, taking no account of survival probability p_s.

8 The utility function used in our model takes negative values, and smaller absolute values mean better levels of utility. As consumption and utility level increase, a numerical value of utility approaches the upper limit, zero, and the corresponding size of a numerical increase becomes smaller. When a progressive tax is adopted, the tax burden for the low-income class decreases, while it increases for the high-income class. Because of the particular form of utility function employed in our analysis, a numerical increase in utility for the low-income class is large, while a numerical decrease in utility for the high-income class is small. Since the social welfare function is evaluated by a simple summation of the utilities of different income classes, the welfare of the low-income class carries great weight with the function in our study.

9 In Japan, it has been determined that the ratio of one-third will be raised to a half in the near future.

10 Progressive taxation promotes capital accumulation under inelastic labor supply. This is verified if a progressive labor income tax is adopted under a pay scale based on seniority, or if a progressive expenditure tax is introduced under the age-consumption profile with an upward slope. This "capital increasing effect" is caused by changing the timing of taxes to occur later in the lifecycle: if labor income or expenditure grows over the lifecycle, households accumulate more assets to maximize their lifetime utilities (see Okamoto (forthcoming) for further details).

References

Arrau, P. (1992) "Endogenous growth in a life-cycle model: the role of population growth and taxation," *Journal of Policy Modeling* 14(2): 167–86.

Asano, S. and Fukushima, T. (1994) "Some empirical evidence on demand system and optimal commodity taxation," *Discussion Papers in Economics and Business*, 94–101, Faculty of Economics, Osaka University.

Aso, Y. (1996) "Effects of social security, taxes and aging of population on capital accumulation," *IPTP Review*, Institute for Posts and Telecommunications Policy (IPTP), Ministry of Posts and Telecommunications, 187–211 (in Japanese).

Atoda, N. and Kato, R. (1993) "Savings and taxation system in the transition to aging Japan," *Tezukayama University Discussion Paper*, J-034, Tezukayama University (in Japanese).

Auerbach, A. J. and Kotlikoff, L. J. (1983a) "National savings, economic welfare, and the structure of taxation," in M. Feldstein (eds), *Behavioral Simulation Methods in Tax Policy Analysis*, Chicago: University of Chicago Press, 459–98.

Auerbach, A. J. and Kotlikoff, L. J. (1983b) "An Examination of Empirical Tests of Social Security and Savings," in E. Helpman *et al*. (eds), *Social Policy Evaluation: An Economic Perspective*, New York: Academic Press, 161–79.

Auerbach, A. J. and Kotlikoff, L. J. (1987) *Dynamic Fiscal Policy*, Cambridge: Cambridge University Press.

Auerbach, A. J., Kotlikoff, L. J., Hagemann, R. P., and Nicoletti, G. (1989) "The economic dynamics of an aging population: the case of four OECD countries," *NBER Working Paper*, 2797.

Auerbach, A. J., Kotlikoff, L. J., and Skinner, J. (1983) "The efficiency gains from dynamic tax reform," *International Economic Review* 24(2): 81–100.

Fullerton, D. and Rogers, D. L. (1993) *Who Bears the Lifetime Tax Burden?*, Washington, DC: The Brookings Institution.

Hatta, T. (1996) "The logic and the problem of a tax structure," in K. Kinoshita and H. Kaneko (eds), *The Logic of a Taxation System in the 21st Century*, Zeimu Keiri Kyokai (Tokyo), 1: 25–58 (in Japanese).

Hausman, J. (1979) "Individual discount rates and utilization of energy using durables," *Bell Journal*, Spring.

Homma, M., Atoda, N., Iwamoto, Y., and Ohtake, F. (1987a) "Pension: aging society and pension plan," in K. Hamada, A. Horiuchi, and M. Kuroda (eds), *Macroeconomic Analysis of the Japanese Economy*, Tokyo University Shuppankai, 149–75 (in Japanese).

Homma, M., Atoda, N., Iwamoto, Y., and Ohtake, F. (1987b) "Life-cycle growth model and sensitivity analysis," *Osaka Economic Papers*, Osaka University, 36(3/4): 99–108 (in Japanese).

Ihori, T. (1987) "Tax reform and intergeneration incidence," *Journal of Public Economics* 33: 377–87.

Ihori, T. (1996) *Public Finance in an Overlapping Generations Economy*, London: Macmillan.

Iwamoto, Y. (1990) "Pension plan and bequest behavior," *Quarterly Journal of Social Security Research*, 25(4): 388–411 (in Japanese).

Iwamoto, Y., Kato, R., and Hidaka, M. (1993) "Public pensions and an aging population," *Review of Social Policy*, 2: 1–10.

Kaldor, N. (1955) *An Expenditure Tax*, London: George Allen and Unwin.

Kato, R. (1998) "Transition to an aging Japan: public pension, savings, and capital taxation," *Journal of the Japanese and International Economies* 12: 204–31.

Lawrence, E. (1986) "The savings behavior of rich and poor: a study of time preference and liquidity constraints," Ph.D dissertation, Yale University.

Noguchi, Y. (1987) "Future public pension and Japanese international performance," *Financial Review*, June (in Japanese).

Okamoto, A. "Stimulating progressive expenditure taxation in aging Japan," forthcoming in *Journal of Policy Models*.

Seidman, L. (1984) "Conversion to a consumption tax: the transition in a life-cycle growth model," *Journal of Political Economy* 92: 247–67.

Seidman, L. (1997) *The USA Tax: a Progressive Consumption Tax,* Cambridge, MA: MIT Press.

Shoven, J. B. and Whalley, J. (1992) *Applying General Equilibrium,* Cambridge: Cambridge University Press.

Summers, L. (1981) "Taxation and capital accumulation in a life cycle growth model," *American Economic Review* 71(4): 547–60.

Tachibanaki, T. (1999) "Japan was not a welfare state, but...," in R. Griffiths and T. Tachibanaki (eds), *From Austerity to Affluence: The Turning-Point in Modern Societies,* London: Macmillan Press.

Data

Economic Planning Agency (1996) *Annual Report on National Accounts 1996,* Printing Bureau of Ministry of Finance, Japan.

Economic Planning Agency (1996) *Economic White Paper 1996,* Printing Bureau of Ministry of Finance, Japan.

The Institute of Population Problems of the Ministry of Health and Welfare (1992) *Population Projections for Japan: 1991–2090* (estimation in September 1992), Japan.

The Japan Cooperative Association (1996) *The Household Expenditure Survey 1995,* Japan.

The Ministry of Health and Welfare (1996) *White Paper on Welfare 1996,* Japan.

8 Pension reform in the UK

From contribution to participation

Ashwin Kumar[1]

8.1 Introduction

In 1997, the state pension problem facing the new UK government was not one of funding but of adequacy.

A series of reforms by the administration of 1979–97 had seen a fall in projected spending on state pensions as a proportion of GDP. Rather than the 'demographic timebomb' of popular perception leading to a funding crisis, the UK was one of few developed countries to face no serious future funding problems in its state pensions. In fact, as a proportion of GDP, state spending on transfers to the elderly was projected to fall by one-third over the next 50 years.

This reduction in future spending arose out of reforms in the 1980s that reduced the future value of both the flat-rate basic state pension and the State Earnings-Related Pension (SERPS). The reforms had also widened the options for individuals making their own private provision.

But those at the bottom of the earnings distribution were least able to deal with the effects of these reforms. First, the basic state pension would no longer guarantee a minimum level of income around the level of Income Support, the main means-tested form of support.

Second, the earnings-related pension, SERPS, which was being reduced in value, by its design already provided least support to lower earners. Third, lower earners were least able to take out the new private pensions (known as personal pensions) because their charging structures tended to be designed for those with more to invest.

Short- and medium-term estimates did foresee the same or a smaller proportion of pensioners reliant on Income Support, probably as a result of cohort effects increasing the average amounts of occupational pension that future pensioners could expect to receive. But the longer-term estimates suggested that the proportion on Income Support would then start to rise as some of the 1980s reforms matured.

One potential effect of a greater proportion of the pensioner population relying in the future on means-tested support might be to discourage voluntary saving on the part of low and moderate earners. Those who perceived, correctly or incorrectly, that they would be unable to save enough to take themselves clear of the thresholds for means-tested support would have a large disincentive to save.

The problem, then, was not how to spend less but how to spend more on the lower paid at the same time as encouraging private saving.

The government's response, *A New Contract for Welfare: Partnership in Pensions*, was published in December 1998.[2] The proposals contained within this document represented a fundamental shift in the concept behind state second tier pension provision in the UK. This shift was from the contributory and earnings-related principle of the 1970s to the wider entitlement of a participatory principle and to the flat-rate benefit principle enshrined in the Beveridge Report of 1942.[3]

This chapter seeks to draw out the implications of the reform proposals, over time and across the earnings distribution and to place them in the wider context of the concepts behind pension provision.

8.2 The current system

8.2.1 Overview of the UK state pension system

8.2.1.1 The pre-1979 position

In the UK, the first tier of state pension provision is the basic state pension, introduced by the postwar government in 1948. Anyone who works and earns above a low earnings threshold[4] for enough years receives a flat-rate pension, currently worth £66.75 per week.

Anyone claiming unemployment benefits, aged 16–18, aged 60 or over, or on sickness benefits receives credits automatically.[5] Anyone who cares for a child under 16 or spends at least 35 hours a week caring for a disabled person for a full year also has their basic state pension rights protected.

In 1975, the government committed itself to uprating the basic state pension in line with the higher of average earnings and prices.

The second tier of UK state pension provision is the State Earnings Related Pension Scheme (SERPS), introduced in 1978. This is an earnings-related pension for employees only. Those who earn more than the low earnings threshold pay National Insurance (NI) contributions as a proportion of their earnings up to a higher threshold.[6]

In return for these earnings-related contributions, employees build up rights in SERPS. The SERPS pension at retirement was to be worth 25 per cent of a person's average earnings between the lower and upper thresholds and the average was to be calculated on the basis of the best 20 years of each person's working life.[7]

Employees could, however, contract out of SERPS. This meant that employees and their employers paid lower NI contributions and instead the employer guaranteed to provide a pension at least as good as under SERPS. The level of the reduction in NI contributions (known as the contracted-out rebate) was calculated to be 'actuarially fair' and to represent the reduced cost to the government of not having to pay that employee their SERPS pension in retirement.[8]

From the state point of view, therefore, contracting out represented the bringing forward of expenditure: the payment of the second tier pension was made during the employee's working life (in the form of lower revenue from NI contributions) instead of during the employee's retirement. From a macroeconomic point of view, if an employee contracted out of SERPS into a funded pension scheme,[9] contracting out represented a switch of government expenditure from an unfunded to a funded pension.

In simple terms, the state pension system as it then stood provided a pension broadly equal to the LEL + 25 per cent of 20-best-years-average earnings. But employees could choose to replace the second part of their state pension with at least an equivalent amount of occupational pension.

8.2.1.2 The reforms of the 1979–97 administration

The 1979–97 administration reformed state pensions on a number of fronts. From 1980, the basic state pension was uprated in line with prices only.[10] Second, for those who retired after 1999, the accrual rate in SERPS was to be reduced from 25 per cent to 20 per cent.[11]

Third, the method of calculating a person's average earnings for SERPS purposes was to change from the best 20 years to all 49 years of the working life. To be phased in one year at a time from 1999, the scheme was to be redesigned so that there was no longer any 'best years' calculation. Instead, the SERPS pension would be 20 per cent of lifetime average earnings between the two earnings thresholds.

The combined effect of these reforms was that SERPS had been transformed into a scheme where, in each year, employees built up SERPS rights of 1/245 of earnings between the lower and upper earnings thresholds.[12] Each year's accruals would be revalued in line with average earnings to the year before reaching State Retirement Age and added together to give the total SERPS pension at retirement.

8.2.1.3 Means-tested support for pensioners

Underpinning the state pension system is means-tested support for those who had failed to build up enough pension during their working life. The main benefit is Income Support, which is currently set at £75 per week for a single pensioner and £116.60 for a pensioner couple.[13] The benefit is withdrawn at a rate of 100 per cent for income up to these levels. Each pound of income from state, occupational, or personal pensions results in the loss of £1 of Income Support.

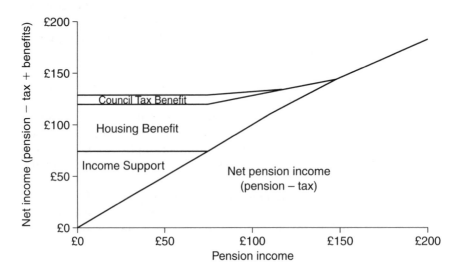

Figure 8.1 Net income of a single pensioner facing rent of £45 per week and council tax of £9 per month[15]

On top of Income Support sits help to pay rents and to pay local taxes (council tax). Any pensioner unit[14] with income up to the Income Support level receives, broadly speaking, the entirety of their rent as Housing Benefit and the entirety of their council tax bill as Council Tax Benefit.

However, for those with income above the Income Support level, Housing Benefit is withdrawn at a rate of 65 per cent, i.e. 65 pence of Housing Benefit is lost for each pound of income above that level. Council Tax Benefit is simultaneously withdrawn at a rate of 20 per cent of income above the Income Support level.

Single pensioners therefore face an effective marginal tax rate of 100 per cent on income up to £75 per week. Those in rented accommodation then face an 85 per cent rate on income above the Income Support level until their Housing Benefit and Council Tax Benefit run out. Those who own their home outright cannot receive Housing Benefit and so face a rate of 20 per cent on income above the Income Support level until their Council Tax Benefit runs out.[16]

8.2.2 *Level of pension provided by the current system*

The value of the state pension for future retirees is falling relative to average earnings for a number of reasons. The basic state pension is being uprated only in line with prices. This effect tends to dominate and results in the total pension expected declining over time. Up to 2027, retirees are also affected by the reforms of the 1979–97 administration restricting the future value of SERPS.

For later retirees the primary driver in changes to the value of SERPS is the movement of the earnings thresholds between which NI contributions are paid and upon which SERPS rights are accrued.

Figure 8.2 shows the expected total state pension under the current system for people who work for 49 years from 16 to 65 and whose earnings go up exactly in line with average earnings throughout their working life.[17] The expected pension is shown in 1999 earnings terms where the expected value of the pension is deflated by the assumed increase in average earnings to show how the pension is expected to vary relative to average earnings.[18]

Where the government achieves its aim of uprating means-tested support for pensioners in line with earnings, the Minimum Income Guarantee (the new name for Income Support for pensioners) is expected to remain constant in 1999 earnings terms. What we see from Figure 8.2 is that under the present system by 2063 we would expect even average earners who rely entirely on the state system to retire below the level for means-tested support.

Looking across the earnings distribution for a particular year produces a similar picture. As we see in Figure 8.3, for the cohort that retires in 2051, a substantial section of the earnings distribution can expect to retire below the level for means-tested support.

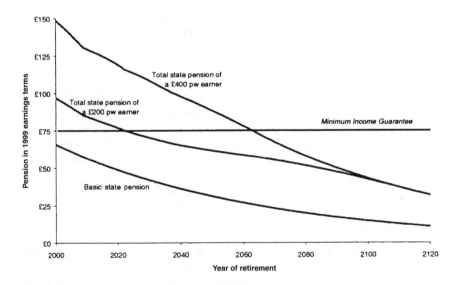

Figure 8.2 Expected pension at retirement under current system, by year of retirement in 1999 earnings terms[19]

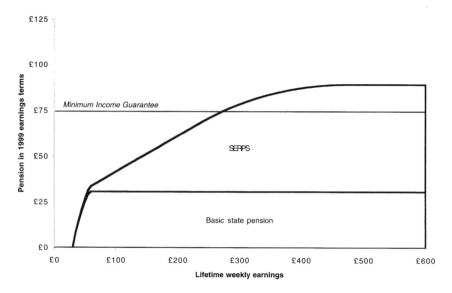

Figure 8.3 Expected pension at retirement in 2051 under current system, by lifetime weekly earnings[20] in 1999 earnings terms[21]

8.3 The pensions Green Paper

8.3.1 The government's proposals

The UK government published its proposals for pension reform on 15 December 1998.[22] The proposals had four main features:

a   The State Earnings Related Pension Scheme (SERPS) to be reformed and renamed the State Second Pension.
b   A commitment to uprate Income Support for pensioners in line with average earnings as funds allow, renaming it the Minimum Income Guarantee.[23]
c   A new form of private pension, called Stakeholder Pensions, to be launched with lower charges and easier access for the lower paid.
d   An improvement in awareness of pensions, including the development of annual statements of projected pension income.

8.3.1.1 The State Second Pension

Expected to commence in 2002, the State Second Pension (S2P) is a reform of SERPS and as such carries over many of its features. For example, the number of working years required to obtain the maximum amount of S2P will be 49 and the rule for inheritance of the rights accrued by a deceased partner are to remain the same as under SERPS.

However, in its purpose the new pension is fundamentally different with its two-stage shift from the earnings-related SERPS to a flat-rate pension. The State Second Pension will differ from SERPS in three key respects:

8.3.1.1.1 £180 PER WEEK UNDERPIN

Anyone earning between the Lower Earnings Limit (LEL) and £180 per week will be treated for S2P purposes as if they were earning £180 per week. The level of this underpin will be uprated each year in line with earnings.

8.3.1.1.2 NEW ACCRUAL STRUCTURE

Earnings between the LEL and the underpin will accrue S2P rights at 40 per cent, i.e. twice the rate under SERPS. This extra generosity for lower earners will be tapered away so that those earning above an upper threshold of around £400 per week will accrue the same rights as they would have done under SERPS.

8.3.1.1.3 CREDITS FOR CARERS AND SOME PEOPLE WITH A LONG-TERM ILLNESS OR DISABILITY.

Anyone caring for a full year for a child of up to five years of age[24] or caring for a disabled person for at least 35 hours a week will receive a credit at the underpin level. Those of the long-term disabled who, by the time they retire, have worked for at least 10 per cent of their working life (usually five years), will receive a credit for each year that they were in receipt of long-term disability benefits.

Figure 8.4a compares the proposed accrual structure with that of SERPS by showing how much an employee would accrue under each system if S2P were introduced in 1999.

Phase 2 of the State Second Pension is expected to be introduced in 2006. Under Phase 2, the benefit paid to those contracted-out of S2P and those who remain in the state scheme will diverge.

Those who do not contract out (referred to as being 'contracted-in') will face a flat-rate accrual structure. Earnings above the underpin will not accrue any pension and everyone will receive the same pension as those at the underpin level.

Figure 8.4b shows the accrual structure if Phase 2 were introduced in 1999.

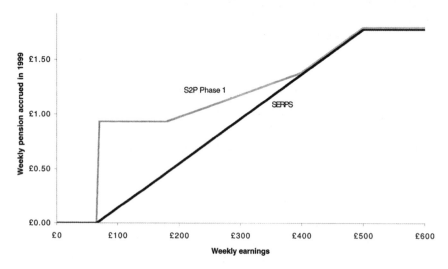

Figure 8.4a Accrual structure of S2P Phase 1 compared with SERPS

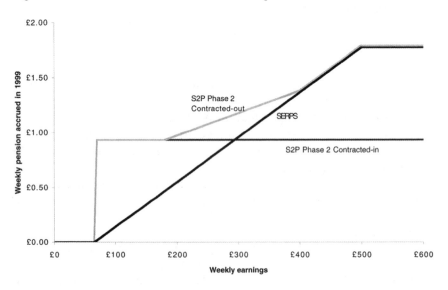

Figure 8.4b Accrual structure of S2P Phase 2

8.3.2 *Long-term effects of the State Second Pension*

8.3.2.1 *Accrual structure*

Whilst the accrual structure looks relatively simple when shown for a single year, the dynamic picture is more complex.

With the LEL and UEL rising with prices, they are falling relative to

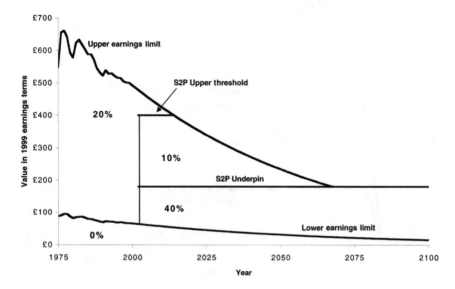

Figure 8.5 NI contributions and S2P thresholds in 1999 earnings terms

earnings. This means that the band of earnings with a 40 per cent accrual rate is widening and, the 10 per cent band of earnings is shrinking.

The effect of these movements in the bands is that all individuals, across the earnings distribution will do better under S2P Phase 1 (or S2P Phase 2 contracted-out) than under SERPS. Further, whether or not a person does worse contracted-in under S2P Phase 2 than under SERPS depends on the width of the relevant bands in the years that they work.

8.3.2.2 Distributional effects

With the State Second Pension to be introduced in 2002, the first cohort, therefore, to have spent a full working life under S2P will retire in 2051. Figure 8.6 shows the lifetime effects across the earnings distribution of S2P for this cohort.

As we might expect from the design of the scheme, S2P will provide substantially higher levels of pension than SERPS at the bottom of the earnings distribution. The extra benefit will be greatest for those earning just above the Lower Earnings Limit and will remain substantial further up the distribution.

For the cohort that retires in 2051, the switch to the flat-rate Phase 2 will not leave higher earners who remain contracted-in much worse off than under SERPS. Those who earn on average more than £370 per week are likely to be no more than £2.50 per week (in 1999 earnings terms)

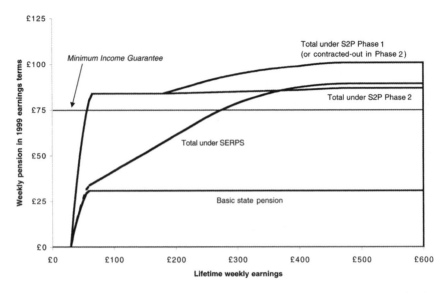

Figure 8.6 Expected pension in 2051 under S2P by lifetime weekly earnings in 1999 earnings terms[25] (see Figure 8.3)

worse off. Those who contract out will be better off than under SERPS all the way up the earnings distribution.

We can also see that anyone who works (or receives S2P credits) for the entirety of their working life will retire with a state pension above the level of the Minimum Income Guarantee, putting themselves above the level of the 100 per cent effective marginal tax rate.

8.3.2.3 Costs and financing

State support for the elderly in the form of state pensions and Income Support for pensioners currently costs 5.4 per cent of GDP. Under current policies, this proportion is projected to fall to 3.6 per cent by 2050. The effect of the proposals in the Pensions Green Paper is to halve this fall so that, by 2050, the government can expect to be spending around 4.5 per cent of GDP on pensioners.

If the extra cost of the State Second Pension were raised entirely from NI contributions, the potential reduction in contribution rates by 2050 would be reduced. Phil Agulnik[26] has estimated that, instead of a fall of 4.25 percentage points in contribution rates, financing the State Second Pension would require the fall to be limited to only one percentage point. However, lower expenditure on means-tested benefits would also allow a 0.6 percentage point fall in income tax rates.

8.3.3 Adequacy of the State Second Pension

The State Second Pension is heavily redistributive. It provides a very large boost to the pensions of the lowest earners and, if financed through NI contributions, will tax those with higher earnings to pay for it. It also ensures that those who work for a full working life will retire above the level of the Minimum Income Guarantee. Has the state pension problem been solved?

The key question to ask is how successful will the new system be at keeping people above the Minimum Income Guarantee level? The Department of Social Security estimated that, had SERPS remained but an earnings-uprated Minimum Income Guarantee been introduced, approximately 1 in 3 pensioners would have had pension income lower than the Minimum Income Guarantee.[27] The State Second Pension was estimated to reduce this proportion to 1 in 4.

Although these estimates are subject to a high degree of uncertainty, it is apparent that, despite the extra generosity of the State Second Pension, substantial numbers of pensioners will still find themselves below the level of the Minimum Income Guarantee.

There are two principal reasons for this. First, the Minimum Income Guarantee is intended to be uprated each year in line with earnings as funds allow. But once in payment, SERPS/State Second Pension is uprated in line with prices only. With both components of the state pension – the basic state pension and the State Second Pension – going up in line with prices once a person has retired, their state pension is losing value relative to the Minimum Income Guarantee.

The hypothetical low earner who works for 49 years and earns between the LEL and the S2P underpin throughout their working life will retire on approximately £84 per week state pension in 1999 earnings terms (see Figure 8.6). Using the Government Actuary's Department assumption of 1.5 per cent real earnings growth, it would take approximately eight years for this pension to fall below the level of the Minimum Income Guarantee (see Figure 8.7). This means that any single lifetime low earner who relies entirely on the state pension will find themselves reliant on the Minimum Income Guarantee by the age of 73.

With an ageing population we can expect in the future a higher proportion of the pensioner population to consist of older pensioners. Because of the reasons highlighted above, older pensioners are more likely to rely on the Minimum Income Guarantee. So we can expect demographic factors to provide an upward push on the proportion of the pensioner population that relies on the Minimum Income Guarantee.

The second reason for the substantial number reliant on the Minimum Income Guarantee is that the State Second Pension is based upon a 49-year working life.

The caring credit will make a huge difference to many women whose

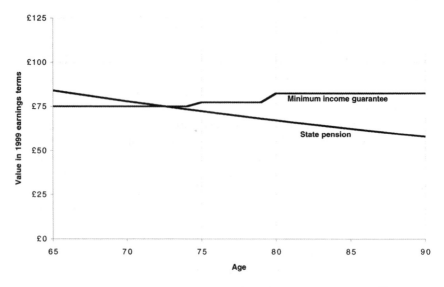

Figure 8.7 Value after retirement of the pension of a lifetime low earner[28]

pensions suffer from broken work records due to years spent caring for children. Approximately 1.7 million women and around 30,000 men[29] will benefit each year because they are caring for children. Around 166,000 female and 48,000 male carers of disabled people will also benefit from a caring credit.[30] So substantial numbers of women who have traditionally lost out on pension entitlement because of caring responsibilities will receive protection under the new system. But despite the caring credits the 49-year rule will ensure that large numbers will accrue less than the maximum S2P possible. From the government point of view, those of concern are people for whom years spent not working or not caring mean that their pension in retirement is less than the level of the Minimum Income Guarantee.

Because the 40 per cent S2P band is widening relative to earnings (see Figure 8.5), the later a year is missed the greater the loss to the final pension. Figure 8.8 shows the pension at retirement under two scenarios – one where the years not accruing S2P rights are at the beginning of the working life and one where the years missed are at the end.

We see that a lifetime low earner[31] who fails to find work for at least the first ten years of his/her life would retire with a state pension less than the Minimum Income Guarantee. A person who becomes unemployed eight or more years before state retirement age and retires entirely on the state pension would also retire below the Minimum Income Guarantee.

Unemployment is used here as an example of non-work activity during which basic state pension rights are preserved but S2P rights are not building up. The same analysis applies equally to a woman who spends

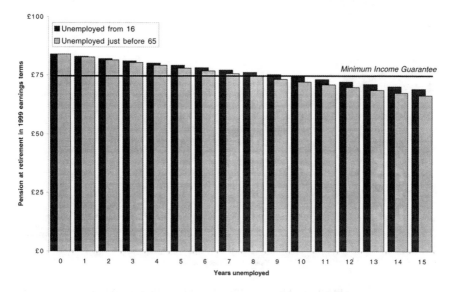

Figure 8.8 Pension at retirement of a lifetime low earner by number of years spent unemployed[32]

time out of the labour market caring for children aged over five and under 16.

In such a position, she would receive Home Responsibilities Protection so that her basic state pension was protected but she would accrue no S2P rights. If, for example, her period of caring for older children began at age 25 then nine years out of work would be enough for her state pension at retirement to be less than the Minimum Income Guarantee.

The two reasons why individuals will still end up with a state pension worth less than the Minimum Income Guarantee do not occur in isolation. So we need to examine their interaction. The question is not simply the amount that a person retires on but, if they do retire above the Minimum Income Guarantee, how many years it takes for them to fall below that level.

Figure 8.9 takes a lifetime low earner who does not work for a number of years from age 25 but has her basic state pension protected during this period. It shows, given differing lengths of time not working, how long after retirement it would take for her state pension to fall below the Minimum Income Guarantee.

It is also possible to model whole-life scenarios.

8.3.3.1 Scenario 1

A woman born in 1986 leaves school at 16, remains inactive until she begins work at 19. She stops work when she has her first child at 25 and

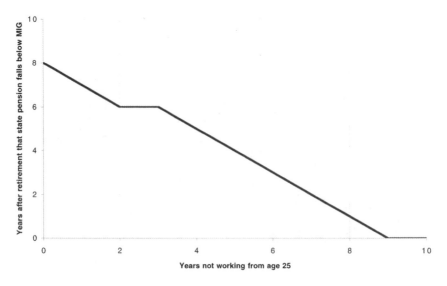

Figure 8.9 The number of years after retirement that the state pension of a lifetime low earner who cares for children older than five from age 25 falls below the Minimum Income Guarantee

has a second at 28. At 35, she returns to work part-time. At 40, she returns to full-time work and works until she is 62 when she becomes inactive until reaching state retirement age in 2051.

Her wages on starting work are £200 per week in 1999 earnings terms and they go up in line with average earnings. When she returns to work part-time in 2021, she earns £90 per week in 1999 earnings terms, rising with average earnings. When she goes full-time in 2025, her wages go up to £180 per week and go up in line with average earnings until she stops work in 2048.

8.3.3.2 Scenario 2

A man born in 1986 leaves school at 16 and remains inactive until he begins work at 19. His wages on starting work are £180 per week in 1999 earnings terms, rising in line with average earnings. At 25, he gets promoted and his earnings go up to £220 per week in 1999 earnings terms. At 40 he gets made redundant and is unemployed for two years. At 42, he finds work at £200 per week in 1999 earnings terms and he continues to work until 55 when he is made redundant once again. He remains unemployed until state retirement age at 65.

	Scenario 1 Single woman	Scenario 2 Single man	Scenario 3 Couple
State pension under SERPS	£48	£52	£100
Gain from S2P	£29	£16	£45
State pension under S2P	£77	£69	£145
Rate of MIG	£75	£75	£116.60
Years after retirement that state pension falls below MIG	2	0	14
In rented accommodation facing rent of £45 pw and council tax of £9 pw:			
Total income (incl. HB + CTB)	£129	£129	£175
Marginal withdrawal rate on further pension income	85%	100%	85%
Owner occupier facing council tax of £9 pw:			
Total income (incl. CTB)	£85	£84	£149
Marginal withdrawal rate on further pension income	20%	100%	20%

Figure 8.10 Income under whole-life scenarios[33]

8.3.3.3 Scenario 3

The two individuals are partners and remain partners in retirement.

8.4 Analysis

8.4.1 Why does the state support the elderly?

Having looked at the effects of the State Second Pension in some detail and given a picture of what state pension provision will look like in 2051, it is appropriate to return to the fundamental questions about pension provision. First and foremost amongst these questions is why does the state provide support to the elderly?

There are two principal answers to this question. The first is that the state wishes to guarantee a minimum standard of living for its elderly citizens and the second is that the state wishes to offer earnings-replacement in retirement.

The first of these approaches can be seen in practice in the Republic of Ireland, the Netherlands or New Zealand where state support for the elderly is flat-rate.[34] Clearly redistributive, such systems are aimed at guaranteeing that all pensioners have a minimum standard of living, often expressed as a proportion of average earnings. The second approach is best exemplified in the systems of France and Germany where, although there is some redistributive element for the lowest earners, the main body of the system is earnings-related.

The second dimension through which to examine pension systems is that of entitlement. Systems vary from the entirely means-tested Age Pension in Australia to the contributory system in Germany to entitlement based on residence tests only in New Zealand and the Netherlands.[35]

8.4.2 *What kind of system does the UK have?*

The current UK system encompasses a combination of these principles. Originally, when introduced in 1948, the state pension was intended to guarantee a minimum standard. Beveridge had been explicit:

> The State in organising security should not stifle incentive, opportunity, responsibility; in establishing a national minimum, it should leave room and encouragement for voluntary action by each individual to provide more than the minimum for himself and his family.[36]

The level of the basic state pension was therefore set just above the level of National Assistance, the means-tested benefit of the time.[37] This parity was broadly maintained until relatively recently. It is only in the last 10

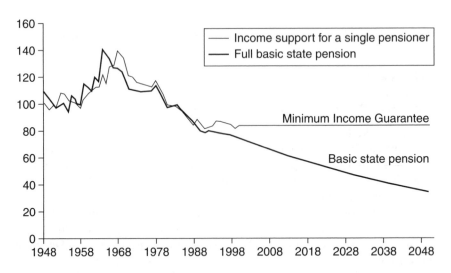

Figure 8.11 Movement of Income Support for a single pensioner and the basic state pension relative to average earnings where Income Support for a single pensioner in 1948 = 100

years that the level of the basic state pension has started to fall consistently below the level for means-tested support.

Entitlement to the basic state pension is drawn widely. In addition to those working (and earning above the LEL), the claimant unemployed, those caring for children up to 16 or for the disabled, those on disability benefits and the low paid on certain in-work benefits, all receive either credits for the basic state pension or protection to ensure that they do not lose entitlement.[38]

The entitlement conditions are sufficiently wide that they cannot be described as purely contributory. In 1995/96, 58 per cent of the working age population had a qualifying year for the basic state pension through paid contributions only whereas 25 per cent did not have sufficient paid contributions but gained either credits or home responsibilities protection so as not to lose entitlement[39] (see Figure 8.12). At a recent seminar,[40] the entitlement conditions were described as being tantamount to entitlement through citizenship. This is overstating the case as, in 1995/96, 17 per cent of the working age population failed either to gain a qualifying year or to be awarded Home Responsibilities Protection in virtue of caring responsibilities.

On top of the basic state pension sits SERPS. Introduced in 1978, it was not the first attempt at an earnings-related concept within UK state pension provision. Its forerunner, Graduated Retirement Benefit, was limited in value and did little to increase pensions.[41] In fact, the 1958 White Paper setting out the scheme stated its first objective as being to 'place the National Insurance scheme on a sound financial basis'[42] rather than to improve pensions.

SERPS on the other hand was substantially more generous. Based on earnings-related contributions, when originally introduced, it was expected to give a pension broadly equal to the LEL + 25 per cent of 20-best-year-average earnings between the LEL and the UEL.

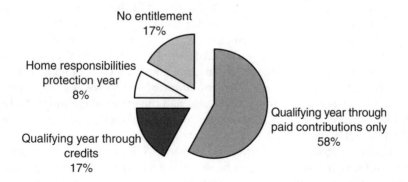

Figure 8.12 Sources of entitlement to the basic state pension in 1995–6 as a proportion of the working age population

As discussed above, the reforms of 1979–97 reduced the future value of the state pension. First of all, uprating of the basic state pension and earnings thresholds was limited to prices only and second the value of SERPS for future retirees was reduced. In general terms, the state pension that can be expected once transitional arrangements have expired is broadly equal to the (lower) LEL + 20 per cent of lifetime average earnings between the LEL and the UEL.

Originally, therefore, the UK system had two components, the first of which was a basic state pension intended to guarantee a minimum standard whose entitlement fell somewhere between the citizenship and the contributory principle. On top of that sat SERPS, a strictly contributory earnings-related pension whose aim was a measure of earnings-replacement. Those who failed the basic state pension entitlement test would end up on means-tested support.

8.4.3 A conceptual view of the reform proposals

The world envisaged by the Pensions Green Paper looks very different. First of all, we will have the basic state pension with entitlement somewhere between the citizenship and contributory principles. However, this will no longer be the guarantor of a minimum standard. As we see from Figure 8.11, if the current uprating policy is continued, by 2051 the basic state pension will be worth 40 per cent of the Minimum Income Guarantee.

Next we will have the State Second Pension. Unlike SERPS its entitlement will not be purely contributory but wider. In addition to those who pay National Insurance contributions, four groups will gain entitlement. The first three have already been mentioned: carers of young children, carers of disabled people and those with a long-term illness or disability who have had some attachment to the labour market.

The fourth group appeared in the March 1999 budget. The Chancellor of the Exchequer announced that there would in the future be a zero rate of National Insurance contributions for those earning above the LEL but less than the Income Tax threshold.[43]

Those earning just above the LEL would continue to accrue entitlement to contributory benefits but neither they nor their employer would pay contributions for them. The intention of the move was to improve work incentives for the low paid. It also had the effect of creating a further break with the contributory principle by creating another group with entitlement but no requirement to pay contributions.

Entitlement to the State Second Pension (S2P) is therefore not purely contributory but wider and can be described as participatory. Three out of the four groups, and the vast majority of individuals, entitled to S2P credits gain this entitlement through participating in activities that society deems in some way to be worthy of support: caring for young children, caring for a disabled person and working in very low paid jobs. The fourth group – the long-term disabled – will only receive credits if they have participated in the labour market (earning above the LEL) for at least 10 per cent of their working life.

In addition to the entitlement of S2P being different from that of SERPS, so is the level of benefit. For those contracted-in, S2P will be flat-rate and it will be set at a level so that those entitled will retire above the Minimum Income Guarantee provided they have worked or received credits for around 40 years.[44]

Once the Pensions Green Paper proposals have been implemented, therefore, the UK will have two flat-rate pensions. The first of these – the basic state pension with its not-quite-citizenship entitlement – will on its own no longer be the guarantor of the minimum standard. On top of this will sit the State Second Pension with its participatory entitlement, wider than under SERPS. Receipt of the two together will enable those who rely on a state pension to retire above the level of means-tested support.

8.4.4 The role of government in the reform proposals

The first question is whether or not it is the role of government to do any more than guarantee a minimum standard of living in retirement. Although that was the limit of Beveridge's ambition, by the late 1960s there was a political consensus that the government should intervene to the extent of providing some earnings-replacement.[45]

In 1999, the consensus has moved the other way. The previous administration was happy to let the value of SERPS fall whereas the current administration has made an explicit commitment to return to a Beveridge-style flat-rate benefit.[46] Thus in the UK we have an answer to our question. In future the role of government in terms of direct support is to provide a minimum standard of living in retirement. It is the responsibility of the individual and/or their employer to make provision beyond that.[47]

Given that the objective of state pension policy is now to ensure that all are able to enjoy a minimum standard of living in retirement, what is the best mechanism for achieving this? There are two principal models. One is the Australian route of an entirely means-tested system and the other is the New Zealand/Netherlands route of a flat-rate pension with entitlement according to the citizenship principle.

In the UK, the Pensions Green Paper envisages using the participatory principle to achieve this objective. It will be those who satisfy the entitlement test of the State Second Pension for enough years who can expect to have a state pension above the level for means-tested support. Those who fail the participatory condition for enough years risk relying on a means-test to achieve the minimum standard.

In principle, therefore, the role for means-testing is greater than in a system where passing the entitlement test of the basic state pension is enough to guarantee a state pension above the level for means-tested support.

8.4.5 Is means-testing a problem?

Means-tested benefits have tended to have lower take-up than insurance-style benefits. This means that a system that relies on a means-test as the guarantor of a minimum standard for a large part of the population is likely to find a number of its elderly short of the minimum standard. Second, knowledge during the working life of the likelihood of having to rely on a means test acts as a disincentive to save because those with very low income face high effective marginal tax rates in retirement.

The government is currently engaged in a take-up campaign to reduce the estimated 600,000 elderly people who are entitled to but do not claim the Minimum Income Guarantee. One can argue that, in principle, a means-tested benefit is always likely to suffer lower take-up than an insurance-style benefit however this could be proved wrong by a successful take-up campaign.

With regard to savings disincentives, it is possible to ask whether those who are likely to end up on means-tested benefits and so might face high effective marginal tax rates are those who might have made additional provision for themselves or not.

It could be argued that some of those not catered for by S2P credits such as the long-term disabled who have never worked could not reasonably be expected to build up private savings or private pensions. Therefore, the existence of the means-test disincentives has no effect for this group. To justify such an argument, one would need analysis of the savings behaviour and assets of those who might fail the participatory test of the State Second Pension.

There is however a further problem that affects those whose income is just above the threshold for means-tested support.

A person who makes voluntary contributions into a private pension scheme defers consumption during their working life and expects to achieve a rate of return on their voluntary saving. In a money purchase pension the rate of return is equal to the growth in the investment fund less fund charges and charges for purchasing an annuity. In a final salary occupational pension scheme, the rate of return is less transparent but is of a similar order of magnitude.

Consider a situation where the level of the state's compulsory pension provision is below the level for means-tested support. In such a scenario, any person whose income is above that threshold would have made some voluntary private pension saving.

Individuals whose level of income in retirement is just above the threshold receive very little more income than if they had not made any voluntary private pension saving. For them the effective rate of return on their voluntary saving (as reflected by the additional income that they receive as a result of their saving) is very low.

This low effective rate of return may have two effects, one economic and one political. Those who can expect to retire with income above the level of means-tested support can expect not to face high effective marginal tax rates. But some of these people may quite reasonably expect that the rate of return on their private saving will be low. This may reduce their desire to defer consumption during their working life and provide a disincentive to making private saving.

The political effect is that those who have made enough voluntary saving to be just above the level of means-tested support but find that they have received a very low effective rate of return may feel aggrieved once they retire. The potential rates of return in marketing material on private pension savings products are likely to have created an expectation of higher levels of return. This may increase political pressure upon government to provide higher levels of non-means-tested support for pensioners.

8.4.6 The future

It is clear that earnings-replacement as a concept in UK state pension provision is no longer a realistic prospect. However, the new objective of guaranteeing a minimum standard can be achieved from a number of directions. For the UK, two directions for the long term present themselves. On the one hand we may see a gradual drift towards a more citizenship based approach. On the other the system might move towards a more heavily means-tested approach.

But in the medium term, two issues remain on the agenda. The first is the question of contracted-out rebates in Phase 2 of the State Second Pension. As things stand, S2P is a flat-rate pension only for those contracted-in. Those who contract out of S2P into an occupational, personal, or stakeholder pension will continue to receive earnings-related rebates based on the Phase 1 level of the State Second Pension.

At the inception of Phase 2, this will provide a clear incentive for those earning above the S2P underpin level to contract out and will have the effect of bringing forward state expenditure from the future to the present as well as shifting it from unfunded to funded pensions. However, the extra rebate paid to those contracted-out compared to the pension paid to those contracted-in is a subsidy to those with private provision.

At the introduction of a scheme that shifts from an earnings-related to a flat-rate pension, such a subsidy ensures that those who earn above the S2P underpin can avoid losing out in terms of pension[48] by contracting out into, for example, a stakeholder pension. It also provides an incentive for moderate and higher earners to embrace a form of provision that makes it simple for them and/or their employer to add to the provision provided by the state.

However if this policy were successful, we may see a higher proportion, and possibly a majority, of those in this earnings range contract out. If this happens, a subsidy to those who are able to arrange private provision for themselves will seem increasingly anachronistic. Future generations will look at the pension system as it then stands, rather than with a memory of the earnings-related Phase 1 of S2P, and will see the arguments for making S2P genuinely flat-rate.

The second issue is that of the Lower Earnings Limit as the earnings qualification level for entitlement to the State Second Pension. As discussed above, the LEL is no longer the earnings level above which National Insurance contributions are paid. It now exists merely as a qualification level for 'contributory'[49] benefits.

At the time of setting a zero rate for NI contributions just above the LEL, Gordon Brown, the Chancellor, was explicit in uprating the LEL at its usual rate (in line with prices) so as to preserve benefit entitlement. But this commitment is made in the context of recent memory of the LEL as the level above which entitlement to certain benefits occurs.

Over time, future generations will wish to examine the issue of entitlement afresh rather than simply with reference to the history of the LEL. It is of course entirely open whether the earnings level for benefit qualification goes up or down. Currently it is falling relative to earnings but budgetary pressure may lead future governments to increase the level. On the other hand, at a recent seminar,[50] a suggestion was made for it to be reduced to equal 16 times the hourly minimum wage.[51] Sixteen is the number of hours of work needed to qualify for in-work benefits such as the Working Families Tax Credit and the Disabled Persons Tax Credit.

If the latter suggestion were taken up, we would see the first example of the entitlement conditions behind the participatory principle being widened. It is conceivable that over the long term this process might continue. In 1999, at the design of the new pension system, society determines that certain groups are participating in 'approved' ways such that they are entitled to non-means tested support in retirement.

This throws up the issue of why other groups are excluded from a similar level of support. Groups that could in the future be considered to have a reasonable claim to participating in activities 'approved' of by society might include those in various forms of training or education.

As society becomes more aware that the State Second Pension is the true guarantor of a non-means-tested minimum standard of living in retirement perhaps the test will not be groups that participate in 'approved' activities but instead groups that society believes should have the chance of a non-means-tested retirement. In such a world, it is conceivable that the participatory entitlement conditions of the State Second Pension might widen towards those of the basic state pension, perhaps partially funded by the withdrawal of the rebate subsidy to contracted-out moderate and higher earners.

If that were to happen, we would reach a situation where we had two flat-rate pensions, both with not-quite-citizenship entitlement, together designed to take individuals over the levels of means-tested support, although with the possibility of substituting one with equivalent levels of private provision. This would be taking us some of the way back to the 1948–60 pension scheme of Beveridge design, although with the added feature of opting out.

An alternative direction towards which we could move is a more means-tested system. It is unlikely that such a move will take place explicitly. Instead, we would see a gradual diminution of the benefits provided by state pensions until, for all practical purposes, the low paid had no option to but to rely on means-tested support in retirement.

One way of going down this road would be to raise the earnings level of the work participation threshold at a faster rate than at present, so that entitlement to the benefits of S2P will reduce. Alternatively, we could find the uprating of the S2P underpin limited by a future government to prices rather than earnings. Similarly, the value of the credit given to carers and the long-term disabled may be reduced.

Each of these measures would undermine the value of S2P to the extent that those who rely entirely on state pensions may no longer find themselves retiring above the level for means-tested support. In time, such a situation could lead to a more explicit embrace of means-testing as the principle behind support for the elderly.

8.4.7 Conclusion

The situation that the current government inherited was in need of reform. The basic state pension, originally intended to provide a minimum standard, no longer did so. SERPS, originally intended to provide earnings replacement, no longer did so. The two together would in the future no longer provide a minimum standard for an increasing proportion of the population.

The government identified that the contributory principle behind SERPS failed to provide for many and set out that its replacement should have a wider more inclusive entitlement.

It also identified guaranteeing a minimum standard as a more important goal than the provision of earnings-replacement. But its mechanism for achieving this goal is not rooted in either the citizenship principle or the means-tested principle. Instead, it sits somewhere in between, although closer to the citizenship principle. As such, it provides enough nourishment to the adherents of both camps that the one thing we can be sure of is that unemployment is not a danger for the pensions pundits of the future.

Disclaimer

Any views expressed in this paper are those of the author and are purely personal. They are not necessarily the views of the UK government.

Notes

1 Thanks go to Donna Ward, Chris Curry and Phil Agulnik for contributions to the discussions and the modelling that went into this chapter. Any views expressed within are those of the author and are purely personal. They are not necessarily the views of the UK government. Note that all benefit rates, thresholds, and earnings levels are specified at the 1999/2000 level unless otherwise stated.
2 Department of Social Security, 1998a.
3 Beveridge, 1942.
4 The lower earnings limit for National Insurance contributions, currently standing at £66 per week.
5 This list of groups who receive credits is not exhaustive. For a full list see Hansard Commons Written Answers, 28 April 1999, Column 166, Answer by Stephen Timms MP to Steve Webb MP at www.parliament.uk.
6 The Upper Earnings Limit for National Insurance contributions, currently standing at £500 per week.
7 During the working life, rights in SERPS are revalued in line with average earnings and, once in payment, the SERPS pension is uprated in line with prices.
8 More recently employees have been permitted to contract out into money purchase pensions provided that the entirety of the contracted-out rebate goes into the fund.
9 In the UK, private sector occupational pension schemes are funded but most occupational schemes for public sector workers are unfunded.
10 According to Nicholas Timmins, Geoffrey Howe, the Chancellor, had also proposed in 1980 that pensions should not rise in line with prices. See Timmins (1996: 375).
11 Instead of the SERPS pension being worth 25 per cent of relevant earnings, it was to be 20 per cent of relevant earnings. The rate was to be reduced gradually so that those who retired from 2009 onwards faced an accrual rate of 20 per cent.
12 For example, a person earnings £20,000 per annum today and due to retire in 2027 would, in the currently year, accrue a SERPS pension of £67.62 per year (£1.30 per week). This would be revalued in line with average earnings to the year before they reach SRA and then be added to the similar amounts accrued from each year that they had worked.
13 Slightly higher rates are payable for older pensioners:

Age	Single pensioner	Pensioner couple
SRA–74	£75.00 per week	£116.60 per week
75–79	£77.30 per week	£119.85 per week
80 and over	£82.25 per week	£125.30 per week

14 A single pensioner or pensioner couple.
15 These amounts are the average faced by Income Support recipients aged 60 or over, expressed in April 1999 prices, to the nearest pound. See Department of Social Security 1998b: 62, 82.

16 In addition to the income tests, there are also capital limits. For each £250 of capital above £3000, one pound of Income Support, one pound of Housing Benefit and one pound of Council Tax Benefit is lost. However, no Income Support is payable if capital is over £8000 and no Housing Benefit or Council Tax Benefit is payable if capital is over £16,000. From April 2001, the lower capital limit will rise to £6000 and the upper capital limit for Income Support to £12,000.

17 These assumptions are clearly not realistic but are used to illustrate the value of the state pension for hypothetical individuals. Later, there is discussion of the impact of years spent outside the labour market.

18 Throughout this chapter the UK Government Actuary's Department assumption that average earnings will rise 1.5 per cent faster than prices is used.

19 Estimated using the Department of Social Security's *LifePen* model that estimates likely pension at retirement given hypothetical earnings, unemployment, and caring profiles.

20 Once again, the assumption is that the individuals concerned work for 49 years and that their earnings go up exactly in line with average earnings.

21 Estimated using the Department of Social Security's *LifePen* model.

22 Department of Social Security, 1998a.

23 The commitment is to increase in line with earnings until the next election and then as funds allow. For the purposes of this chapter, I assume that this level of increase is achieved.

24 The credit will go automatically to those in receipt of child benefit for a child of up to five years. Child Benefit is a universal benefit payable for every child and almost always goes to the mother of the child.

25 As in Figure 8.3, the assumption behind this chart is that individuals work for 49 years from 16 until State Retirement Age and that, through their working lives, their earnings go up in line with average earnings. Estimates generated using the *LifePen* model.

26 Agulnik (1999: 19–22).

27 See Hansard, Commons Written Answers, 22 February 1999, Col. 160, Answer by Stephen Timms MP to Frank Field MP at www.parliament.uk. These estimates were produced by extrapolating beyond the normal modelling range of the PENSIM model and are thus subject to a high degree of uncertainty.

28 See note 13 for Minimum Income Guarantee rates.

29 Family Resources Survey, 1997/8.

30 Department of Social Security: Lifetime Labour Market Database containing a 1 per cent sample from the National Insurance Recording System taken in February 1997. This is the estimate of individuals with a qualifying year for the basic state pension from Invalid Care Allowance NI credits only.

Note: Income Support (IS) Carer premium recipients are not included in this total because the May 1995 number of Income Support recipients also in receipt of Invalid Care Allowance (ICA) was 119,000 (Department of Social Security 1998b: 40). This is the same as the number of recipients of the IS Carer premium in February 1995 (Department of Social Security 1999: 71). This suggests that at the time all IS Carer premium recipients were also on ICA.

31 A lifetime low earner is a person who earns between the LEL and the S2P underpin throughout their working life.

32 Estimated using the *LifePen* model.

33 MIG = Minimum Income Guarantee, HB = Housing Benefit, CTB = Council Tax Benefit, all figures in 1999 earnings terms, estimates generated using the Department of Social Security's *LifePen* model.

34 For a discussion of pension systems in ten OECD countries, see Johnson 1998.

35 Residence test based entitlement is often referred to as entitlement based on citizenship.
36 Beveridge (1942: 6–7).
37 The basic state pension on introduction on 5 July 1948 was £1.30 (26s 0d) and National Assistance for a single person was £1.20 (24s 0d) (Department of Social Security 1989).
38 See note 5.
39 Department of Social Security: Lifetime Labour Market Database containing a 1 per cent sample from the National Insurance Recording System.
40 Debate of the Age, 9 April 1999.
41 Contributions were paid whilst working. Each £7.50 in contributions paid by a man and £9 paid by a woman between 1961 and 1974 (regardless of the year in which the contribution was paid) is today worth 8.67p per week in pension.
42 Cm 538, HMSO, 1958, quoted in Timmins 1996.
43 The Income Tax threshold currently stands at £4335 per annum or £83 per week.
44 As discussed above, the number of years not paying contributions or receiving credits that can be sustained whilst still retiring above the Minimum Income Guarantee depends on the year that contributions/credits are missed (see Figure 8.8).
45 The Bill to introduce SERPS was given an unopposed second reading in the House of Commons. See Timmins (1996: 349).
46 Note, however, that Beveridge believed in flat-rate contributions for a flat-rate benefit.
47 This point relates only to direct support. The government does see as part of its role taking action to make it easier for individuals to take on this responsibility. Both the introduction of the stakeholder pension and reducing the number who expect to rely on means-tested benefits aim to do just that.
48 Although they may have to pay higher contributions than otherwise to fund the scheme.
49 These benefits cannot be described as purely contributory as entitlement is wider. Groups other than those who pay contributions also enjoy entitlement.
50 Debate of the Age, 9 April 1999.
51 The minimum wage is currently £3.60 per hour so this would mean an LEL of £57.60.

References

Agulnik, Phil (1999) 'The Proposed State Second Pension and National Insurance', in Phil Agulnik, Nicholas Barr, Jane Falkingham and Katherine Rake (eds), *Partnership in Pensions? Responses to the Pensions Green Paper*, CASEpaper 24, Centre for Analysis of Social Exclusion, London School of Economics.

Beveridge, Sir William (1942) *Social Insurance and Allied Services*, Cm 6404, HMSO.

Department of Social Security (1999) *Income Support Statistics Quarterly Enquiry February 1999*, Analytical Services Division.

Department of Social Security (1998a) *A New Contract For Welfare: Partnership in Pensions*, Cm 4179, London: The Stationery Office.

Department of Social Security (1998b) *Social Security Statistics 1998*, Leeds: Corporate Document Services.

Department of Social Security (1998c) *Contributions and Qualifying Years for Retirement Pension 1995/96 Vol. 2*, Analytical Services Division.

Department of Social Security (1989) *Social Security Statistics 1989*, London.

Disney, Richard, Emmerson, Carl, and Tanner, Sarah (1999) *Partnership in Pensions: An Assessment*, London: Institute for Fiscal Studies.

Johnson, Paul (1998) *Older Getting Wiser*, London: Institute for Fiscal Studies.

Rake, Katherine, Falkingham, Jane, and Evans, Martin (1999) *Tightropes and Tripwires: New Labour's Proposals and Means-testing in Old Age*, CASEpaper 23, Centre for Analysis of Social Exclusion, London School of Economics.

Seminar organised as part of Age Concern's Debate of the Age, 'Pensions or penury in the new millennium?', 9 April 1999 at the London School of Economics.

Timmins, Nicholas (1996) *The Five Giants – A Biography of the Welfare State*, London: Fontana.

9 Reform of the public pension system in Germany[1]

Kai A. Konrad and Gert G. Wagner

Abstract

This paper studies the current status in the German pension system and discusses the various reform proposals. It concludes with a short evaluation of the recent pension reform of 2001.

9.1 A brief history

Entering the new millennium, Germany can look back on more than 100 years of a public pension system. The system originated in 1889 as part of Bismarck's policy of establishing a public social security system which was an answer to the pressing social and political situation. He tried to remedy the political conflict and to satisfy to some extent the demand for protection from risks that emerged with the arrival of a large working class that had no chance to develop institutions to cope with these risks. The pension system was initially designed mainly as disability insurance, with the major share of contributions used for work disability pensions. The system was available to and mandatory for a limited group of the workforce, the replacement rate provided by the system for those who reached the (at that time rarely attained) age of 70 years was rather low, and the system was partially funded (see, e.g. Lampert 1996).

The history of reform of the system during the last 100 years was smooth and, for most parts, unidirectional. First, the types of workers required to participate in the system systematically expanded with time. Today (in 2001) mandatory participation in the public pension system encompasses almost all groups of earners with the exception of some groups of self-employed professionals and civil servants,[2] without provisions to opt out even for higher income employees.[3] Reforms established in 1999 continued and finally completed this process: criteria have been tightened by which activities are considered self-employed, forcing some further groups of self-employed individuals into the public pension system. This latest reform was intended as a reaction to the current trend of individuals in several professions to opt out of the public pension system by ending their employment relationship with a firm and, instead, working for this firm on a freelance "self-employed" basis, without actually changing their job characteristics as regards their actual responsibilities.

Second, the contribution rate and the replacement rate have both risen several times since the system was established. Important changes were the reduction in the retirement age from initially 70 to 63 and 60 for men and women, respectively,[4] and adjustment rules for pensions that tied the pension benefits to the growth of wages. It is only in recent years, as it has become more and more transparent that the future financial viability of the system requires reform, that some of these reforms have been reversed. For instance, the reform in 1992 made pension increases a function of net wages instead of gross wages, and the reform that was to be implemented in 1999 aimed at changing retirement age in several steps back to 65 in the first decade of the new millennium.[5]

Third, when the German pension system was established, it was intended as a (partially) funded system. The funded part of the system rapidly vanished. Hyperinflation in the 1920s and a currency reform after World War II would have eliminated any funds in any case. Today, the system is fully pay-as-you-go, with an annual budget of 447bn DM in 2000[6] (*Rentenversicherungsbericht* 2001, Übersicht A13) financed by contributions as a percentage of labor income (19.1 percent of insured earnings in 2001) and federal transfers paid from the general tax revenue of about 137bn DM in 2001 (*Finanzbericht* 2001: 19).

While we were writing this survey, a reform has been enacted which will become effective in 2002. Major elements of this reform are a reduction of the pay-as-you-go financed replacement rate by about 2 percentage points, and the re-introduction of elements of partial funding of old-age pensions. Starting in 2002, selected types of savings in pension funds and some other savings activities will receive child-dependent and income dependent governmental matching subsidies; the amount of savings can be deducted from taxable income, and returns on these savings are tax exempt up to the time when retirement age is reached. However, the tax deductible amount of savings is limited to 1 percent of annual income in 2002 (capped), and this percentage is to increase bi-annually to 4 percent of income (also with a cap) in 2008.[7]

It is well-known that the introduction of a pay-as-you-go financed public pensions system benefits the "first generation:" those who are old and close to retirement when the system was introduced pay little or no contributions but receive pensions for the rest of their life. This "first-generation benefit" accrues not only if a pension system is introduced, but also whenever the existing system is expanded.

For instance, persons who have already completed a major part of their working life gain if the replacement rate of the system is increased: these persons paid only few contributions up to that point. They then pay higher contributions for the rest of their working life, but will receive higher old-age pensions during their whole retirement.

Similarly, persons who are working benefit if, for a given replacement rate, the group of contributors increases. The amount needed to finance the currently retired is paid for by a larger working population. Hence, these workers' contributions rate is reduced. But at the same time, for a given replacement rate, the present value of their receipts in terms of future pensions remains unchanged.[8]

The continuing reforms that increased the group of participants in the social security system, increased the replacement rate, and reduced the retirement age can be seen as a process that granted each generation some "first-generation advantage," and this effect was probably important for generating a political climate of broad acceptance for this system. The "first-generation gift" makes current generations vote in favor of an introduction or expansion of an unfunded pension system if they believe that the expansion is indeed permanent, especially if the growth rate of the wage bill exceeds interest rates.

The political economy of the "first-generation gift" effect makes it surprising that it took about 100 years until the system had managed to grow to its present maximum size, and the recent reversal in this trend is even more surprising. The process of granting first-generation gifts must come to an end if the growth rate of the sum of wages falls short of the interest rate. In the case of a stationary pay-as-you-go pension system the internal rate of return of the pay-as-you-go system equals the growth rate of the sum of wages. The internal rate of return of the system is smaller than the capital market interest rate, implying that workers who make contributions to this system get less than if they save in the capital market or buy an (almost perfect) old-age and disability insurance contract. The difference between these returns implies that generations in the mature state of the pension system receive a present value of pensions that is smaller than the present value of their contributions. The difference is an implicit tax, which serves to finance the interest on the "first-generation gift." As is well-known, such implicit taxes have substitution effects, and induce workers to generate less income in the official labor market. Indeed, there is a maximum limit to the pension system, given that the system is financed by pay-as-you-go. As with any tax, a Laffer curve argument can explain why the system has a maximum limit.[9]

9.2 Why was reform needed?

The discussion of a crisis in the social security pension system is an almost universal problem in OECD countries and social security reform is discussed in all industrialized countries. Its main cause is demographics. The size of the problem differs from country to country, depending on the country's demography, the replacement rate, retirement age, and the method of finance. A survey for European countries is, for instance, provided by Boldrin, Dolado, Jimeno and Peracchi (1999).

The German situation has been described in more detail and with great precision by several authors. For a comprehensive and comparative analysis see, e.g. Sinn (1999a, 1999b). The population in Germany is shrinking rapidly, life expectancy is increasing, and the unemployment rate is high. For a given pay-as-you-go system with a given retirement age this implies that there are fewer workers per pensioner at each time, and for a given replacement rate, this increases contribution rates.

Due to these demographic developments, the internal rate of return that a married male earns by participating in the mandatory pay-as-you-go pension system in Germany was estimated to be about 3.5 percent for those born in 1930 and this rate continuously dropped to 1.2 percent, 0.6 percent and 0.3 percent for those born in 1960, 1970, and 1980, respectively (see Schnabel 1998), if the labor market characteristics are unchanged. This low internal rate of return of the pension system would not be a problem if the pay-as-you-go system were a minor budget share. However, the total annual budget of the German public pension system is about the same size as the annual budget of the federal government. (Note that the German pension system is not part of the federal government activities, but is organized separately.)

The financial burden that is imposed by the pay-as-you-go system can be visualized by the time paths of contribution rates without reform (see, e.g. Sinn and Thum 1999). The most recent and most sophisticated version of estimates is the computational general equilibrium model by Hans Fehr (1999). Figure 9.1 illustrates the various estimates of contribution paths for the present system. The most notable facts are the sharp increase in contribution rates from 19.1 percent in 2001 to about 30 percent of gross labor income in 2040.

These contribution rates do not include the huge transfers from the general federal budget to the pension system that amount to about one quarter of total social security old age pensions. A large share of the contribution rate is similar to an implicit tax on labor income, because the internal rates of return for the current working generation and their children are much lower than the capital market rate of return, and because the current system also redistributes between different types of workers within each generation. The rate of this implicit tax has been calculated for a "representative" worker for Germany by Thum and von Weizsäcker (1999). They find that with the current system the implicit income tax is about 8 percent for the representative worker born in 1940, and rises to 19 percent for the representative worker born in the year 2000. From a theoretical point of view, these calculations most likely underestimate the true effects as they are not based on a general equilibrium model that takes into account the effects of extremely high tax rates on official labor income and tax evasion. Indeed, adding to these implicit taxes the substantial marginal labor income tax rates and other components of social security payments that are similar to an implicit tax (e.g. public health insurance[10])

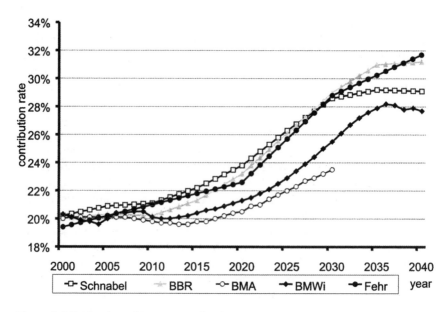

Figure 9.1 Projection of future contribution rates

Sources: Sinn and Thum (1999) and Fehr (1999).

Note: Schnabel: Schnabel (1998), medium scenario; BBR: Besendorfer, Borgmann and Raffelhüschen (1998); BMA: Sozialbeirat (1998); BMW: Wissenschaftlicher Beirat beim Bundesministerium für Wirtschaft (1998), (scenario 2); Fehr: Fehr (1999).

the disincentives could be massive, and, depending on the elasticity of the tax base, the system may simply become unsustainable.

Summarizing, the demographic trend of shrinking population size in Germany reduces the internal rate of return of the pay-as-you-go pension system far below the market rate of interest. At the same time the system has grown to a size at which contributions become a major share of workers' budgets. Accordingly, there will be growing labor market disincentives of the implicit tax which make a reform of the system useful.

9.3 Reform proposals

Consider the various parameters that influence a pay-as-you-go financed pension system.

1 As has been discussed by many researchers, technological progress and economic growth are beneficial but do not help to reduce the contribution rate if the replacement rate is fixed.

2 An increase by higher fertility rates (induced, for instance, by an aggressive family policy) could raise the internal rate of return in the long run. However, such a policy is unlikely, and given that the system faces

major problems in the next 40 years, the effects of this policy are felt too late to solve this problem.

3 A considerable increase in female labor participation would reduce the contribution rate, but only temporarily. The impact would be similar to an expansion of the system, just like adding a further group of the working force that starts paying contributions now and earns pensions only later. However, an increase of female labor force participation could help to understand the problems of the next 40 years.

4 The effects of temporary immigration are similar. Only a permanent inflow of immigrants and the induced growth of the workforce would increase the attractiveness of the system permanently, just like a permanent increase in the birth rate. However, the size of such immigration inflow had to be large in order to have a considerable impact on the contribution rate. Börsch-Supan and Winter (1999) report that in the next few decades an inflow of about 800,000 immigrants per year would be needed to fully compensate for population aging, which would be about 2.5 times the current net immigration which is already very high by European standards.

5 With respect to the contribution rate, an increase of the retirement age (which reduces the number of recipients and increases the number of contributors) would be more effective than lowering the replacement rate. However, an increase in retirement age is most difficult because one cannot set the effective age of retirement by law. Effective retirement depends on labor market conditions, and a disability pension is an alternative pathway into effective retirement.

6 Given the problems of increasing the retirement age, the most obvious way to reduce the contribution rates is to reduce the replacement rate of current and future pensioners. Of course, this is not without problems, because the current elderly expected to receive the present replacement rate, and adjusted their private savings accordingly. It was too late for them to revise their intertemporal allocation of income. However, a reduction in pensions of the current generation is one of the few ways to make this generation share the burden of pension reform and should therefore be considered as a reasonable goal.

7 An extensive academic discussion took place about the possibility of an efficiency enhancing transformation from a pay-as-you-go financed system to a fully (or partially) pre-funded system. This intellectual debate started with a paper by Breyer (1989) who showed that, essentially, the transition from an unfunded pension system to a fully funded system cannot be achieved as a Pareto improvement. Breyer's insight is the same as Mats Persson's (2001) who points out that unfunded systems make a bonus to the first generation, and, when returning to a funded system, this bonus must be repaid by someone.

Some authors (e.g. Homburg 1990; Raffelhüschen 1993; and Breyer and Straub 1993) argued, however, that, due to endogenous labor supply, proportional contribution rates to an unfunded social security system involve an excess burden which is absent in a funded system. If these welfare losses could be avoided, the welfare gains could be used to compensate the generations for paying the bonus to the first generation. These approaches assume that the welfare losses incurred in the present system by making the contribution rate proportional to income is a necessary element of a pay-as-you-go financed pension system that would disappear in a funded system.

The proportionality of contributions to a pay-as-you-go system with flat pensions and the involved welfare losses in these models is not an intrinsic element in pay-as-you-go systems. It is a result of intragenerational redistribution. Fenge (1995) pointed out this fallacy, showing that a welfare improving transition from pay-as-you-go to a funded system is not viable in a system that avoids intragenerational redistribution, by making pensions a function of contributions (which is – more or less – the case in Germany).

This was not the end of the discussion. For instance, Belan, Michel, and Pestieau (1998) consider an endogenous growth model in which macroeconomic spillovers from capital investment is the "growth engine." They argue that the economy is undercapitalized in this case, and transition from an unfunded to a funded system could be welfare improving because it increases capital accumulation. Fenge and von Weizsäcker (1999) argue that partial transition to an at least partially funded compulsory system could be more powerful than a fully unfunded system in addressing Coate's (1995) Samaritan dilemma problem that arises in economies in which individuals receive a governmentally guaranteed minimum income. A last example of this type of result is Demmel and Keuschnigg (1999) who consider an economy in which a monopoly union pursues an inefficient wage policy that leads to unemployment. They argue that proportional (or progressive) labor income taxation aggravates the inefficiency, and this inefficiency would be reduced in a funded system.

All these proposals rest on the assumption that there is a given inefficiency in the economy and claim that a transition from pay-as-you-go to a funded system reduces or eliminates this inefficiency. While the arguments here are more indirect than with the original contribution by Homburg (1990), we have to ask whether the inefficiency is generically linked to the pay-as-you-go financing of the pension system. In the few contributions we briefly discussed above, it seems to be straightforward to correct the inefficiency without making a transition from a pay-as-you-go system to a funded system. A more extensive review of this discussion can be found in Bach and Wiegard (1999).

This discussion suggests that there is no Pareto-improving transition from a pay-as-you-go system to a funded system. Accordingly, the discussion about transition and about the appropriate transition path is mainly a discussion that is about intragenerational and intergenerational redistribution. This observation may explain the heat in the public debate.

Before the most recent pension reform took place in June 2001 several policy proposals were discussed in Germany. But, first of all, the government as well as the unions seem to believe in the positive effects of a significant decrease of open unemployment. Low unemployment rates (like in the US or the Scandinavian countries) will increase the contributions which are paid to the pension system, will increase labor force participation of women, will attract immigrants, and will increase the effective retirement age. Nevertheless there will be an unavoidable increase in the contribution rate which is considered as not acceptable (see Wagner 1999).

The most radical reform proposal (advocated by many economists and the Prime Minister of Saxony, Kurt Biedenkopf, see, e.g. Biedenkopf and Miegel (1997)) is to cut down the public pension system to a flat-rate pension ("basic pension"). Individuals could then decide on whether they would like to increase private savings on a voluntary basis. Many other reform proposals are similar to the proposal made by the scientific advisors of the Ministry of Economics who advocated essentially to keep a pay-as-you-go system, but, in order to level the contribution rate over the next 25 years, to build up reserves in the next few years by raising the contribution rate above what is needed to finance the current pensions. This view has been supported also by Sinn (1999a) and Fenge and von Weizsäcker (1999) as well as by the Council of Economic Advisors (Sachverständigenrat zur Begutachtung der wirtschaftlichen Lage).

These reform proposals differ somewhat in their assumptions regarding some structural parameters, e.g. the adjustment of retirement age, the growth rate of wages, immigration, and, in particular, the path of repayment of the gift that was received by the "first generation." The conservative government which was in power until 1998 intended to reduce the replacement rate in a slow adjustment process that would have taken more than 10 years, in line with the interests of the current elderly voters who are more inclined to vote conservative. The current government which draws more strongly on younger voters did cut down the replacement rate instantly in the year 2000 by an adjustment of pensions that, for some time, proceeded slower than net wage increases. Further reform steps of the new government are discussed in the final section.[11]

The current working population is most heavily burdened by all reform proposals. A move toward a funded system that takes place within the next 20 to 30 years imposes a double burden on the current working generation, having to pay contributions to the pensions paid to the retired, without receiving a transfer from their children themselves. The size of the burden of the children of the current working generation depends on the different types of reform. For instance, the speed of transition to a funded system determines which generation is burdened more heavily.

In addition to these intergenerational issues, the reform proposals differ with respect to their intergenerational redistributional impact. For instance, the German pay-as-you-go system has always been financed by contributions proportional to wage income plus governmental transfers from general tax revenue. A tax reform in Germany in 1999 has increased the share of transfers from general tax revenue considerably in order to reduce the contribution rate. This reform was meant to redistribute the burden of financing old-age pensions from employed workers to other groups in society (self-employed, civil servants, unemployed, retired). However, the extent to which such a transition could occur is limited. At present, more than 25 percent of the federal budget is used for such transfers to the pension system and accounts for about the same percentage of the pension bill there.[12]

9.4 Guidelines for partially funded systems

All over the world reform proposals for a transition from pay-as-you-go to (partial) pre-funding mainly differ with respect to the allocation of the burden of financing the bonus that has been made to the first generation when introducing the pay-as-you-go system, or to subsequent generations, when expanding the system. Whether and how a (partially) funded pension system is introduced is mainly a matter of intergenerational redistribution, and economics does not give clear-cut advice on such matters (cf. Breyer 2001). However, if such a system is introduced, this needs to take care of a number of design issues.

We will only discuss the problems of partially funded old-age retirement payments because this reform feature is the most challenging one. It is important to note, however, that measures for increasing the effective age of retirement, restructuring widows' payments and other kinds of redistribution elements, and last but not least, the rules for paying contributions are most important keystones of a reform package as well (see Wagner 1999). We will also abstain from a discussion of potential macroeconomic problems with funded systems (see Wagner *et al.* 1999).

9.4.1 Political economy risks

An important consideration is the political economy risk. As is well known, the political decision about introducing a pay-as-you-go system is strongly biased in favor for such a system, as many voters would belong to the "first generation" that wins from such an introduction. Accordingly, if a funded system exists, there is strong political pressure to divert the accumulated funds and use them directly or indirectly on the current generations and to re-introduce a pay-as-you-go system.

In order to reduce such political risks, it can be useful to accumulate funds in a privately organized system (Sinn 1999b). Also, privatized funds may operate more efficiently than funds managed by a governmental bureau, and we would like to subscribe to this view.

There are certainly some design questions of how to organize such a private system (Holzmann and Palacio 2000). For instance, similar to existing regulation in insurance markets and banking, some consumer protection may be discussed. Much can be learnt from insurance markets, in particular about the dangers of regulatory capture. But on the other hand, one needs to think about the problems of fraud and gambling by fund managers, and some experience with pension fund regulation in other countries can be usefully applied.

9.4.2 Design of a private system

The introduction of a funded system with privately managed funds raises a number of design questions. For instance, should the pension system be mandatory, or should the system be voluntary? If the system is voluntary, should the government subsidize individual savings? Should it be possible to borrow against the future pensions? Should participants be able to allocate their savings freely between different types of assets? Should funded pension savings be paid out when individuals enter their retirement period, or should transformation of accumulated savings into annuities be mandatory when retirement age is reached? Many of these questions are related to a simple fundamental trade off in a modern welfare state that makes the answers to most of these questions ambiguous, and we consider this trade off somewhat closer.

9.4.2.1 Flexibility and the Samaritan's dilemma

Individuals will always be entitled to have some means-tested basic income or basic consumption level which they either earn for themselves, or receive as a transfer from the rest of society. Individuals may pursue strategies by which they end up with little or no wealth when being old. For instance, individuals who do not have much income anyway may decide not to save for old-age consumption. If they consume the present value of their lifetime-income before they enter retirement, they receive social subsistence benefits from society. This may be advantageous even if it leads to a very uneven consumption pattern over a lifetime, because the elicited subsidy yields an increase in expected lifetime income.

For similar reasons, individuals who know that they receive subsistence payments if they have no income when old have an incentive to gamble, even if the gamble is not actuarially fair. Suppose some individuals have wealth x when entering retirement, and assume that this wealth is higher than the guaranteed minimum subsistence consumption level y. The individuals can simply consume x and have utility $u(x)$ in retirement. Alternatively, they can buy highly risky assets that yield either 0 or $10x$ with probabilities 90 percent and 10 percent, respectively. Hence, this gamble is fair, and risk averse individuals would not accept it. However, individuals who can rely on a guaranteed minimum subsistence consumption level $y>0$ may still choose to gamble, even if they are risk averse. They will, if

$0.9u(y) + 0.1u(10x) > u(x)$ which is always the case for x sufficiently close to y. Hence, individuals may put all their retirement savings at risk, and modern capital markets would provide the means to do this most elegantly and with almost no transaction cost. Of course, this behavior is inefficient. The transfer to these individuals must be paid by other individuals. In a symmetric world, all individuals contribute in financing these transfers, and all individuals will lose from such behavioral incentives. Welfare losses are generated because the individuals' expected income is unchanged but their consumption allocation becomes risky. Welfare losses in this allocation are equal to the individuals' risk bearing cost in this example.

These are two variants of Buchanan's (1975) Samaritan's dilemma, that has been re-emphasized in Coate (1995), and is the main efficiency argument for compulsory retirement plans and compulsory insurance. Similarly, to avoid the second type of Samaritan's dilemma, individuals must be persuaded not to gamble. To do this, individuals' portfolio choices must be controlled and tightly regulated.[13]

Of course, such stringent regulation regarding the size of savings, and the portfolio composition have their costs. One type is monitoring cost. A second type of cost is the welfare loss from distortions that a regulatory regime is likely to generate. Individuals' preferences and their future earnings expectations are typically private information. Hence, it will typically be difficult to devise a mandatory regime in a way that does not impose binding restrictions on some individuals and constrains them to some consumption plan which differs from their first choice. Someone who anticipates that he or she will have access to major income flows when he or she will have passed the average retirement age should not be forced into mandatory savings. Persons also differ with respect to their risk aversion and with respect to their information as regards investment alternatives. Accordingly, a uniform mandatory portfolio composition will force individuals into allocations that are suboptimal.

However, the trade off does not end here. Individuals and the market are ingenious in bypassing any regulatory constraint. For instance, if individuals can borrow against their pension entitlements, any mandatory savings plan could simply be compensated by an appropriate reduction in other savings, or appropriate borrowing. Hence, to escape from the Samaritan's dilemma, borrowing against accumulated pension funds must be ruled out. Of course, this will be difficult and costly. Suppose this borrowing would be illegal. An illegal market could emerge that caters to this demand, most likely causing the usual additional burden which characterize illegal markets.[14]

With modern capital markets and access to fancy derivative instruments, it is even more difficult to rule out gambling. Any regulatory regime that has some "bite" will have high enforcement cost, high indirect cost from making individually desired transactions illegal, and high cost from constraining individuals away from their first best consumption. It seems not unlikely to us that extremely tight regulation generates welfare losses that outweigh the benefits from solving the Samaritan's dilemma.

9.4.2.2 Governmentally subsidized savings

Alternatively, the government may try to induce voluntary savings and a "reasonable" portfolio composition. What comes to mind here are governmental subsidies to voluntary savings plans that provide an appropriate portfolio management. Indeed, such instruments seem to be quite popular in the US (for some discussion see Mitchell 2002). The following example can explain why such savings plans are popular and, at the same time, why such a policy may seriously reduce welfare.

Consider first a situation in which the Samaritan's dilemma is absent. Suppose a person lives for two periods, the working period 1, and the retirement period 2, and has utility of private consumption

$$U(x_1, x_2) = u(x_1) + u(x_2)$$

with x_i consumption in period i. Let the capital market rate of interest be zero, for simplicity. Suppose the individual has income m that accrues in period 1. It can allocate this income between consumption x_1 and x_2, and, in a *laissez-faire* situation, it would allocate equal shares between the periods: $x_i = m/2$. We denote savings by k. If all saving k is subsidized, with s the constant subsidy rate, this will typically increase savings, such that $u'(m - k) = (1 + s)u'(k(1 + s))$. Of course, this intertemporal allocation is distorted.

If there is an upper limit as regards the amount of z that is subsidized, and if the individual has access to perfect capital markets, the budget constraint becomes $m + sz = x_1 + x_2$. The intertemporal distortion disappears. However, such a (lump-sum) transfer from the government to the individual is expensive in a world in which tax revenue cannot be collected without an excess burden.

If only a certain type of saving is subsidized (e.g. stock market investment, but not housing), and if there is no limit to the maximum amount of savings that is subsidized, this will lead to distorted investment incentives. It will distort the intertemporal allocation and will crowd out non-subsidized forms of private saving, even if they have a higher gross return than the subsidized savings instruments. Hence, restricting subsidies to a subset of assets generates further distortions. Again, if there is a sufficiently low upper limit for subsidized savings, the intertemporal distortion vanishes. However, two types of welfare cost remain: the excess burden of collecting the taxes needed to make the transfers, and the distortions in savings composition.

Consider now whether governmental subsidies can alleviate the

Samaritan's dilemma problem. Suppose again that there is a governmentally guaranteed minimum income y in each period. Instead of allocating m equally between periods, the person may spend all income in period 1 and rely on welfare, receiving a transfer equal to y in period 2. This choice is made if

$$u(m) + u(y) > u(m/2) + u(m/2).$$

For y sufficiently close to m, this condition is fulfilled, even if u is strictly concave.[15] This outcome describes the Samaritan's dilemma situation.

Assume now that the government subsidizes a particular retirement plan, such that each USD put into this plan receives some governmental subsidy equal to s, up to a maximum saving, say,

$$\frac{m}{2} \geq z.$$

The individual could save now and obtain utility

$$u\left(\frac{m}{2} + \frac{sz}{2}\right)$$

in both periods, by appropriate transactions in the capital markets. Indeed, it may be true that

$$2u\left(\frac{m}{2} + \frac{sz}{2}\right) \geq u(m) + u(y).$$

However, if the individual has access to a perfect capital market, whether the Samaritan's dilemma applies depends on whether

$$2u\left(\frac{m}{2} + \frac{sz}{2}\right) \geq u(m + sz) + u(y).$$

The individual can achieve utility

$$2u\left(\frac{m}{2} + \frac{sz}{2}\right)$$

by borrowing $(1 + s)z$ on the private capital market, spending all income in the first period, using the payments $(1 + s)z$ to pay back the loan, and rely on welfare in period 2. This possibility arises especially if the contribution plan is not automatically annuitized and paid out at the beginning of retirement age.

The example makes clear that saving through savings plans can be offset by borrowing, and that individuals may have a strong incentive to do this. In particular, without introducing capital market restrictions and if pension plans are not automatically annuitized, they may be of rather limited help for overcoming the Samaritan's dilemma. But, on the other hand, any general restriction on portfolio choice constrains other groups of individuals and also generates welfare losses. Summarizing, governmentally subsidized savings plans are not a straightforward instrument to deal with the Samaritan's dilemma.

9.5 Conclusions

This chapter highlights that reform of pension systems is mainly a matter of redistribution between the currently retired generation, the current workforce, and their children, between high income earners and low income earners, between those currently paying into the system and those who do not, and between families with many children and families with few children. Political economy aspects will be essential in predicting and understanding the reform outcome.

Apart from this, the chapter has highlighted a fundamental trade off as regards regulation in a funded pension system and discussed why we think regulation will not be able to effectively address the Samaritan's dilemma in its various guises, regardless whether this regulation will impose mandatory contributions to a funded pension system and stringent portfolio regulation, or whether the government may try to solve the problem by tax incentives.[16]

Notes

1 We thank Toshihiro Ihori and Marcel Thum for valuable information, discussion and comments, and Rainer Möhlenkamp for valuable research assistance. Of course, the usual caveat applies.
2 Civil servants' pensions are calculated according to different rules and are paid from current tax revenue. In other words, there is a second, smaller scale pay-as-you-go system that finances civil servants' pensions.
3 The system is capped. Earnings exceeding a certain limit (*"Beitragsbemessungsgrenze"*) are not included in the insurance system. Workers do not pay contributions on this portion of their earnings. In 1999 this limit was DM 8500, and DM 7200 in former East Germany.
4 The current rules are complicated. For instance, the regular retirement age for men was 63 for male individuals who were in the system for at least 35 years, and 65 for others. Long-term unemployment and disability also has an impact on individuals' eligibility to retire earlier. Apart from this, earlier or later retirement was possible and had an impact on the replacement rate. Rules for individuals retiring after 2000 are less generous (see e.g. *Sozialgesetzbuch* 1999: 35–41).
5 Due to early retirement rules (e.g. for long-term unemployed), the current average retirement age was as low as age 59.5 in 1998 (Börsch-Supan and Winter 1999).

6 Including 28bn DM of the mining fund (Knappschaftliche Rentenversicherung).

7 See, e.g. BMA, Die neue Rente, http://www.bma.bund.de/frame.asp?u=/de/asp/
   broschueren/index.htm).

8 This is strictly true only if the system has a replacement rate that follows gross
   wages. If, as is the case in Germany, the replacement rate follows net wages,
   there is a countervailing effect, because the replacement rate of the pensioners
   increases due to lower contribution rates for the employed.

9 Breyer (1994) has made this Laffer curve argument in a simple full information
   model with exogenously assumed proportional contributions. But of course,
   the thrust of the argument also applies in an incomplete information context
   with a government that chooses the optimal mechanism to elicit contributions.
   In this context, Konrad (1995a) has considered the role of public investment
   for the maximum size of the public pension system, and Konrad (1995b) has
   analysed the impact of international social security tax competition with
   mobile workers. He shows that worker mobility increases the incentives for
   public infrastructure investment and reduces the incentives for public education investment.

10 At present, German mandatory public health insurance is highly redistributive.
   While most benefits of public health insurance are independent of income,
   health insurance contributions are proportional to income, up to an upper
   limit. Currently the average contribution rate is about 13 percent of gross labor
   income (below a certain limit), and an increasing trend is apparent. Accordingly, from the perspective of individuals, this amounts to an implicit marginal
   income tax of about 13 percent.

11 For voter shares in recent elections, see, e.g. http://www.statistik-bund.
   de/wahlen/eutabalt/eutab19.html

12 Another element of intragenerational redistribution in social security has been
   highlighted in a paper by Breyer and von der Schulenburg (1987). They consider parents who care about the utility level of their children, but unlike Barro
   (1974), consider heterogenous families. Consider two types of families. Let the
   parents be about 45 years old in both families. Suppose one family has one
   child, whereas the other family has more children, and suppose both parents
   care about the earning capacity of their children. Independent of whether
   Barro's bequest motive is operative or not, the fathers of the two types of
   families care quite differently about possible reforms of the social security
   system, since the effects differ for the two types of families if they have different numbers of children.

13 In a recent paper, Homburg (1999) shows that forced savings as a share in
   labor income may be a poor instrument to cope with the Samaritan's dilemma
   if one takes into account that labor income itself is endogenous. Forced savings
   may then drive some individuals into a poverty trap even during the working
   stage of their life, because they are able to earn enough to make ends meet, but
   their incentives to earn are not strong enough to make them earners if they
   also have to contribute to a social security system.

14 Some of these costs are expected penalty costs on the demand side and on the
   supply side, increased transaction cost from the lack of public protection,
   reduced market transparency, and inefficient enforcement of contracts in these
   markets.

15 This minimum income of an n-person household in Germany is approximately
   45 percent of such households' average net income.

16 It may be a surprise that the new government which is more in favor of progressive taxation that the old government will not achieve its goal of lowering
   the replacement rate by a change in the income tax treatment of pensions. At

present, the treatment of pensions for income taxation is complicated in Germany. Only about 25–30 percent of the amount of each individual public pension is considered taxable income. Given that the German marginal income tax is zero in the range between DM0 and about DM13,000 for singles and between DM0 and about DM26,000 for married couples, if pensioners have no other major source of income, they do not pay income tax on their pensions if they do not exceed DM42,000 per year. This is puzzling, because a major share of contributions to social security is essentially tax free. Compared to conventional aims of income redistribution, a regular tax treatment of pensions may be more appealing than a general downward adjustment of the replacement rate. Still, a drastic increase in the tax burden on social security pensions is unlikely to happen. One reason could be government's concerns about the opposition of the elderly voters against a regular tax treatment.

References

Bach, Stefan and Wiegard, Wolfgang (2001) "Public finance," in Klaus F. Zimmermann (ed.), *Frontiers in Economics*, Heidelberg: Physica.

Barro, Robert J. (1974) "Are government bonds net wealth?," *Journal of Political Economy* 82: 1095–117.

Belan, Pascal, Michel, Philippe, and Pestieau, Pierre (1998) "Pareto-improving social security reform," *Geneva Papers on Risk and Insurance Theory* 23(2), 119–25.

Besendorfer, D., Borgmann, C., and Raffelhüschen, B. (1998) "Ein Plädoyer für intergenerative Ausgewogenheit: Rentenreformvorschläge auf dem Prüfstand," *ifo Studien* 44: 209–31.

Biedenkopf, Kurt H. and Miegel, Meinhard (1997) *Von der Arbeitnehmer-zur Bürgerrente – Das Konzept der Grundsicherung im Alter*, Bonn.

Börsch-Supan, Axel (1998) "Zur deutschen Diskussion eines Übergangs vom Umlage- zum Kapitaldeckungsverfahren in der gesetzlichen Rentenversicherung", *Finanzarchiv* 55: 400–28.

Börsch-Supan, Axel and Winter, Joachim K. (1999) "Pension reform, savings behavior and corporate governance," mimeo, University of Mannheim.

Boldrin, Michele, Dolado, Juan J., Jimeno, Juan F., and Peracchi, Franco (1999) "The future of pensions in Europe," *Economic Policy* 29: 289–320.

Breyer, Friedrich (1989) "On the intergenerational pareto-efficiency of pay-as-you-go finance pension systems," *Journal of Institutional and Theoretical Economics* 145: 643–58.

Breyer, Friedrich (1994) "Voting on social security when labor supply is endogenous," *Economics and Politics* 6(2): 119–30.

Breyer, Friedrich (2001) "Why funding is not a solution to the 'social security crisis'?," *DIW Discussion Paper*, 254.

Breyer, Friedrich and Graf v.d. Schulenburg, Matthias (1987) "Voting on social security: the family as decision-making unit," *Kyklos* 40(4): 529–47.

Breyer, Friedrich and Straub, Martin (1993) "Welfare effects of unfunded pension systems when labor supply is endogenous," *Journal of Public Economics* 50: 77–91.

Buchanan, James M. (1975) "The Samaritan's dilemma," in E. S. Phelps (ed.), *Altruism, Morality and Economic Theory*, New York: Russel Sage Foundation, 71–85.

Coate, Stephen (1995) "Altruism, the Samaritan's dilemma, and government transfer policy," *American Economic Review* 85(1): 46–57.

Demmel, Roland and Keuschnigg, Christian (1999) "Funded pensions and unemployment," *Finanzarchiv* 56 (forthcoming).

Fehr, Hans (1999) "Pension reform during the demographic transition," mimeo.

Fenge, Robert (1995) "Pareto-efficiency of the pay-as-you-go pension system with intragenerational fairness," *Finanzarchiv* 52(3): 357–63.

Fenge, Robert and von Weizsäcker, Robert K. (1999) "To what extent are public pensions Pareto-improving? On the interaction of means tested basic income and public pensions," *CESifo Working Paper*, 197.

Finanzbericht 2001, Bonn: Bundesministerium für Finanzen.

Holzmann, Robert and Palacio, Robert (2000) "Symposium on key issues in introducing pre-funded pension schemes," in Schmollers Jahrbuch *Journal of Applied Social Science Studies* 120(3): 309–11.

Homburg, Stefan (1990) "The efficiency of unfunded pension schemes," *Journal of Institutional and Theoretical Economics* 146(4): 47.

Homburg, Stefan (1999) "Compulsory savings in the welfare state," mimeo.

Kirner, Ellen, Meinhardt, Volker, and Wagner, Gert G. (2000) "Problems of providing income security in old age cannot be solved merely by changing the mode of financing," *Economic Bulletin* 37: 275–84.

Konrad, Kai A. (1995a) "Social security and strategic inter-vivos transfers of social capital," *Journal of Population Economics* 8: 315–26.

Konrad, Kai A. (1995b) "Fiscal federalism and intergenerational redistribution," *FinanzArchiv*, N.F. 52(2): 166–81.

Lampert, Heinz (1996) *Lehrbuch der Sozialpolitik* 4. Auflage; Heidelberg: Springer.

Mitchell, Olivia (2002) "Managing pensions in the 21st century: design innovations, market impact, and regulatory issues for Japan," this volume.

Persson, Mats (2001) "Five fallacies in the social security debate," this volume.

Raffelhüschen, Bernd (1993) "Funding social security through Pareto-optimal conversion policies," *Journal of Economics*, Suppl. 7: 105–31.

Rentenversicherungsbericht (2001) "Bericht der Bundesregierung über die gesetzliche Rentenversicherung, insbesondere über die Entwicklung der Einnahmen und Ausgaben, der Schwankungsreserve sowie des jeweils erforderlichen Beitragssatzes in den künftigen 15 Kalenderjahren gemäss § 154 SGB VI," Bundesdrucksache 14/7639.

Schnabel, Reinhold (1998) "Rates of return of the German pay-as-you-go pension system," *Finanzarchiv* 55: 374–99.

Sinn, Hans-Werner (1999a) "Pension reform and demographic crisis: why a funded system is needed and why it is not needed," *CESifo Working Paper*, 195.

Sinn, Hans-Werner (1999b) "The crisis of Germany's pension insurance system and how it can be resolved," *CEPR Working Paper*, 2175.

Sinn, Hans-Werner and Thum, Marcel (1999) *Gesetzliche Rentenversicherung: Prognosen im Vergleich*, München: ifo Diskussionsbeiträge, ifo Institut.

Sozialbeirat (1998) *Gutachten des Sozialbeirats zum Rentenversicherungsbericht 1998 und Stellungnahmen zu einigen weiteren Berichten zur Alterssicherung*, Bonn.

Sozialgesetzbuch (1999) "Sechstes Buch (VI) Gesetzliche Rentenversicherung," http://www.bma.bund.de/download/gesetze/SGB6.htm

Thum, Marcel and von Weizsäcker, Jakob (1999) "Implizite Einkommensteuer als Messlatte für die aktuellen Rentenreformvorschläge," mimeo, University of Munich.

Wagner, Gert G. (2000) "Perspektiven der Alterssicherung," in R. Hauser (ed.) *Die Zukunft des Sozialstaats*, Berlin: Beiheft 8 der Zeitschrift für Wirtschafts- und Sozialwissenschaften, 113–66.

Wagner, Gert G., Kirner, Ellen, Leinert, Johannes, and Meinhardt, Volker (1999) "Fully funded insurance – no panacea for social security for the elderly," *Economic Bulletin* 36: 37–44.

Wissenschaftlicher Beirat beim Bundesministerium für Wirtschaft (1998) *Grundlegende Reform der gesetzlichen Rentenversicherung*, Bonn: Bundesministerium für Wirtschaft.

10 Pension systems and labor force participation in the Nordic countries

Fredrik Haugen, Erik Hernæs, and Steinar Strøm

10.1 Introduction

This chapter gives an overview of the structure of the pension systems in Denmark, Finland, Norway and Sweden, and the most important of the recent changes in these systems. In all the Nordic countries, the public pension component plays an important role. These public pension systems are of pay-as-you-go type, and are in all countries set to encounter financial problems in the not so distant future. Some recent changes aimed at meeting this problem are described, but the chapter includes no discussion of the financial situation of the public pension systems. The emphasis in the chapter is on the institutional arrangements and the ensuing labor supply incentives for older persons. The chapter also includes a brief overview of labor force participation of older persons in the Nordic countries.

The situation in Norway has been treated most extensively. For Norway, we also recount the results of two recent analyses of the impact of an early retirement system, which was introduced in 1989.

10.2 Institutional aspects

10.2.1 Norway

10.2.1.1 History

In 1937, the first mandatory old age pension insurance was implemented in Norway. The system was universal in the sense that everyone was included. It was restricted to persons with relatively low income. The age of eligibility was set to 70 years. In 1957 the means testing was lifted and co-ordination with government pensions introduced. An earnings based component was added to the basic pension in 1967 and the age of eligibility was lowered to 67 years.

Pensions are financed through taxes levied on employers and employees as percentages of total earnings and on the self-employed as a percentages of their income. There exists a central pension fund, but it is not required that this should meet future net expected obligations. The system is based on yearly contributions from the government.

10.2.1.2 The current old age pension system

The system as it appears today is a three-tier system. The first tier is a mandatory public pension system that includes all Norwegian citizens. The second tier is occupation-based, creating a distinct difference in pension benefits received between those who have occupation-based pensions and those who do not. The last tier is private pensions. These latter pensions are individual insurances where people save for their own retirement.

10.2.1.3 The public old age pension system

The mandatory public pension system has two main components. One component is a minimum pension, paid to all persons who are permanently residing in the country. The pension is reduced proportionally with less than 40 years of residence.

The other main component is an earnings-based pension. A crucial parameter in the system, used for defining contributions as well as benefits, is the basic amount. The basic amount (G) in 1998 was NOK44,413 (as of June 2002, US$1 is approximately NOK7.6).

The earnings-based pension depends on the basic pension and the individual's earnings history in several ways. Each year, earnings exceeding the basic pension are divided by (G) to give pension "points" for that year. Earnings above 12 times G do not give points, and earnings between 6 and 12 times G (8 and 12 times before 1992) are reduced to one third before calculating pension points. The yearly calculated points are then multiplied by a supplementary pension rate of 0.45 (points obtained after 1992 are multiplied by a rate of 0.42) and the average yearly points over the 20 best years are calculated. These points multiplied by G give the earnings-based component, and adding 1G gives the total public pension. If a person has had less than 40 years with earnings above the basic pension, the earnings based pension is reduced proportionally.

The public pension system also has a number of additional regulations, which we will only briefly recount here. First, since we are still in the process of phasing in the public pension system established in 1967, a special "overcompensation" program is in operation for persons born before 1928. Second, there is a supplementary pension for those without or with a low earnings based pension component, giving a minimum pension level of 1.605 times the basic pension. Because of the supplementary pension, income below 2.344 times the minimum pension does not contribute to the total public pension. Third, there is co-ordination of the pensions for married couples, mainly resulting in a reduction of the couples' joint pension compared to the sum for two single persons.

Keeping 1994 regulations constant, the maximum future pension level will be 4.75 times (G), i.e. NOK180,080. This pension level requires 20 years with earnings of at least NOK456,960 (12G) and another 20 years with earnings of at least NOK38,080 (1G in 1994). Although there is a re-distributive effect of the tax system also for pre-retirement earnings, this effect is much stronger after retirement. For pre-retirement earnings up to around NOK100,000, after-tax pension is actually higher than after-tax earnings. Also, the after-tax public pension curve is fairly flat, implying a strong re-distributive effect. The replacement level implied by the public pension curve falls from 1.0 at an income level of 2.344G (below that level income does not influence the public pension). At earnings just allowing the maximum pension, the replacement level is between 0.3 and 0.4.

10.2.1.4 Government sector pensions

State and local government employees have co-ordinated occupation-based pensions, so that benefits will be the maximum of the public and the government pension. The government pension is based on the earnings level immediately prior to retirement and not on the previous earnings history. The pension is 66 percent of their gross income the year prior to retirement up to 8 times G (the same basic amount as in the public system) and, up to May 2000, 22 percent of income between 8 and 12G. As in the public system, income under 1G does not count. The maximum government sector pension up to May 2000 was thus 6.16 times G, giving a replacement ratio at that level of 0.51. With effect from May 2000 earnings between 8 and 12G count as earnings up to 8G, increasing maximum pension to 66 percent of 12G.

10.2.1.5 Private sector occupation based pensions

In the private sector 36 percent of the workforce is covered by occupation-based pensions, from which benefits are received "on top" of the public pension without any reduction (NOU 10 1998: 66–7). For employers to receive tax deductions for contributions, there are regulations, implying that the pension should include all employees and that the eligibility age is at least 65.

10.2.1.6 Earnings testing of pension benefits

Pensioners in the public pension system (previously employed in the private sector), who continue to work in a different job from the one they had when they retired, will have their pension reduced if earnings from work exceed a certain level. The same happens to pensioners in the government sector who start working in other jobs in the government or local government. However, if the government pensioners get a job in the private sector their income does not influence their pension. For pensioners aged 70 years or more there are no reductions in benefits regardless of what system one receives pension benefits from.

10.2.1.7 Private pensions

In addition, there are private pensions. These pensions are based on personal savings made during working life. The savings are tax deductible and widespread. In 1996 a total of 167,000 individuals received tax reductions due to private pension savings.

10.2.1.8 Early retirement

Finally, in 1989 employers and unions negotiated an early retirement scheme (AFP). Under this scheme, persons working for employers who are participating (in 2001 about 43 percent of private employees and all employees of central and local government) and meeting individual requirements can retire at an earlier age than the normal 67. The age at which persons become eligible for AFP has been gradually lowered since the first agreement in 1989. Table 10.1 gives a summary of this.

The pension under the AFP scheme is calculated in much the same way as the ordinary pensions except for some differences due to the age at which one chooses to retire and the sector one is working in. Individuals working in the private sector who choose to retire early get the public pension as described above and an additional tax-free AFP lump sum of NOK 11,400 a year.

In the government sector, both state and local, the rules are different. First of all the occupation-based pension is part of the AFP scheme from the age of 65. Second, the AFP lump sum is different. Retired people between 62 and 65 get a taxable AFP lump sum of NOK 20,400 a year, otherwise they follow private sector rules. From the age of 65, when they receive occupation-based pensions, they do not get the AFP lump sum. The pension level is as it would have been from age 67, had the person continued until that age in the job they held at the time of early

Table 10.1 Eligibility for AFP and age limit

Introduced	Age limit
January 1989	66 years
January 1990	65 years
October 1993	64 years
October 1997	63 years
March 1998	62 years

Table 10.2 AFP and replacement ratios in different sectors. 1997

Income	Replacement ratio in private sector	Replacement ratio in government sector (62–64 years)	Replacement ratio in government sector (65–66 years)
1G	2.21	2.40	1.89
2G	1.22	1.32	1.04
3G	0.96	0.98	0.94
4G	0.84	0.84	0.85
5G	0.76	0.76	0.80
6G	0.71	0.71	0.78
7G	0.67	0.68	0.79
8G	0.65	0.66	0.80
9G	0.61	0.62	0.76
10G	0.57	0.58	0.72
11G	0.55	0.56	0.68
12G	0.52	0.53	0.65

Source: Haugen (2000).

retirement. Individuals who have taken out AFP are not allowed to start working in another AFP-company later on.

Calculations reported in Table 10.2 show that the replacement ratio, defined as the net pension income divided by the net income when working, for retired persons from the government and private sector aged 62 to 64 is marginally different. This indicates that the net effect of the two different AFP lump sums is approximately the same. When the retirees are 65 or 66, however, there is a marked difference. Government sector employees are compensated to a significantly higher degree than their counterparts in the private sector. For mid- and high-income persons, the difference in replacement ratio is between five and fifteen percentage points when we compare the two groups. The difference for high-income individuals will increase with the change in pension calculation in May 2000, allowing all income up to 12G to give a pension at 66 percent, takes effect.

The tax rules are different between pension benefits and labor income. For a given income level, retired persons generally face lower taxes compared to working people. The difference in marginal tax is smaller the higher the income.

In 1992 there was a tax reform in Norway. This reform had significant effects on the degree to which persons were compensated when they retired. Table 10.3 reports the replacement ratio of persons receiving pension in the public pension system in 1991 and 1992.

Table 10.3 shows that the reduction in disposable income, if an individual decided to retire, was considerably larger in 1992 than in 1991. The main reason was the change in taxation rules in 1992. This tax reform lowered taxes on wage incomes and made it more profitable to work.

Table 10.3 Tax reform and replacement ratios in the public pension system

Income	Replacement ratio 1991	Replacement ratio 1992	Difference 1991–2
1G	1.93	1.86	−0.07
2G	1.06	1.03	−0.03
3G	0.88	0.86	−0.02
4G	0.77	0.74	−0.03
5G	0.73	0.68	−0.05
6G	0.74	0.65	−0.09
7G	0.77	0.65	−0.12
8G	0.78	0.64	−0.14
9G	0.75	0.60	−0.15
10G	0.73	0.57	−0.16
11G	0.70	0.54	−0.16
12G	0.68	0.52	−0.16

Source: Haugen (2000).

When trying to model the retirement decision, different economic incentive measures are used (see Lumsdaine and Mitchell 1999, for reference). Replacement ratios, or work income and income as retired, are often used in models attempting to find out why people retire. If the focus of study is on the timing of the retirement decision, Social Security Wealth and Social Security Wealth Accrual are alternative variables often used.

Social Security Wealth is defined as the discounted value of future pension benefits if one retires at a given age. Social Security Wealth Accrual is what an individual gains by postponing retirement by one period (months or years). Defining t as month, $t \in [63_1, 66_{12}]$, 66_{12} as month 12 when aged 66, 63_1 as month 1 when aged 63 and so forth and r as discount factor, we can write Social Security Wealth and Social Security Wealth Accrual more formally as:

$$SSW(t) = \int_t^{66_{12}} AFP(t) \cdot e^{-r(t-63_1)} \tag{1}$$

$$SSWA(t) = SSW(t+1) - SSW(t) \tag{2}$$

In Norway Social Security Wealth declines sharply if retirement is postponed. Calculations using information from Norwegian administrative registers of individual earnings and pension benefits rights give us Figure 10.1. The figure illustrates Social Security Wealth and Social Security Wealth Accrual for individuals who were eligible for early retirement in Norway in the period 1993–7 when the eligibility age was 64 years. The graphs are based on calculation of Social Security Wealth and Social Security Wealth Accrual for each month between 63 to 67 years by using formulae (1) and (2). Comparing voluntary retirement when an individual is 63 years and 11

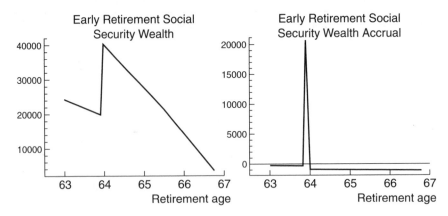

Figure 10.1 Early retirement Social Security Wealth and Social Security Wealth Accrual with eligibility at age 64

months with retirement when becoming eligible for pension benefits at the age of 64 will, as Figure 10.1 shows, lead to a large increase in the Social Security Wealth. After the month the individual becomes eligible the Social Security Wealth Accrual is negative until the individual reaches the standard retirement age of 67 years.

The decline in Social Security Wealth when postponing retirement after the month an individual becomes eligible would seem to make it difficult to rationalize a retirement decision between the early and standard retirement age. Studies of take-out dates in Norway do however show that a considerable part of those eligible for AFP that actually retire do not retire at the earliest possible occasion. In a study of married males that became eligible for early retirement during 1993 or 1994, Røgeberg (2000) shows that a fraction of 29.7 percent retired during the first year after becoming eligible. Of these more than two-thirds retired during the first two months. A further 9.5 percent retired between 1 and 2 years after becoming eligible, making the total fraction of retirees 39.2 percent two years after eligibility.

This may reflect changes in other factors than the economic. Changes in an individual's health conditions or changes in family situation (e.g. retirement of spouse) could lead to retirement. However, it may also indicate that the Social Security Wealth is not a measure used by all individuals in the retirement decision.

Another factor that may influence retirement timing is calendar time. If an individual's Social Security Wealth is not the decisive factor in the retirement timing decision, it is possible that individuals, if they have decided to retire, make the transition at a date that is "convenient." This could for instance be in connection with holidays or when a new calendar year starts. In Table 10.4 we have reported the actual takeout-months of

Table 10.4 Observed retirement months of new early retirement retirees in 1995

Month	Frequency	%
January	724	14.6
February	317	6.4
March	306	6.2
April	350	7.1
May	364	7.3
June	434	8.8
July	808	16.3
August	504	10.2
September	398	8.0
October	309	6.2
November	253	5.1
December	191	3.6
Total 1995	4951	100

all individuals who took early retirement in 1995. The data are collected from administrative registers of the early retirement scheme. It is evident from Table 10.4 that there are some seasonal variations in the retirement pattern.

That less than half of those eligible take early retirement in spite of the fall in SSW after eligibility is probably due to the fairly low replacement rate, particularly for persons with high earnings. For these persons, pension income will appear low, and it is still an advantage to be in work in spite of a high effective tax rate.

10.2.2 Sweden

In 1913, the first compulsory old-age system was implemented. It consisted of two parts; a means-tested basic pension, and a supplementary pension related to individual contributions. The Swedish system was the first pension system in the world to cover all citizens, regardless of occupation. In 1994 the Swedish Parliament decided that the Swedish pension system should be reformed. We will look at both the old system, and the new system, which came into effect in 1999.

Until 1999 pensions in Sweden consisted of two formally different pensions, the national basic pension ("folkpensionen") and a supplementary pension ("allmän tillägspension – ATP"). All Swedish citizens and all persons living in Sweden with at least three years' residence are entitled to a basic pension. There is a proportionate reduction in the basic pension received if the time of residence in Sweden is below 40 years. The basic pension is related to the basic amount (BA), an amount decided each year by the government. In 1995, the BA was SEK34,986, and the annual wage of an average production worker was SEK189,488. A single old-age pensioner received 96 percent of the BA in basic pension. Individuals with low, or no, ATP are entitled to a special supplement (Palme and Svensson 1999).

The ATP is earnings-related. It is constructed in a three-step procedure, which has much in common with the Norwegian system described above. The first step is to determine the pension-rights income for each year from the age of 16. Income above 7.5BA is not included in pension-right income. The second step is to calculate the average pension points. This is done by dividing the pension-rights income with the corresponding year's BA to obtain the pension points for each year. The average pension point is the average from the individual's best 15 pension point years. Finally, the ATP is calculated applying the following formula:

$$ATP = 0.6 \cdot AP \cdot \min\left(\frac{N}{30}, 1\right) \cdot BA, \tag{3}$$

where AP is individual average pension points and N is the number of years registered with pension points greater than zero. As the formula indicates, to be entitled to full ATP the number of years with pension points has to be at least 30. In 1995 the maximum pension in the Swedish pension system was SEK170,032 (Palme and Svensson 1999: 16).

In addition to the ordinary pension, around 90 percent of the work force in the private sector and all in public sector have centrally bargained occupation-based pensions. As in Norway there are different pension funds within the private and the public sector. The different funds have different rules regarding benefit level and at what time the pension is paid out.

The standard retirement age in Sweden is 65. Still there is a possibility of retiring as early as age 61. This age limit was 60 until 1998. If the individual chooses to retire prior to the age of 65, he or she will be penalized with having less pension-income. The monthly pension benefit is permanently reduced by 0.5 percent for each month of early withdrawal. For example, if the individual retires at 61 compared to retiring at the age of 65, the permanent reduction is 24 percent. On the other hand, if the individual decides to postpone retirement, the pension income is increased with 0.7 percent for each month of postponement. It is possible to delay retirement until 70, which means that an individual retiring at 70 gets a 42 percent higher pension compared to what he or she would have got had he or she retired at 65 (Palme and Svensson 1997).

Swedish data show that early retirement is quite uncommon. At 31 December 1997 there were approximately 20,700 individuals aged 60–64 who drew early retirement pension. Most of them were aged 64. The main reason is believed to be the permanent reduction in pension benefits (NOU 1998: 19).

As noted above, in 1994 the Swedish parliament decided to reform the pension system and in 1999 the new system came into effect. The main changes are: earnings from the entire lifecycle are counted when the individual's pension is determined, rather than only the best 15 years. The pension is related to the real growth in the economy – rather than price indices. Life expectancy influences the individual pension, that is, increased life expectancy and lower economic growth rates decrease individual pension income at a given retirement age.

There are special phasing-in rules for individuals of different cohorts regarding how they are influenced by the new system. Individuals born in 1934 or earlier receive benefits from the old system described above. Those born in the period 1935–53 receive a combined pension from both systems, and those born after 1953 receive benefits entirely from the new system.

The new national pension is based on the individual's total lifetime income. Income every year from the age of 16 is contributing to the final pension. Hence, both earnings each year and the number of working years are important factors when calculating the final pension. However, only earnings up to an annual income ceiling of 7.5 times the basic amount (BA) are pension carrying. Any non-work income on which one has paid tax, for example sick pay, parental benefits, and unemployment benefits, is also pension entitling.

Each month, an amount equivalent to 18.5 percent of the pension-carrying income is drawn in the form of a pension fee. Of this, 16 percent contributes to the financing of today's pensioners. In return for this money, the individual will be allocated a pension entitlement stating that the system owes it money. This money is repaid in form of a pay-as-you-earn pension (PAYE-pension) when the individual retires. The remaining 2.5 percent is deposited in an individual premium reserve pension (PR-pension) account. The individual can choose in what funds this money should be invested. The size of the PR-pension depends on how well the chosen funds develop.

An individual can retire whenever he or she wants after the age of 61. However, the accumulated pension will be calculated dependent on the expected remaining living years. Hence, delaying retirement could raise the pension considerably. There is also an option of part-time retirement. It is possible to choose a pension take-out rate of 75, 50 or 25 percent from age 61.

In addition there is a guaranteed pension that provides a basic cover for individuals with no or low income. This pension is not paid out before the individuals are 65 years old. Most people will receive pension benefits in addition to those received through the new national pension system. People may have an occupation-based pension through work or private pension savings. These pensions do not reduce the national pension.[2]

10.2.3 Denmark

As the first of the Nordic countries, Denmark introduced a pension system in 1891. Today the Danish system is one of Europe's strictest systems when it comes to early retirement (Pedersen and Smith 1996). A national old age pension is available today to all citizens from the age of 67, irrespective of their former labor market status. The system is made up of a general earnings-dependent pension, an extra pension that is income independent, occupation-based pensions and individual pensions. So far, these pension schemes, except for the individual pensions, have not been used in the design of the early retirement scheme. If one chooses to stay in work after the standard retirement age, the pension rises at a rate of 5 percent every half year until age 70. It follows that persons retiring at 70 get a 30 percent higher pension compared to retirement at age 67 (Rapport fra en arbeidsgruppe 1997: 83).

The general pension has as its purpose to secure a minimum income. It is independent of the previous income record, and paid to all persons permanently residing in the country. There is a minimum requirement of three years of residence. 40 years yields full general pension, and fewer years reduce the pension proportionally (NOU 1998: 19).

Second, there is a mandatory extra pension (ATP) introduced in 1964. The ATP is administered entirely by the parties of the labor market, with the government being left out. All working individuals, employers, persons on labor market training, persons receiving unemployment benefits, etc., is part of the system, which is independent of income history. The amount of ATP-benefits received depends on the number of years the membership fee has been paid, which is the same regardless of income. When people retire, they all receive the same benefits, which is the same annual payout given that they have been members for the same number of years.

In addition there are occupation-based pensions. These are the result of wage agreements or are agreements that are company specific. Individuals working in a company with such an agreement are automatically covered by it.

Finally there are personal pensions were people save for their retirement. Individual pensions are collectable from the age of 60.

10.2.4 Finland

In 1937, Finland commenced an old-age pension system. There are two separate systems in Finland, a residence-based national pension system ("Folkepensjonssystemet") and an earnings-related pension system. Voluntary pensions, whether employer-based or industry-wide supplementary pensions or personal pension arrangements, are of minor importance in Finland. The national pension is meant to secure everyone a minimum income, and was earlier divided in two separate parts, a basic pension and an extra pension. In 1997 the two parts were merged into one national pension, which is calculated according to number of years of residence. Benefits are indexed to consumer prices. A minimum of three years of residence is required to gain rights to this pension, and 40 years gives the maximum national pension. Fewer years reduce the pension proportionally. The eligibility age is 65 years.

National pension benefits depend upon how much earnings-related pension one is receiving. If the earnings-related pension exceeds a certain amount, no national pension is paid out (NOU 1998: 19). The national pension is a compound of different benefits. Old age-, early-retirement-, disability- and individual early-retirement pension are all elements of the national pension (Rapport fra en arbeidsgruppe 1997: 80).

The earnings-related pension system is different in the private and the public sector. The law governing these pensions came into effect in the private sector in 1962. Private sector employees had previously been covered by the national pension system and by voluntary firm specific pension schemes. Now benefits in the earnings-related pension system depend upon earnings and work history. The level of old-age pension in the private sector is determined by multiplying 1.5 percent of a person's wage by the number of years of service. To reduce the incentive of early retirement, income earned after age 60 earns 2.5 percent. The maximum pension represents 60 percent of the average pay, and to obtain full old-age pension 40 years of service is required (Lilja 1996). Until 1996 the average pay was calculated from the income the last four years of each employment contract. Each job one has had counts, and they are all part of the final calculation of pension benefits. However, a reform in 1996 changed this to the last 10 years. The new calculation method will be gradually introduced up to 2006. The scope of the reform was to encourage people to stay longer in work and at the same time lower the expenses.

Contributions to the system are collected from both employers (current average 16.8 percent of wages) and employees (4.7 percent). Future changes in the system will be shared equally between the two parties.

The private-sector earnings-related system is partially funded. Funding is collective but based on individual pension rights. Currently the main pre-funding rules are as follows: a part of the old-age pension benefits, payable after age 65, is funded for each employee. Funding takes place between ages 23–54, so only benefits accrued during those years are (partially) funded. Funds only affect contributions. When an individual receives a pension, its funds are used to pay the part of the pension benefit that was pre-funded. The rest comes from the pay-as-you-go part, the so-called pooled component in the contribution rate. Funding in the public sector is of much less importance. The state has very small funds (Lassila and Valkonen 2000).

In the public sector the pension is calculated by multiplying 2.0–2.2 percent of the salary by the number of years of service. Full pension is earned after 30 years of service, and it represents 60 percent of the average pay. Pension rights for both private and public earnings-related pensions are not affected by labor force participation after becoming eligible for, and receiving, the old-age pension. Persons working after 65 years of age receive 1 percent higher pension for each month they stay in their job. The rule applies to both pension systems.

In addition, there is the possibility of early retirement. Early old-age pension, introduced in 1986 in the private sector, can be drawn from age 60. The pension is permanently reduced by 1/2 percent for each month short of age 65. The reduction is permanent in the sense that when the pensioner attains ordinary retirement age, the pension remains at the reduced rate. People that retire when 60 years of age will lose 30 percent of their pension compared to retirement at age 65. Public-sector early retirement pension was introduced in 1989 for employees between the ages of 58 and 62. In neither sector were there any limitations for a person receiving early retirement to enter the labor market again.

10.2.5 Summary and comparison

A comparison of the pension systems in the Nordic countries shows that there are important differences between the countries, both with regards to the size of benefits received, the age of eligibility, and the flexibility of the different schemes. Generally speaking the public systems are of two different types, the universal systems that covers all individuals, and systems restricted to the working population. A summary of the different characteristics of the universal systems in the Nordic countries is given in Table 10.5. In Table 10.6 and in Table 10.7 the systems restricted to working individuals are summed up.

The degree to which individuals are compensated when they retire is an important factor in the retirement decision, both because it influences whether the individuals are able to maintain their living standard and because the cost of continuing working is high. Replacement ratios calculated by OECD (1998), reveal that there are significant differences in compensation among the Nordic countries. The OECD-replacement ratios are calculated somewhat differently from replacement ratios in Haugen (2000) in that they are based on gross earnings and pension benefits,[3] whereas replacement ratios in Haugen (2000) are based on net earnings. Figure 10.2 illustrates the differences in replacement ratios amongst the Nordic countries. It is evident that the Swedish system is the most generous. Consequently, the economic incentives to retire are stronger in Sweden than in the other Nordic countries.

Another aspect accounted for in Figure 10.2 is that the replacement ratios in all Nordic countries, except Finland, are higher for those with low earnings than those on high earnings. This is a result of several factors. The existence of flat pension components (universal pensions) and income

Table 10.5 Mandatory basic pension

Country	Coverage	Retirement age	Basic pension	Financing
Norway	All citizens	67 years	Yes, 40 years of residence for full pension	Pay-as-you-go. Integral part of the National budget. Tax on employers' and employees' and contributions from the government
Sweden	All citizens	65 years	Yes, 30 years of residence for full pension	Pay-as-you-go. Integral part of the National budget. Tax on employers' and employees' and contributions from the government
Denmark	All citizens	67 years	Yes, 40 years of residence for full pension	Pay-as-you-go. Integral part of the National budget. Tax-financed
Finland	All citizens	65 years	Yes, but is reduced with high mandatory extra pension	Pay-as-you-go. Integral part of the National budget. Tax on employers' and employees' and contributions from the government

Source: NOU 1998: 10.

Table 10.6 Other non-mandatory extra pensions

Country	Coverage	Compensation	Payments	Financing
Norway	1 Occupation-based pensions, either statutory, based on wage agreements or company-internal arrangements 2 Private pensions, tax-favored	1 Most commonly based on payments (tax-favored) 2 Deposit based	1 Employers. Government contributes with favorable tax rules 2 Personal payments. Government contributes with favorable tax rules	1 Fund or life insurance company 2 Pension insurance, individual fund accounts with investment choice
Sweden	1 Occupation-based pensions based on wage agreements 2 Private pensions	1 Based on payments 2 Deposit based	Personal payments	1 Funded, pay-as-you-go in local government sector 2 Pension insurance
Denmark	1 Supplementary occupation-based pension based on wage agreements or company-internal arrangements 2 Private pensions	1 Deposit based 2 Deposit based	1 Tax related to income from employers and employees 2 Personal payments	1 Insurance based or pension funds 2 Pension insurance
Finland	Very few due to mandatory extra pension with no income ceiling			

Source: NOU 1998: 10.

Table 10.7 Mandatory extra pensions

Country	Coverage	Offered by	Compensation	Payments	Financing
Norway	All working, unemployed and insured	The government	Based on payments, 40 years for full pension, calculated from 20 best years, income ceiling	Tax on employers and employees, government contribution	Pay-as-you-go. Integral part of the National budget
Sweden	All working, students, military service and unemployed	1 The government through a supplementary pension until 1999 2 The government through a distribution system and premium reserve pension system from 1999	1 Based on payments, 30 years for full pension calculated from 15 best years, income ceiling 2 Distribution system with contribution-based elements and premium reserve pension system with individual fund accounts	1 Tax on employers (since 1995) and employees, government contribution 2 16% to distribution system and 2.5% to own accounts with optional fund manager	1 Pay-as-you-go, with buffer fund. 2 Pay-as-you-go distribution system and individually funded premium reserve pension
Denmark	Statutory, mandatory extra pension to all workers, unemployed and employers	Independent institution owned by the parties of the labor market	Dependent upon hours of work and number of membership years	Negotiated amount, employer/government pay 2/3 and employees pay 1/3	Funded in collective fund.
Finland	Statutory, mandatory extra pension to all workers, self-employed, sailors and farmers (cover 95% of workforce)	Independent work pension system monitored by the government. Administered by the parties of the labor market	Based on payments, no income ceiling. 40 years for full pension. Maximum compensation is 60% of average income	Negotiated tax from employers (18–21.1%) and from employees form 1992 (4.3% in 1997)	Partially funded, collective funds

Source: NOU 1998: 10.

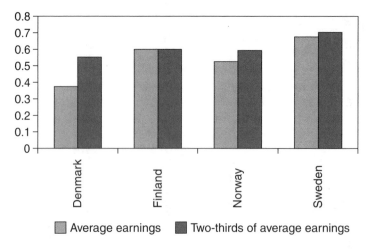

Figure 10.2 Replacement rate by earnings level for a single worker 1995
Source: OECD 1998.

ceilings in calculation of pension rights are the main reasons. Tax systems benefiting those with low incomes contribute further to this fact. This feature of the pension systems indicates that they have a redistributive effect between high- and low-earners.

There has been a clear tendency for the expected pension replacement rates to change over time. According to Table 10.8 the replacement ratio actually fell in Norway and Sweden between 1975 and 1995, whereas in Denmark it rose by about 14 percentage points in the same period. However, if we expand the comparison period to 1960 it is evident that all the systems have become much more generous over time. A rise in replacement ratio of more than 20 percentage points in all the Nordic countries lowers the economic risk of retiring considerably, and thus the retirement incentive becomes stronger.

Table 10.8 Expected old-age pension gross replacement rates

	1961	1975	1995
Denmark	35.9	42.3	56.2
Finland	34.9	58.6	60.0
Norway	25.3	61.2	60.0
Sweden	53.8	77.1	74.4

Source: OECD (1998).

10.3 Exit routes for elderly persons

The exit routes from full-time jobs for older workers are:

– part-time work, eventually combined with transfers from the government,
– out of labor force, eventually combined with transfers from the government,
– disability pension,
– retirement, either through early company-specific retirement programs or through mandatory pension programs.

Economic as well as non-economic aspects are influencing the retirement decision. The most important economic variable is the replacement ratio. It is also important for the decision of when to retire if and how early retirement is penalized. Because most people are married or cohabiting one should pay attention to how the decision to retire early among married men may be affected by the working status of the wife. Wives tend to be some years younger than their husbands. If the couple likes to enjoy common leisure, we would expect them to reduce their working commitments at the same time. If more emphasis is put on consumption levelling one may on the contrary expect the wife to increase her working effort when her somewhat older husband retires.

Business cycles may also affect the decision to retire. In recessions the firms may put pressure on older workers to retire early, either because the firm need to do some downsizing or because they like to replace older workers with younger, and most likely, more productive workers.

In addition to the economic variables there is certainly a battery of non-economic variables such as health that are important when explaining retirement decisions.

10.3.1 Norway

In Table 10.9 we report the labor force participation rate for males and females aged 40–54 and 55–66. We observe that the participation rate of males at their core working age, 40–54, has been quite stable since 1972. Males aged 55–66, however have drastically reduced their participation rate from 81 percent in 1972 to percentages ranging in the 60s in the 1990s. The decline started in the early 1980s and may be due to the fact that Norway entered a recession in the early 1980s. After a short-lived booming economy, the Norwegian economy entered a new and even harder and long-lasting recession in the late 1980s. As mentioned above, in 1989 an early retirement scheme was introduced. Thus business cycles, the introduction of an early retirement program and a trend in the economy towards more production of services relative to the manufacturing of

Table 10.9 Persons in the labor force by sex and age, as percentage of all in each group, Norway

| Years | Males | | Females | |
	40–54	55–66	40–54	55–66
1972	93.4	81.0	54.5	40.1
1973	93.8	81.1	56.9	39.5
1974	93.7	80.5	56.4	39.1
1975	94.6	79.6	59.5	41.9
1976	95.3	81.1	64.2	43.8
1977	95.2	81.6	64.9	45.5
1978	95.7	80.9	68.3	46.6
1979	95.6	80.1	70.0	47.3
1980	93.9	79.1	72.0	46.9
1981	94.4	78.2	74.6	48.4
1982	95.2	77.8	75.2	48.4
1983	94.2	75.5	75.2	48.5
1984	94.0	74.7	77.4	48.4
1985	94.0	74.0	77.0	49.3
1986	94.0	72.5	79.5	49.7
1987	93.6	71.9	81.1	50.3
1988	92.9	71.0	81.6	49.9
1989	93.1	69.6	80.0	48.7
1990	92.4	67.4	80.3	49.1
1991	91.9	66.5	80.3	49.9
1992	91.3	66.2	79.4	49.7
1993	90.5	65.7	79.9	49.4
1994	91.3	65.2	80.4	50.3
1995	91.9	66.0	81.0	51.9
1996	91.5	67.0	82.5	53.8
1997	91.7	68.3	83.9	54.6
1998	91.9	69.0	83.8	55.5
1999	91.4	68.8	84.3	55.9
2000	91.0	69.2	84.2	56.7

Source: NOS Labour Market Statistics.

goods may explain the decline of participation among older male workers in Norway.

For females we observe that the participation rate has increased drastically for women aged 40–54. Fewer children, higher education, and a trend in the economy towards more production of services may be important reasons for this increase in labor market participation. However, it is interesting to note that there has been a marked upward trend also in labor market participation among older women, apart from the recession years in the late 1980s. After the 1980s, cohort effects (note the development for younger females) may have counteracted a fall in labor force participation for older women like that as observed for males. The most obvious explanation behind this trend for females is the change in the industrial structure in the economy, away from production of manufacturing goods towards higher production of services. Norway became an oil and gas producer and exporter in the 1970s, which, for several reasons, had a negative impact on traditional manufacturing industries and a positive impact on the demand for services. It should also be noted that because of the working history of females in the cohorts now approaching the early retirement age there are fewer that qualify for full pensions than their male counterparts. With the cohort effects, which can be read from the table, this is set to change substantially over the years to come with increasing labor market experience and accumulation of pension rights among older women.

To examine further the impact of the early retirement program (AFP) on the Norwegian labor market, we have analyzed:

1   What would have happened to the labor market participation if the AFP scheme had not been introduced?
2   If the AFP scheme is a substitute for disability pension or if it is a new and independent exit route out of the labor force.

The analyses are done within the econometric framework of competing risk models.

10.3.1.1 *Effects of early retirement on labor market participation*

As noted above an early retirement program was introduced in 1989. Here we will report some results of an econometric investigation of the impact of this program on labour market participation among older workers. Individuals have been followed on a quarterly basis from 1988-II until 1999-IV. This period covers a period of recession with increasing and high unemployment by Norwegian standards. In the early 1990s the recession ended and the Norwegian economy has since then experienced a steady increase in employment.

The data set is a rotating sample, increasing in size from 12,000 to 20,000 over the observation period. Thus, the total sample contains 481,371 observations.

Each individual is allowed to move between three states: employment, unemployment, and out of the labor force.

Let $[Y_j(t+1)\,|\,Y_i(t)]$ denote the event that an individual transit from state i in period t to state j in period $t+1$, $i, j = 1, 2, 3$.

1   State 1 is employment.
2   State 2 is unemployment.
3   State 3 is out of labor force.

The probability of transiting from state i in period t to state j in period $t+1$, is given by

$$\Pr[Y_j(t+1)\,|\,Y_i(t)] = \frac{\exp(\alpha_{ij}^* + x(t)\beta_{ij}^*)}{\displaystyle\sum_{k=1}^{3} \exp(\alpha_{ik}^* + x(t)\beta_{ik}^*)}$$

$$= \frac{\exp(\alpha_{ij}^* - \alpha_{i3}^*) + x(t)(\beta_{ij}^* - \beta_{i3}^*))}{1 + \displaystyle\sum_{k=1}^{2} \exp(\alpha_{ik}^* - \alpha_{i3}^*) + x(t)(\beta_{ik}^* - \beta_{i3}^*))} \qquad (4)$$

By letting $\alpha_{ij}^* = \alpha_{ij}^* - \alpha_{i3}^*$; $\beta_{ij}^* = \beta_{ij}^* - \beta_{i3}^*$, we get

$$\Pr[Y_j(t+1)\,|\,Y_i(t)] \equiv \varphi_{ij}(t+1)$$

$$= \frac{\exp(\alpha_{ij} + x(t+1)\beta_{ij})}{1 + \displaystyle\sum_{k=1}^{2} \exp(\alpha_{ik} + x(t+1)\beta_{ik})}\,; \text{ for } i, j = 1, 2, 3 \qquad (5)$$

We note that

1   All coefficients are normalized against the destination state $j = 3$, which is out of the labor force.
2   Coefficients vary across originating as well destination states.
3   $x(t)$ is a vector of observed, explanatory variables such as individual characteristics like age and education, and aggregate variables like local unemployment rates, vacancy rates, etc.

From the definitions of the α-s and the β-s, we have

$$\varphi_{i3}(t+1) = \frac{1}{1 + \displaystyle\sum_{k=1}^{2} \exp(\alpha_{ik} + x(t+1)\beta_{ik})} \qquad (6)$$

The model is estimated on the Norwegian data briefly described above. The estimated model is used in out-of-sample predictions and the estimated model tracks very well observed paths. More details concerning data, model, and estimation results can be found in Brinch, Hernæs, and Strøm (2001).

Among the covariates are dummies that are set equal to 1 if the individual is eligible for the early retirement program (AFP) introduced in Norway in 1989, and with a gradual decrease in the eligibility age during the observation period (Table 10.1). By setting all dummies equal to zero from 1999 and onwards we may simulate the impact of abolishing the early retirement program, AFP, on future labor market participation. By abolishing AFP, the retirement age is kept equal to the ordinary retirement age of 67. It should be noted that not all individuals retire when they become eligible for early retirement. Typically, the higher the education level is, the later the individual retires.

Here we report the impact on the labor market in 2005-IV of abolishing AFP in 1999-IV. Focusing on older people, aged 55–67, we find that the abolishment of AFP increases the participation rates among males from 72 percent (in the baseline projection) to 83 percent. Among females in the same age cohorts the increase is from 62 percent to 67 percent. These results imply that abolition in 1999 of the early retirement program may increase the total labor force in 2005 by as much as 2–3 percentage points.

10.3.1.2 A new exit route?

When the AFP scheme was introduced in 1989, the aim of the reform was that the new scheme would give tired workers a more "dignified" exit route out of the labor force. Up until the introduction of AFP both long-term unemployment and disability rates were growing, and AFP was one of the means introduced to reduce this trend. Hence, the scheme was intended to be a less socially stigmatizing substitute to the other exit routes available for the age groups covered by the reform.

Using data from a number of administrative registers, we have estimated a competing risk hazard rate model to study the substitution effects of the AFP program (Haugen and Røed 2001). Our data allows us to trace individuals' main labor market activity month-by-month through our period of study. We observe exits from the labor market due either to early retirement or to disability pension or long-term sickness. From the Norwegian population we have sampled all individuals eligible for AFP in the period 1993 to 1997. This particular period is chosen because the eligibility age was constant at 64 years throughout the period. Our sample used for estimations consists of 38,500 individuals.

One of the registers we have access to is the Social Security income database, and this gives us the opportunity to calculate both individuals' expected incomes from continuing to work and their expected benefits if they retire early or if they get disability benefits. In addition to economic benefits information we have information about the firm the individuals worked in, the individuals' sickness history (to capture state of health) and a wide range of other control variables including educational attainment, private wealth, spouse characteristics and region of residence.

10.3.1.3 Results

To be entitled to retire through the disability retirement scheme you need a statement from a doctor saying that you are no longer able to work. This feature of the disability scheme makes it non-voluntary. You need to have a reduced working ability to be able to retire, and not all workers in the age group in question have this. Voluntary early retirement on the other hand is available to all workers that meet the individual requirements and work in an AFP-affiliated firm. Furthermore, since the economic benefits received in the two different schemes are by all practical means the same, one could expect that most individuals eligible for it would prefer the AFP-scheme. As noted above, when introducing the scheme it was argued that it would give individuals a more dignified route out of the labor force. This argument indicates that disability retirement is thought of as a socially less accepted exit route.

However, this need not be the view held by the majority of Norwegian population. In the last decades disability retirement has become increasingly more common, and it might be argued this has made it less socially stigmatizing than the government think it is. In addition, it is possible that some individuals think of disability retirement as a "better" retirement path because you need have a medical condition to be eligible. AFP retirement could signal that you retire because you are tired of working or think you have a boring job, which for some individuals could be less acceptable than a health reason.

As we have in our data a control group of individuals that meets the individual requirements for eligibility for early retirement, but does not work in an AFP-affiliated firm, we are able to study the differences in behavior between two groups where one has the option of voluntary early retirement and the other has not. By controlling for a lot of different individual characteristics, we try to isolate the effect of the AFP-reform. That is, we try to control for factors that are due to differences between individuals rather than the effects of working in different firms. If we manage to do this we can more convincingly interpret our results as causal effects of the AFP-reform. It will of course never be possible to do this perfectly due to the heterogeneity of the labor force, but we believe the richness of our control variables is at least helping to control some of the heterogeneity.

We should thus be able to study whether the disability retirement probability pattern is different between the AFP-eligible group and the non-eligible control group. Our estimated results show that the probability of an exit from voluntary retirement is around 8 percent when the AFP-eligible get the opportunity to retire. After the first period of eligibility the transition probability to AFP stays between 2 and 5 percent. As Figure 10.3 illustrates, the probability for a transfer to disability pension declines somewhat for the group of AFP-eligible when they become eligible for AFP compared to the group of non-eligible. Although the results presented in Figure 3 indicates a substitution effect from the introduction of the AFP-scheme, the effect is modest and not comparable with what was expected when the scheme was introduced.

In sum this means that the substitution effects between disability pension and voluntary early retirement are small. The introduction of an early retirement scheme has provided a new and independent possibility

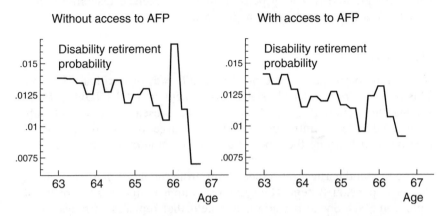

Figure 10.3 Estimated transition rates for a mean worker with and without affiliation to an AFP-firm

of exit for workers that would otherwise have worked until the normal retirement age. Our estimates suggest that the new scheme has led to a reduction in the labor participation rate among older workers that could be as large as 50 percent.

10.3.2 Sweden

In addition to the previously described national old-age pension scheme, there are two other pathways to early retirement in Sweden: the partial retirement pension and the disability pension. A partial retirement pension allows workers aged 60 and older to reduce their hours of work and receive a benefit to compensate for lost earnings. To qualify, the worker has to fulfill some requirements, the most important being that he or she has to have at least 10 years of pension-rights earnings after age 45. The benefit is 65 percent of the lost earnings due to reduced work.

The most common way of leaving the labor market before the normal retirement age is through disability pension. According to Palme and Svensson (1997), in 1994, 37 percent in the male age group aged 64 and 35 percent in the corresponding group of females received full-time disability pension. The pension consists of the same two parts as the old-age pension, the basic pension and the income related ATP, and is calculated in the same way. However, the reduction in pension due to early take out does not apply. Disability pension can be drawn at 16. A medical assessment from a physician is required to qualify.

Between 1970 and 1991, it was possible to receive disability pension for labor market reasons. The requirement for receiving such disability benefits was that the insured individual was more than 60 years old and did not qualify for unemployment insurance.[4] Almost half of the people aged 60–4 who were granted disability pension in 1985, received disability pension for labor market reasons (Wadensjö 1996).

10.3.3 Denmark

In 1976, the participation rate of men aged 65 was higher than 75 percent. This rate was reduced to less than 30 percent in 1998 (NOU 1998: 19). During the period from 1976 up until the present day, several public arrangements were introduced that gave large population groups the possibility of learning the labor market before the official retirement age of 67.

The first and earliest retirement route from the labor market is through the social pension system. The system as it appears today is the result of a reform in 1984. Social pension is a benefit that replaces earnings when a person cannot maintain a "normal" association with the earnings market. There are five tiers to the system: the highest, the intermediate, the augmented ordinary, and the ordinary early retirement pensions, and the disability grants.

The highest class is available to people under 60 whose capacity for work has been reduced almost to nil. Intermediate early retirement pension is available to those aged 60 whose capacity for work has been reduced to less than one-third of the normal level, and those between 60 and 66 whose capacity is almost zero. Eligibility for these two classes is decided on health grounds. To be eligible for ordinary early retirement pension an individual has to have his or her work capacity reduced to half the normal level, both based on health criteria and social criteria, or he or she has to be aged between 50 and 60 and meet social or health criteria, provided that rehabilitation to full capacity is deemed impossible. Lastly, individuals are entitled to a disability grant if they have a normal income from work but are eligible on health grounds to early retirement pension at the highest or intermediate level (Pedersen and Smith 1996). In 1997, there were about 270,000 pensioners on social pension. Of these, 34 percent were in the age group 60 to 66.

In 1979, a scheme for related-market-related early retirement known as the "post-employment wage" ("Efterlønsordningen – PEW") was introduced. No health criteria have to be met to enter the scheme, but there was an age limit of 60 years. Eligibility depends on a minimum of 20 years' (out of the last 25) membership of a recognized unemployment insurance fund. Today around 75 percent of the workforce are members of such a fund (NOU 1998:19). Compensation under the PEW is restricted upwards to 90 percent of the unemployment benefits and it is reduced to 82 percent after 30 months. In 1997 there were 30,300 persons who were granted PEW. Of these, 59 percent of the new beneficiaries were 60 years old and 11 percent were 61 years. 70 percent of those eligible had used the opportunity when they reached the normal retirement age of 67.

In 1995, the PEW was reformed to also include the opportunity for a part-time PEW. The reduction in work has to be at least one quarter of the number of hours worked prior to PEW take out. The scheme has not become especially popular, and in June 1998, 1500 persons received these benefits.

10.3.4 Finland

As in the other Nordic countries, disability pension is the most common early exit route from the workforce. Earnings-related ordinary disability pension has been available since 1962 in the private sector. A full disability pension is paid if the reduction in work capacity is considered to be at least three-fifths, and a partial disability pension is paid if the reduction is considered to be between two-fifths and three-fifths. In principle the pension is calculated in the same way as the normal old-age pension.

Early disability pension was introduced in the private sector in 1986 and in the public sector in 1989. This pension is granted to those aged 55–64 with a long working career behind them, provided that their work capacity has been permanently reduced to such an extent that they cannot be expected to continue at the same place of work and in their present job. The reason for not being able to continue in their present job does not have to be medical. The same rules as in the case of ordinary disability pension are applied when calculating the size of the pension.

In addition there is the possibility of part-time pension. This pension is payable to workers between the ages of 58 and 64 with a long working history, who are not receiving any other pensions and are reducing their number of work hours. The benefits received cover 50 percent of the lost earnings.

10.3.5 Comparison

In Table 10.10 we report the participation rate for older male workers. We observe that the reduction in participation rate is particularly strong in Finland. This may be due to the fact that Finland entered a much deeper recession than the two other countries in the late 1980s and beginning of the 1990s.

Table 10.10 Participation rate for older male workers

	1971	1995	1995–71
Finland	73.2	46.0	−27.2
Norway	83.3	72.3	−11.1
Sweden	84.6	54.9	−14.3

Source: OECD (1998).

Table 10.11 Estimates of the average age of transition to inactivity among older
workers, males 1970–95

	Males				
	1970	*1980*	*1990*	*1995*	*Decrease 1995–70*
Denmark	66.3	64.5	63.3	62.7	−3.6
Finland	62.7	60.1	59.6	59.0	−3.7
Norway	66.5	66.0	64.6	63.8	−2.7
Sweden	65.3	64.6	63.9	63.3	−2.0

Source: OECD (1998).

Table 10.12 Estimates of the average age of transition to inactivity among older
workers, females 1970–95

	Females				
	1970	*1980*	*1990*	*1995*	*Decrease 1995–70*
Denmark	62.0	61.0	59.9	59.4	−2.6
Finland	60.6	59.6	59.4	58.9	−1.7
Norway	66.2	61.5	63.0	62.0	−4.2
Sweden	62.5	62.0	62.4	62.1	−0.4

Source: OECD (1998).

In Tables 10.11 and 10.12 we report the average age of transition from work to inactivity for males and females, respectively. Denmark and Finland predominate with the most marked reduction from 1970 to 1995 for males, while Norway has had the most marked reduction for females. However, it should be noted that the age of female inactivity has always been the highest in Norway compared with the other Nordic countries.

10.4 Conclusion

In all the Nordic countries the pension systems are dominated by a public pension component. These public pension systems are re-distributive in that the replacement level falls with income. Up to 1975, the replacement rate increased, but since then it has increased only in Denmark, and has remained fairly constant in the other Nordic countries.

In all the Nordic countries, there are numerically important exit routes before the official retirement age at 65 or 67. Male related force participation has declined. At the time of writing male labor force participation in the age group 55–64 is above the OECD average in Norway and Sweden, and below the OECD average in Denmark and Finland (OECD, 2000). Analyses for Norway indicate that an early retirement program that was introduced in 1989 has opened up a new exit route in that country. A simulation indicates that overall labor force participation might have been decreased by 2–3 percentage points. This clearly illustrates the impact on financial incentives in influencing labor force participation of elderly persons.

Notes

1 This is part of the project *Ageing Economic Society* funded by the *Economic and Social Research Institute, Government of Japan*, and we gratefully acknowledge generous support.
2 Source: Brochure from the Swedish pension authorities. http://www.pension.nu/pdf_nya/spraken/engelska.pdf
3 A more detailed description of the assumptions underlying the calculated replacement ratios is given in Box III.1, OECD (1998: 17).
4 Workers were generally entitled to unemployment insurance for 1 year and 9 months.

References

Brinch, C., Hernæs E., and Strøm, S. (2001) "Labour supply effects of an early retirement program," *CESifo Working Paper* 463.

Haugen, F. "Insentivvirkninger av skatte-og pensjonsregler," (2000) *Arbeidsnotat 2/2000*, Frischsenteret, Oslo.

Haugen, F. and Røed, K. (2001) "Early retirement and economic incentives – evidence from a quasi-natural experiment in Norway," Memoranda, University of Oslo.

Lassila, J. and Valkonen, T. (2000) "Prefunding in a defined benefit pension system – the Finnish Case," *Discussion Paper* 741, The Research Institute of the Finnish Economy.

Lilja, R. (1996) "Microeconomic analysis of early retirement in Finland," in E. Wadensjö (ed.), *Leaving the Labour Market Early in the Welfare State – Development over Time*, in part 2 of E. Wadensjö (ed.), *The Nordic Labour Markets in the 1990s*, North-Holland: Elsevier, 157–73.

Lumsdaine, Robin L. and Mitchell, Olivia S. (1999) "New developments in the economic analysis of retirement," in O. Ashenfelter and D. Card (eds) *Handbook of Labor Economics*, Vol. 3, Elsevier Science B. V.

NOS (1991–2000) "Labour Market Statistics," Norway: Statistics.

NOU (1998) "Fleksibel pensjonering," *NOU 1998: 19*.

NOU (1998) "Fondering av Folketrygden?," *NOU 1998: 10*.

OECD (1998) "The retirement decision in OECD countries," *Economics Department Working Paper*, 202, Paris: OECD.

OECD (2000) "OECD Employment Outlook," Paris: OECD.

Palme, M. and Svensson, I. (1999) "Social security programs and retirement in Sweden," in J. Gruber and D. Wise "Social security programs and retirement around the world," NBER Conference Report, Chicago University Press.

Pedersen P. J. and Smith, N. (1996) "Duration analysis of the decision to retire early," in E. Wadensjö (ed.), *Leaving the Labour Market Early in the Welfare State – Development over Time*, in part 2 of E. Wadensjö (ed.), *The Nordic Labour Markets in the 1990s*, North Holland: Elsevier, 131–55.

Rapport fra en arbeidsgruppe (1997) "Analyse av fleksible pensjonsordninger og endringer i besteårsregelen," Norway: Ministry of Health and Social Affairs.

Røgeberg, O. J. "Married men and early retirement under the AFP scheme," Memoranda 02/2000, University of Oslo.

Wadensjö, E. (1996) "Early exit from the Swedish labour market," in E. Wadensjö (ed.), *Leaving the Labour Market Early in the Welfare State – Development over Time*, in part 2 of E. Wadensjö (ed.) *The Nordic Labour Markets in the 1990s*, North Holland: Elsevier.

11 Public pension reform and welfare in an economy with adverse selection

Hideki Konishi

Abstract

The welfare consequences of the recent major proposals for public pension reform, prefunding, coverage reduction, and privatization, are analyzed, taking account of adverse selection in annuity markets. Prefunding is shown to reduce the premium for private annuities and improve the welfare of every individual if the economic growth rate is lower than the interest rate. A higher replacement ratio is shown to increase the premium for private annuities and reinforce the relative cost advantage of public pensions. The analytical results give an economic rationale to maintaining a large pay-as-you-go program even in the situation of the economic growth rate being lower than the interest rate. Also examined are the welfare effects when incorporating the amortization of the unfunded pension debt, as well as the necessity of imposing a minimum coverage regulation on private annuity contracts when privatizing the public program.

11.1 Introduction

For these decades the economies in most of the industrial countries have been growing at slower rates than the interest rates and the populations are getting older. Under such economic and demographic conditions, their public pension programs are requiring more contributions than ever. One of the reasons is attributed to the pay-as-you-go financial schemes and several reform plans are controversially proposed. In this chapter I will focus on the following three major proposals: prefunding, coverage reduction, and privatization.

These proposals share the same idea that in a graying society longevity insurance should be provided by the market rather than the government. Prefunding proposals attempt to switch the financial scheme from pay-as-you-go to fully-funded. Coverage reduction proposals advocate to reduce the replacement ratio of the public program and make private annuities play as important a role as public pensions when people finance their after-retirement consumption. Privatization proposals often mean more than abolishing the public program in the sense that the necessity of compulsory participation in private annuity plans is commonly emphasized there.[1]

Theoretically, we can say that the background of these proposals is in a large part built upon what we call the Golden Rule criterion. This insists that long-term economic welfare is improved by reducing intergenerational income transfer if and only if the interest rate is higher than the economic growth rate (the population growth rate plus the growth rate of per worker wage income).[2]

We cannot *a priori* presume, however, that the market provides less costly longevity insurance whenever the economic growth rate is lower than the interest rate. Asymmetric information about longevity risks between the insurer and the insured may cause the failure of annuity markets due to adverse selection. In the literature it is explained as an economic rationale for compulsory public pension programs.[3] Recent empirical studies also claim that the expected present value of annuity payouts noticeably falls short of the cost of premiums on average and adverse selection explains roughly half of the discrepancy.[4]

Taking adverse selection into consideration, I will focus on the following two questions in the first part of this chapter:

1   Is the Golden Rule criterion still valid?
2   Will the above-mentioned three proposals result in qualitatively the same welfare consequence?

If annuity markets are well organized with complete information, the three proposals have qualitatively the same welfare effect. First, privatization and prefunding produce no difference in their economic impacts because a fully-funded public pension program merely displaces exactly as much "private" capital as the "public" capital it brings into being (Samuelson 1975: 541). Second, we can judge whether or not to maintain a public pension program by simply comparing the (internal) rate of return on public pensions with that on private annuities. In a steady state, the internal rate of return on pay-as-you-go financed public pensions is equal to the economic growth rate while the rate of return on private annuities is determined by the interest rate. If the economic growth rate is lower than the interest rate, a pay-as-you-go public pension program provides more costly longevity insurance and long-term economic welfare increases as its coverage decreases.

Under asymmetric information, however, private annuities are priced according to the distribution of longevity risks in the market. Since individuals with higher longevity risks demand more annuities, longevity risks distribute in the market in such a way that puts higher weight on higher risks in comparison to their distribution in the population. Informational asymmetry, therefore, makes private annuities incur the cost of adverse selection, i.e. they are priced higher than the actuarially-fair level. A key to understanding the welfare consequences of the three reforms is how different impacts they have on the distribution of longevity risks in annuity markets.

When taking adverse selection into consideration, it is useful to view the Golden Rule criterion from two distinguished standpoints: one concerning the choice of financial schemes and the other the choice of replacement ratios. Prefunding proposals are associated with the first category, whereas privatization and coverage reduction are concerned with the second.

With regard to the choice of financial schemes, I will show that the Golden Rule criterion survives even with adverse selection. Prefunding improves the economic welfare in the long run if and only if the economic growth rate is lower than the interest rate. The welfare gains are shown to come from two sources. One is the increased internal rate of return on public pensions as discussed under complete information. The other is, as shown, the reduced premium for private annuities, which prefunding makes possible by changing the distribution of longevity risks in the market.

With respect to the choice of replacement ratios, on the other hand, I will show that the Golden Rule criterion loses its validity when adverse selection occurs. The reason is that a higher replacement ratio increases the premium for private annuities by changing the distribution of longevity risks in annuity markets. As a public program provides more coverage, only individuals with higher longevity risks continue to demand private annuities supplementally and private annuities come to require a higher premium. This implies that a larger public pension program strengthens its cost advantage relative to private annuities, and due to such an external effect, even a fully-funded public program is no longer neutral to the long-run economic welfare in contrast to the discussions assuming complete information. Further, the introduction of a pay-as-you-go public pension program can be justified from the point of economic welfare even in the situation of the economic growth rate being lower than the interest rate, if the replacement ratio is appropriately high.

Since the scale of a public pension program affects the distribution of welfare among individuals having different longevity risks, the optimal replacement ratio depends on how the society evaluates it. When employing the Rawlsian social welfare function, for example, I will demonstrate that if a public pension program is to be introduced to the society at all, its replacement ratio should be so large as to induce the lowest-longevity-risk individuals to demand no private annuities. It is also shown that under the utilitarian social welfare function even a fully-funded program should not be introduced if its replacement ratio is small. These results suggest that coverage reduction proposals may be the worst among the three and can be even worse than the *laissez-faire* in terms of long-term economic welfare.

Due to pay-as-you-go financing, the three reforms bring about the well-known transition problem of how to amortize the implicit debt of the current unfunded program. The welfare gains realized for future generations may be offset by the losses that the generations during the transition period must bear. I will show that prefunding produces no welfare gains for future generations when the unfunded obligations are financed by additional wage taxes. Concerning privatization and coverage reduction, on the other hand, I will demonstrate that abolishing a pay-as-you go public program can never be optimal in light of the Rawlsian social welfare function, no matter how small the economic growth rate is relative to the interest rate.

The recent privatization proposals quite commonly emphasize the necessity of introducing a minimum coverage regulation on private annuities, under which every individual must contract at least as much coverage as a mandatory minimum.[5] Behind such an argument there is a paternalistic or merit-goods view, which considers it necessary and desirable for the government to prevent people from saving too little for their retirement. In the second part of this chapter, assuming rational individuals instead, I will discuss the desirability of a minimum coverage regulation from the standpoint of efficiency.

To enforce a minimum coverage regulation, I will consider two alternative institutional arrangements, one forcing individuals to cover the minimum within a single annuity contract and the other allowing diversification across multiple contracts. The analysis sheds light on their difference in terms of the information about longevity risks conveyed to annuity firms. With single contract restriction, annuity firms can regard their customers who contract more coverage than the mandatory minimum as the types of relatively high longevity risks. Thus they will discriminate annuity premiums between minimum and extra coverage. I will show that a mandatory private program with single contract restriction is equivalent to a fully-funded public program in terms of economic welfare. In the absence of a single contract restriction, on the other hand, no additional information about longevity risks is delivered to annuity firms and private annuity contracts equally incur the cost of adverse selection. In this case a minimum coverage regulation reduces the premium by changing the distribution of longevity risks in the market in such a way that puts higher weight on lower longevity risks. I will show that a mandatory private program without single contract restriction improves the welfare of every individual unless the mandatory minimum is too high for the lowest-longevity-risk individuals in the society.

In a related study, Abel (1986) analyzed the impact of a public pension program on the cost of adverse selection in an overlapping generations model with consumers having private information about their uncertain lifetimes. The model employed here simplifies his model by ignoring bequest motives and capital accumulation. His analysis is elegantly formulated and provides novel economic implications about the effects of a public pension program on the distribution of steady-state welfare and capital accumulation. From a realistic point of view, however, we have to say that his analysis faces a severe limitation in that it focuses only on a fully-funded infinitesimally-small public pension program. In contrast, this chapter addresses currently controversial issues concerning the optimal size of a pay-as-you-go financed public pension program, the welfare effect of prefunding the program, and the desirability of introducing a minimum coverage regulation on private annuity contracts when privatizing the program.

Regarding the organization of this chapter, Section 2 presents a model of adverse selection. The impacts of a public pension program on the cost of adverse selection are then examined in Section 3 as well as the welfare effects. Section 4 lastly considers the welfare effect of a minimum coverage regulation, with Section 5 summarizing the results of this chapter.

11.2 Price competition model of annuity markets

Two types of models have been frequently used to investigate the adverse selection problem in insurance markets. Rothschild and Stiglitz (1976) and Wilson (1977) proposed one type which includes non-linear price discrimination. In this model, each insurance company prepares a non-linear schedule of insurance policies (or several packages of insurance coverage and premiums) which are tailored to meet the needs of various types of individuals, and each individual chooses the most desirable option from the prepared menu. In the separating equilibrium, providing that the schedule is skillfully designed to induce individuals with different risk characteristics to choose different policies, each individual's private information will be revealed by his or her choice, although the equilibrium is not generally guaranteed to exist.[6]

The other frequently used type is the non-discriminatory model of insurance markets, which assume that each insurance firm offers a uniform unit premium and individuals can purchase as much coverage as desired at the premium. The competitive pressure drives the cost of premiums down in equilibrium such that every insurance company breaks even (see Pauly 1974, Jaynes 1978, and Abel 1986 among others). The equilibrium is pooling in the sense that each insurance company charges a unit premium to match the average risk exhibited among customers.

The monitoring assumption is considered to be the crucial difference between these two types of models. Because individuals are naturally permitted to purchase policies from multiple insurance companies, the coverage that a customer purchases from a particular company is not necessarily equal to the total amount of coverage needed. It is obviously the latter information, however, that each insurance company needs in order to infer the risk characteristics of each customer. In the Rothschild-Stiglitz-Wilson model, it is implicitly assumed that insurance companies can perfectly and costlessly monitor the total amount of coverage held by each customer; an assumption that essentially enables them to tie an individual to a single contract. But as Jaynes (1977) showed, when the assumption of costless monitoring is dropped, neither a separating nor a pooling contract can produce equilibrium in this model. In the non-discriminatory model, on the other hand, it is contrastingly assumed that each insurance company cannot monitor the total coverage held by individuals and thus cannot infer their risk characteristics from its sales. In this situation, a natural form of competition will be price competition, i.e. competition in unit premiums with no restrictions put on coverage levels.

We will here employ the non-discriminatory price competition model to describe private annuity markets. Though the price discrimination model admittedly captures some of the important properties of insurance markets, as far as actual annuity markets are concerned, individuals do not appear to be limited to a contract with a single company or face any severe restrictions on the coverage they purchase. Monitoring each customer's total coverage is far from being perfectly achieved and it does incur costs; and in fact, such information does not appear to be exchanged costlessly among insurance companies.

Let us consider a small open economy with two generations overlapping each period. People live two periods at the longest, earning a wage income only when young. The population of each young generation grows at a constant rate of n; the real wage income per worker does at a constant rate of g, and the real interest rate on capital is fixed at r.

Individuals face uncertain lifetimes. They live the first period for sure but their survival in the second period is uncertain. There are h types ($h \geq 2$) of individuals distinguished by their probability of survival θ_i, $i = 1, 2, \ldots, h$, such that $0 < \theta_1 < \theta_2 < \ldots < \theta_h < 1$. The survival probabilities are private information to individuals but their distribution is commonly known. A type-i individual refers to a young individual holding θ_i. The share of type-i individuals in each generation is denoted by $s_i \in (0, 1)$, where

$$\sum_{i=1}^{h} s_i = 1.$$

The average survival probability is denoted by

$$\hat{\theta} := \sum_{i=1}^{h} s_i \theta_i.$$

A mandatory public pension program imposes contribution taxes on wages at a tax rate of τ and provides benefits to the old at a replacement ratio of β. An individual who earns a wage income W when young pays a contribution tax τW and will receive a public pension βW when old if alive.

The contribution–benefit ratio, $\phi := \tau/\beta$, represents the cost of insuring a unit of after-retirement consumption through a public pension program. If the program is run on a fully-funded basis ϕ is equal to $\phi^{FF} := \hat{\theta}/(1+r)$, which we call the actuarially-fair premium hereafter. If it is on a pay-as-you-go basis, on the other hand, ϕ is equal to $\phi^{PAYG} := \hat{\theta}/(1+\gamma)$, where γ denotes the real economic growth rate, i.e. $\gamma := (1+n)(1+g) - 1$. As well known, a fully-funded program can provide less expensive longevity insurance if and only if the interest rate is higher than the economic growth rate, which produces the basis of the Golden Rule criterion mentioned in the introduction.

To focus on the adverse selection problem and simplify the analysis, we do not assume the bequest motives and specify the lifetime expected utility of a type-i individual as

$$U_i = \frac{1}{1-\sigma} C_1^{1-\sigma} + \frac{\delta\theta_i}{1-\sigma} C_2^{1-\sigma},$$

where C_1 and C_2 denote respectively the consumption at the first and second period of his or her lifetime; δ is the discount factor ($\delta > 0$), and it is assumed that $\sigma \geq 0$. To finance the second period consumption, individuals can purchase private annuities at a unit premium p or save in the capital market at the fixed interest rate r. One unit of private annuities insures a unit of second period consumption if the insured is alive but provides nothing if dead. As is clarified later, the absence of bequest motives induces no individual to save in the capital market in equilibrium.[7] For this reason, we will continue with the analysis by assuming that type-i individual chooses his or her demand for private annuities A_i to maximize the utility

$$\frac{1}{1-\sigma}[(1-\tau)W - pA_i]^{1-\sigma} + \frac{\delta\theta_i}{1-\sigma}[A_i + \beta W]^{1-\sigma}$$

subject to $A_i \geq 0$ when his or her labor income is W. The demand function then exhibits the form of $A_i = \alpha_i W$, where

$$\alpha_i := \max\left\{\frac{1-\tau-\rho_i\beta}{p+\rho_i}, 0\right\}$$

and

$$\rho_i := \left(\frac{p}{\delta\theta_i}\right)^{1/\sigma}.$$

Clearly, the demand for annuities decreases with the contribution tax rate as well as with the replacement ratio but increases with the survival probability.

A representative annuity firm, which is assumed to be risk neutral, invests the collected annuity premiums into the capital market to pay annuities to the annuitants who will be alive in the next period. Denoting $R := 1/(1+r)$, when the per worker wage income is W its expected discounted profit is written as πW, where

$$\pi := \sum_{i=1}^{h} (p - R\theta_i) s_i \alpha_i. \tag{1}$$

Due to price competition, the equilibrium premium is sufficiently lowered to make every annuity company break even as long as $\alpha_h > 0$.[8] If $\alpha_h = 0$, however, no one demands annuities and the market degenerates.

Let us denote the equilibrium premium by p^* and the associated equilibrium values of other variables by attaching asterisks, such as α_i^* and ρ_i^*. Because $p^* = R\theta_h$ if only type-h individuals purchase annuities, the market does not degenerate if and only if $\alpha_h > 0$ for $p = R\theta_h$, the condition of which is reduced to

$$\tau + (R/\delta)^{1/\sigma} \beta < 1. \tag{2}$$

When τ and β satisfy (2), the equilibrium premium under price competition is defined as

$$p^* := \min \{p \mid \pi \geq 0\}. \tag{3}$$

Noting that under (2) $\alpha_i > 0$ if $p \leq R\theta_i$ and that π is continuous in p, the existence of p^* is guaranteed when (2) is met. The existence is verified because $\pi < 0$ when $p \leq R\theta_1$ and $\pi > 0$ when p is larger than but sufficiently close to $R\theta_h$.

Since $\pi^* = 0$, the equilibrium premium can be expressed as

$$p^* = R \sum_{i=1}^{h} \theta_i \lambda_i^*, \tag{4}$$

where

$$\lambda_i^* := s_i \alpha_i^* / \sum_{i=1}^{h} s_i \alpha_i^*. \qquad \lambda_i^*$$

represents the share of annuities purchased by type-i individuals in equilibrium. (4) shows that the equilibrium premium is equal to the discounted expected value of survival probabilities calculated according to their distribution not in the population (s_i's) but in the market (λ_i^*'s).

Recall that α_i^* increases with θ_i, which implies that λ_i^*/s_i becomes larger as θ_i is higher. Hence we find that p^* satisfies

$$\phi^{FF} < p^* \leq R\theta_h. \tag{5}$$

The first inequality shows the cost of adverse selection. Annuities are priced higher than the actuarially-fair level so that individuals with low longevity risks must pay expensive premiums in the light of their own risks. The second inequality implies that private annuities are less costly means to finance after-retirement consumption than savings in the capital market (i.e. $p^* < R$), which assures, as we mentioned earlier, that no individual save in the capital market in equilibrium.

The definition of the equilibrium given by (3) allows us to regard the equilibrium premium as a function of τ and β, which we denote by $p^* = p^*(\tau, \beta)$. This function is not necessarily continuous everywhere due to the kink of the annuity demand and the discrete distribution of survival probabilities. But we can claim that p^* is strictly increasing in τ and β when at least two different types of individuals demand annuities.[9] This is intuitively because in reaction to the increases in τ and β individuals with higher longevity risks reduce their demands for annuities in smaller proportions and thus higher longevity risks come to have larger weights in the market. Indeed, as long as $\alpha_i > 0$, the elasticities of annuity demands are obtained as $-(\partial \alpha_i/\partial \beta)/\alpha_i = \rho_i/(1 - \tau - \rho_i)$ and $-(\partial \alpha_i/\partial \tau)/\alpha_i = 1/(1 - \tau - \rho_i)$, both of which are decreasing in θ_i. For example, given a fixed contribution–benefit ratio, consider the impact of introducing an infinitesimally small public pension program on the equilibrium premium. If the utility function is logarithmic ($\sigma = 1$), we can obtain it as

$$\frac{\mathrm{d}p^*}{\mathrm{d}\beta} = \frac{p^{LF} - \phi^{FF}}{\hat{\alpha}^*} > 0, \tag{6}$$

where p^{LF} denotes the premium at the *laissez-faire* equilibrium, $p^*(0, 0)$, and $\hat{\alpha}^*$ represents the average of α_i^*'s, i.e.

$$\hat{\alpha}^* = \sum_{i=1}^{n} s_i \alpha_i^*.$$

11.3 Public pension reform and welfare

To examine the validity of the Golden Rule criterion, we propose two different standpoints of its interpretation; one concerning the optimal financial scheme under a fixed replacement ratio and the other concerning the optimal replacement ratio under a fixed financial scheme. The Golden Rule criterion insists in terms of the first standpoint that if and only if $r > \gamma$, prefunding improves the long-term welfare irrespective of the replacement ratio. In terms of the second, on the other hand, it insists that if and only if $r > \gamma$, the replacement ratio of a fully-funded program has no long-term welfare effect, a reduction in the replacement ratio of an unfunded program monotonically increases the long-term economic welfare, and its optimal replacement ratio is equal to zero. We will now consider how these propositions should be modified in the presence of adverse selection.

11.3.1 Financial schemes

In an equilibrium with fixed τ and β, a type-i individual enjoys the utility $U_i = v_i^* W^{1-\sigma}$, where W is the wage income and $v_i^* := \{(1 - \tau - p^*\alpha_i^*)^{1-\sigma} + \delta\theta_i(\alpha_i^* + \beta)^{1-\sigma}\}/(1 - \sigma)$. Substituting the definition of α_i yields

$$
v_i^* = \begin{cases} \dfrac{1}{1-\sigma}(1 - \tau + p^*\beta)^{1-\sigma}\left(\dfrac{p^* + \rho_i^*}{\rho_i^*}\right)^\sigma & \text{if } \theta_i > \dfrac{p^*}{\delta}\left(\dfrac{\beta}{1-\tau}\right)^\sigma \\[2ex] \dfrac{1}{1-\sigma}\{(1 - \tau)^{1-\sigma} + \delta\theta_i\beta^{1-\sigma}\} & \text{otherwise,} \end{cases} \tag{7}
$$

the upper expression on the right-hand side of which is associated with the case of purchasing private annuities in equilibrium.

We will first consider the steady state welfare effect of prefunding under a fixed replacement ratio ($\beta > 0$).[10] Because $\tau = \phi\beta$ and $\phi^{FF} < \phi^{PAYG}$ in the case of $r > \gamma$, the welfare effect can be identified as that of reducing τ with β fixed. Wherever $p^*(\tau, \beta)$ is differentiable, the effect of a marginal change in τ on the utility of a type-i individual is then obtained as

$$
\frac{dv_i^*}{d\tau} = -(1 - \phi\beta - p^*\alpha_i^*)^{-\sigma}\left(1 + \alpha_i^*\frac{\partial p^*}{\partial \tau}\right) < 0, \tag{8}
$$

the sign of which follows from $\partial p^*/\partial\tau > 0$. Accordingly, prefunding improves welfare if and only if $r > \gamma$, which establishes the validity of the Golden Rule criterion in terms of the optimal financial scheme.

Since $\partial p^*/\partial\tau > 0$, the analysis shows that prefunding produces welfare gains by reducing the premium for private annuities as well as by reducing the contribution taxes. In the literature some sources of long-term welfare gains from prefunding have been pointed out such as the promotion of capital accumulation and the alleviation of labor market distortions. Our result demonstrates another source; it helps alleviate the inefficiency from adverse selection in annuity markets.

11.3.2 Replacement ratios

11.3.2.1 Small programs

We will consider next the steady state welfare effect of changing the replacement ratio under a fixed financial scheme. Plugging $\tau = \phi\beta$ into (7) and differentiating it, we obtain

$$\frac{dv_i^*}{d\beta} = \begin{cases} (1 - \phi\beta - p^*\alpha_i^*)^{-\sigma}\left[p^* - \phi - \alpha_i^*\dfrac{dp^*}{d\beta}\right] & \text{if } \theta_i > \dfrac{p^*}{\delta}\left(\dfrac{\beta}{1 - \phi\beta}\right)^{\sigma} \\[4mm] \delta\theta_i\beta^{-\sigma} - \phi(1 - \phi\beta)^{-\sigma} & \text{otherwise,} \end{cases} \quad (9)$$

wherever $p^*(\tau, \beta)$ is differentiable.

To begin with, let us suppose that the replacement ratio is so low that every individual purchases private annuities supplementally. The upper expression on the right-hand side of (9) captures the welfare change for each individual in this case. Focusing on the bracketed terms, we can decompose the welfare effect into two. The one is the effect associated with the term $p^* - \phi$ in the bracket, which represents the relative cost advantage of providing longevity insurance publicly. If $p^* > \phi$, the public system can supply less expensive insurance than the market. An increase in the replacement ratio thus benefits every individual. The other is associated with the term $-\alpha_i^*(dp^*/d\beta)$ in the bracket, representing the increased cost of adverse selection. Since $dp^*/d\beta = \partial p^*/\partial\beta + \phi(\partial p^*/\partial\tau) > 0$, through this effect a higher replacement ratio deteriorates the utility of each individual proportionally to his or her demand for private annuities. If $p^* > \phi$ is the case, therefore, these two welfare effects trade off each other; otherwise a reduction in β makes every individual better off.

Paying special attention to the case of $p^* > \phi$, we obtain two implications for public pension reform, both of which demonstrate that the Golden Rule criterion is no longer valid concerning replacement ratios.

The first implication is that the replacement ratio of a fully-funded program is never neutral to the steady state welfare. It affects the equilibrium premium for private annuities and influences the distribution of welfare among individuals. To illustrate this point, suppose that the public pension program is small and the utility function is logarithmic. When evaluated at $\beta = 0$ and $\sigma = 1$, (9) is reduced to

$$\frac{dv_i^*}{d\beta} = (1 - p^{LF}\alpha_i^*)^{-1}\left[p^{LF} - \phi - \frac{\alpha_i^*}{\hat{\alpha}^*}(p^{LF} - \phi^{FF})\right], \quad (10)$$

where we make use of (6). Since $p^{LF} > \phi^{FF}$ and $\phi = \phi^{FF}$, the introduction of an infinitesimally small fully-funded program improves the welfare of type-i individuals if and only if they demand private annuities less than the average. Due to the presence of such a distributional effect, therefore, we need some social welfare function to evaluate an infinitesimal introduction of a fully-funded public program. If we employ the utilitarian social welfare criterion, for example, aggregating the marginal utilities in (9) yields

$$\sum_{i=1}^{h}\frac{dv_i^*}{d\beta}s_i = (p^{LF} - \phi^{FF})\sum_{i=1}^{h}\frac{s_i(\hat{\alpha}^* - \alpha_i^*)}{\hat{\alpha}^*}\frac{1}{1 - p^{LF}\alpha_i^*} < 0,$$

the sign of which follows from

$$\sum_{i=1}^{h} s_i(\hat{\alpha}^* - \alpha_i^*) = 0.$$

This demonstrates that even a fully-funded program cannot be justified from the utilitarian point of view when its replacement ratio is small.

The second implication is that contrary to what the Golden Rule criterion insists regarding replacement ratios, a pay-as-you-go financed program ($\phi = \phi^{PAYG}$) can be beneficial to some individuals even if $r > \gamma$ (and hence $\phi^{PAYG} > \phi^{FF}$). The condition that the interest rate exceeds the economic growth rate is insufficient to justify abolishing a pay-as-you-go financed public system on the ground of Pareto improvements. To illustrate this point, let us employ the Rawlsian social welfare function to evaluate the distribution of welfare among individuals. As we can see from the definition of v_i^*, it is the changes in the utility of a type-1 individual, i.e. the individual with the highest mortality risk, that the social judgement should be attributed to. Assuming the logarithmic utility ($\sigma = 1$), then, the condition for improving the Rawlsian social welfare is obtained from (10) as

$$\phi < \left(1 - \frac{\alpha_1^*}{\hat{\alpha}^*}\right) p^{LF} + \frac{\alpha_1^*}{\hat{\alpha}^*} \phi^{FF}.$$

Since the right-hand side is larger than ϕ^{FF}, the Rawlsian view may justify introducing a small pay-as-you-go financed program even though $r > \gamma$.

11.3.2.2 Large programs

We will next consider a large public pension program. When a program is large, it may make every individual better off. To see this, look at the bracketed terms on the right-hand side of (9) and recall the trade off in welfare brought about by a higher replacement ratio. On the one hand, the relative cost advantage of a public program (i.e. $p^* - \phi$) increases as the replacement ratio becomes higher, because private annuities charge a higher premium. The welfare loss associated with the cost of adverse selection (i.e. $\alpha_i^*(dp^*/d\beta)$) may decrease, on the other, because individuals demand private annuities less as the replacement ratio becomes higher.[11] The former gain is thus more likely to overweigh the latter loss as the program becomes larger. It is noted, however, that individuals with relatively low longevity risks will stop purchasing annuities. In such a case the public pension coverage may be too much for them and the program may reduce their welfare. This implies that not only the relative cost advantage but also the divergence of longevity risks among individuals matters to whether or not a large public pension program can make every individual better off.

Taking the case of a fully-funded program, Table 11.1 shows the results of numerical calculations concerning the effects of its replacement ratios on the equilibrium premium and welfare. This simulation assumes two types of individuals, a logarithmic utility function, and $R = \delta = 0.5$. There are considered three different distributions of longevity risks (cases 1, 2, and 3). The replacement ratios also take three levels ($\beta = 0$, 0.4, 0.7). A new notation $d := (p^* - \phi^{FF})/p^*$ measures the discrepancy between the equilibrium premium and actuarially-fair one.

Comparing between cases 1 and 2, the actuarially-fair premiums are equal but case 2 has a higher *laissez-faire* equilibrium premium due to the increased spread in the distribution of longevity risks. Also, looking at the value of d for $\beta = 0$, we notice that case 3 has a *laissez-faire* equilibrium premium less distorted from the actuarially-fair level in comparison with the other cases, owing to the decreased spread in the distribution of longevity risks.

The last two rows of this table show the welfare effects. Both types of individuals are made better off in cases 1 and 2 when the replacement ratios are as large as to induce type-1 individuals to quit purchasing private annuities (respectively the cases of $\beta = 0.7$ and 0.4). In case 3, in contrast, no Pareto improvements are realized at any of the three replacement ratios. This is because the adverse selection distortion is relatively small in comparison to the other cases.

11.3.2.3 Optimal replacement ratios

To begin with, we will examine the conditions under which every individual is made better off by abolishing a public pension program. Since a higher replacement ratio makes private annuities more expensive, (9) demonstrates that a public pension program reduces the welfare of every individual if it lacks the relative cost advantage over private annuities. In fact, a public pension program should be abolished if its contribution–benefit ratio satisfies $\phi > p^{LF}$.[12] The reason is quite simple. Since p^* is increasing in β, a public program can never provide less costly longevity insurance than the market if $\phi > p^{LF}$.

According to the Golden Rule criterion, the optimal replacement ratio of a pay-as-you-go financed program is equal to zero if $r > \gamma$. This condition does not necessarily imply that $\phi^{PAYG} > p^{LF}$, however. Let us measure the adverse selection distortion at the *laissez-faire* equilibrium by $d^{LF} := (p^{LF} - \phi^{FF})/p^{LF} > 0$. The condition of $p^{LF} > \phi^{PAYG}$ is then reduced to $r > \gamma + (1 + r)d^{LF}$, with which we can justify abolishing a pay-as-you-go public program on the ground of long-term Pareto efficiency. Conversely, if $r \leq \gamma + (1 + r)d^{LF}$ holds, some social welfare function can justify keeping a pay-as-you-go public program in the society. Taking the Rawlsian social welfare function, for instance, the socially optimal replacement ratio β^{OPT} is obtained as follows.[13]

$$\beta^{OPT} = \begin{cases} [\phi + (\delta\theta_1/\phi)^{-1/\sigma}]^{-1} & \text{if } \phi < p^{LF} \\ [p^{LF} + (\delta\theta_1/p^{LF})^{-1/\sigma}]^{-1} \text{ or } 0 & \text{if } \phi = p^{LF} \\ 0 & \text{otherwise.} \end{cases} \tag{11}$$

According to (11), the socially optimal replacement ratio exhibits a jump with respect to contribution–benefit ratios and as far as being positive it assures the coverage of private annuities that a type-1 individual would purchase at the premium of ϕ in the absence of a public program. Since p^* increases with β, when $\phi \leq p^{LF}$ the optimal replacement ratio is large to the extent that it induces type-1 individuals to purchase no private annuities.

The reason for the optimality of such a large replacement ratio comes from the fact that due to the increasing effect on the premium for private annuities a higher replacement ratio does not have a monotone impact on the welfare of each individual. Figure 11.1 shows how replacement ratios change the welfare of an individual relative to the *laissez-faire*, taking three cases of $\phi > p^{LF}$, $\phi = p^{LF}$, and $\phi < p^{LF}$. The schedules are shaped such that the welfare is decreasing in the range of small or large replacement ratios while increasing in the range of medium ones. This does not happen without adverse selection. Suppose that individuals do not differ in their survival probabilities. We then necessarily obtain downward-sloping, horizontal, and upward-sloping schedules of welfare in the respective cases.

Since the welfare of each individual changes like Figure 11.1, the optimality of a large program is not limited to the Rawlsian social welfare function but applies to a broad class of social welfare functions. We can say rather generally that a public pension program should assure a high replacement ratio to some extent if it is to be introduced to society at all.

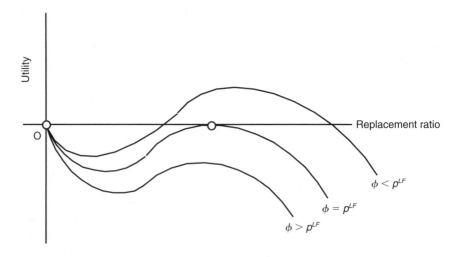

Figure 11.1 Replacement ratio and utility

In the literature few authors have pointed out the importance of maintaining a large public pension program. Diamond (1977) argued in his seminal article on social security analysis that a compulsory public pension program must be sufficiently close to the desired package such that a sizable fraction of the population need not purchase supplementary private insurance policies. It is noted that his argument is based on an exogenous premise that a compulsory program can save transaction costs such as those for administration and advertising.[14] In contrast, our argument is based on the endogenous economies of scale in that a larger replacement ratio increases the cost of adverse selection and makes private annuities less attractive as a means to insure against longevity risks.

Pauly (1974) developed another argument for a large public program in his seminal article on moral hazard and adverse selection. He emphasized the informational externalities of a large public insurance program within a model of adverse selection consisting of two hidden types of individuals. Our model is partly an extension of his model. He argued that a large program enables insurance firms to distinguish the types of individuals and charge the high-risk type actuarially fair because it induces only the high-risk type to purchase private insurances. The numerical calculation in Table 11.1 illustrates his points. When only type-2 individuals purchase annuities, we have $p^* = 0.45$ and, as cases 1 and 2 show, Pareto improvements are achieved. Table 11.1 also demonstrates, however, that the welfare gains from such externalities are limited by the magnitude of adverse selection distortions. As case 3 shows, even if the replacement ratio is as large as to crowd out the low-risk individual from the market, the introduction of such a public pension program is not necessarily Pareto superior to the *laissez-faire*. Moreover, as previously shown, if the contribution–benefit ratio satisfies $\phi > p^{LF}$, the introduction of any public pension program is Pareto inferior to the *laissez-faire*.

Table 11.1 Numerical calculations ($R = \delta$, $= .5$, $\sigma = 1$)

$(\theta_1, \theta_2 s_1)$ β	Case 1 (.5, .9, .5)			Case 2 (.3, .9, .33)			Case 3 (.5, .9, .8)		
	0	*.4*	*.7*	*0*	*.4*	*.7*	*0*	*.4*	*.7*
p^*	.372	.408	.450	.398	.450	.450	.306	.328	.450
ϕ^{FF}	.35	.35	.35	.35	.35	.35	.29	.29	.29
d	.058	.141	.222	.120	.222	.222	.052	.116	.356
α_1^*	.242	.046	0	.148	0	0	.294	.010	0
α_2^*	.376	.171	.017	.351	.143	.017	.457	.252	.030
v_1^*	−.378	−.373	−.370	−.307	−.288	−.335	−.329	−.328	−.316
v_2^*	−.453	−.461	−.441	−.483	−.482	−.441	−.365	−.375	−.385

11.3.3 Amortization of the unfunded obligations

11.3.3.1 Financial schemes

Prefunding, however, faces a serious problem of what is called the "double burden:" in addition to the contributions for their own retirement, generations after the reform (at least during some transition period) must bear the burden of financing the unfunded pension debt accumulated so far. Such additional burdens may be so large as to outweigh or offset the long-term welfare gains discussed in the previous subsections. We will examine this point by incorporating taxes to finance unfunded pension obligations into the model.

Suppose that the government amortizes the unfunded obligations by imposing a proportional wage tax on all the generations after the reform. Let μ be such a constant wage tax rate. If $r > \gamma$ and the wage per worker is W_1 when the financial scheme is switched, the present discounted value of tax revenues is written as

$$\sum_{t=1}^{+\infty} \mu W_1 [(1+\gamma)/(1+r)]^{t-1} = \mu(1+r)W_1/(r-\gamma)$$

in per-worker terms at the timing of the reform. The amount of implicit pension debt is, on the other hand, equal to $\phi^{PAYG}\beta W_1$. Equating these, μ must satisfy $\phi^{PAYG}\beta = \mu + \phi^{FF}\beta$, which implies that each generation incurs the same tax burdens before and after the reform. As long as the unfunded pension debt is amortized in this fashion, therefore, prefunding can produce no welfare gains for future generations.[15]

11.3.3.2 Replacement ratios

As well as prefunding, coverage reduction and privatization bring about similar transition problems. Suppose that the economy satisfies $r > \gamma$ and the government reduces the replacement ratio of a pay-as-you-go financed program from the current level β_1 to some level β. The pension benefits promised in the old program must be secured to the retired at the timing of the reform, however, which requires the government to finance the loss in contribution taxes amounting to $\phi^{PAYG}W_1(\beta_1 - \beta)$. As in the above, assume that it is financed by imposing a proportional wage tax perpetually after the reform. If we let W_1 be the per-worker wage income when the reform is taken into action, the required wage tax rate μ must then satisfy

$$\sum_{t=1}^{+\infty} \mu W_1 [(1+\gamma)/(1+r)]^{t-1} = \phi^{PAYG}W_1(\beta_1 - \beta).$$

Accordingly, we obtain $\mu = (\phi^{PAYG} - \phi^{FF})(\beta_1 - \beta)$ and each generation bears the total tax burdens proportional to the wage income by

$$\mu + \phi^{PAYG}\beta = \phi^{FF}\beta + (\phi^{PAYG} - \phi^{FF})\beta_1 \tag{12}$$

Look at the right-hand side. The first term represents "variable" tax burdens associated with the changes in the replacement ratio, showing that a marginal reduction in the replacement ratio reduces the total tax burdens by the amount of ϕ^{FF}. The second term, on the other hand, represents "fixed" tax burdens associated with the finance of unfunded obligations, which each generation cannot avoid even when the program is privatized. Since $p^* > \phi^{FF}$, we can say that even if being financed on a pay-as-you-go basis under the condition of $r > \gamma$, public pensions always hold a relative cost advantage over private annuities when the unfunded obligations must be financed by wage taxes.

Now let us consider the socially optimal replacement ratio. Suppose that $r > \gamma$. Making use of (12) and plugging $\tau = \phi^{FF}\beta + (\phi^{PAYG} - \phi^{FF})\beta_1$ into (7) instead of $\tau = \phi^{PAYG}\beta$, the optimal replacement ratio of a pay-as-you-go financed program is derived under the Rawlsian social welfare function as follows.[16]

$$\beta^{OPT} = \frac{1 - (\phi^{PAYG} - \phi^{FF})\beta_1}{\phi^{FF} + (\delta\theta_1/\phi^{FF})^{-1/\sigma}} \tag{13}$$

In contrast to the case without taking account of the unfunded obligations, β^{OPT} is now always positive since public pensions hold a relative cost advantage over private annuities.[17] The abolishment of a public pension program, therefore, can never be justified from the Rawlsian point of view, no matter how small the economic growth rate is relative to the interest rate.

11.4 Mandatory minimum coverage

11.4.1 Two alternative institutional arrangements

The recent privatization proposals advocate more than abolishing the public program. They propose quite commonly to establish a private mandatory system that forces every individual to obtain minimum coverage within private annuity contracts.[18] One reason for the necessity of introducing minimum coverage comes from the paternalistic or merit–goods point of view; the government should help imprudent individuals from failing to save sufficient retirement funds. The analysis here will appraise it from another point of view: the alleviation of adverse selection.

Suppose that the government introduces a minimum coverage regulation, under which each worker must contract annuity plans to cover at least as much as a fixed amount of after-retirement consumption.[19] Two alternative ways to enforce minimum coverage can be considered; one is to force every individual to contract at least the minimum within a single contract and the other is to permit every individual to diversify it among multiple contracts. These institutional arrangements will make a difference in terms of the information about longevity risks conveyed to annuity companies through the amounts of contracted coverage.[20] If the regulation is implemented with single contract restriction, annuity companies can distinguish between contracts for minimum coverage and those for extra coverage, and deduce that individuals contracting extra coverage have relatively high longevity risks. Accordingly, annuity plans for minimum coverage will be priced differentiatedly from those for extra coverage. If the diversification across multiple contracts is allowed, on the other hand, annuity companies, being unaware of the total coverage purchased by each customer, can obtain no additional information and hence every annuity plan will be priced uniformly.[21]

11.4.2 *Minimum coverage with single contract restriction*

Suppose that each worker with a labor income W must purchase at least αW units of annuities. We will call α a mandatory coverage ratio. Since with single contract restriction annuity firms can discriminate premiums, let p^M be the premium for an annuity contracted for minimum coverage and p^E be that for extra coverage. Then, a type-i individual chooses his or her demand for extra coverage A_i^E to maximize the expected utility

$$\frac{1}{1-\sigma}\left[(1-p^M\alpha)W - p^E A_i^E\right]^{1-\sigma} + \frac{\delta\theta_i}{1-\sigma}\left[\alpha W + A_i^E\right]^{1-\sigma},$$

which yields $A_i^E = \alpha_i^E W$, where $\alpha_i^E := \max\{(1 - p^M\alpha - \rho_i^E\alpha)/(p^E + \rho_i^E),0\}$ and $\rho_i^E := (p^E/\delta\theta_i)^{1/\sigma}$. Competition drives annuity firms to break even with respect to each type of contract. Invoking (4), it follows that in equilibrium the unit premium for minimum coverage is set actuarially fair as

$$p^M = \phi^{FF}$$

since every individual contracts the same coverage, whereas the unit premium for extra coverage is determined such that

$$p^E = R\sum_{i=1}^{h}\theta_i\lambda_i^E,$$

where

$$\lambda_i^E := s_i \alpha_i^E / \sum_{i=1}^{h} s_i \alpha_i^E.$$

It is now clear that in terms of economic welfare, the minimum coverage regulation enforced with single contract restriction is equivalent to a fully-funded public pension program if the mandatory coverage ratio and replacement ratio are the same. Every individual is forced to participate in a public or private program providing actuarially-fair longevity insurance and may purchase supplementary private annuity plans that incur the cost of adverse selection. Applying the results obtained in the previous section, we can clarify the welfare effects of such a mandatory private program as follows.

First, a higher mandatory coverage ratio increases the annuity premium for extra coverage and thus charges the distribution of welfare in favor of individuals having relatively high longevity risks. Second, a minimum coverage regulation may make every individual better off if its mandatory coverage ratio is so large as to induce individuals having the lowest longevity risk to contract no extra coverage. Third, under the Rawlsian social welfare criterion, the optimal mandatory coverage ratio is positive and can be identified as the optimal replacement ratio of a fully-funded program obtained from (11).

11.4.3 Minimum coverage without single contract restriction

Without single contract restriction, annuity firms cannot infer the respective types of their customers from the sales and hence annuities can be just uniformly priced. Given a mandatory coverage ratio and a unit annuity premium, a type-i individual with a labor income W chooses his or her demand for annuities A_i to maximize the expected utility

$$\frac{1}{1-\sigma}[W - pA_i]^{1-\sigma} + \frac{\delta\theta^i}{1-\sigma}A_i^{1-\sigma}$$

subject to $A_i \geq \alpha W$. The demand function is derived as $A_i = \alpha_i W$, where $\alpha_i := \max 1/(p + \rho_i), \alpha\}$. Together with this new definition of α_i, the equilibrium premium p^* is defined in the same fashion as (3), which allows us to regard p^* as a function of α, i.e. $p^* = p^*(\alpha)$. As in the case of a public pension program, $p^*(\alpha)$ is continuous and differentiable almost everywhere.

Remember that, as we have seen in (4), $p^*(\alpha)$ is equal to the discounted expected value of survival probabilities calculated according to the distribution of annuity demands in the market. It is then clear that $p^* = \phi^{FF}$ if every individual is bound to the regulation and $p^* = p^{LF}$ if no individual is. We can further claim that the equilibrium premium satisfies

$$\phi^{FF} \le p^* \le p^{LF}$$

and a higher mandatory coverage ratio reduces it wherever only some individuals are bound to the regulation.[22] This is intuitively because individuals bound to the mandatory minimum will have relatively low longevity risks and a higher mandatory coverage ratio raises the market share of annuities purchased by such individuals. The impacts on annuity premiums are thus quite contrasting between the cases with and without single contract restriction.

We will now examine the welfare effects. Suppose that not all but some individuals are bound to the regulation. In contrast to the case with single contract restriction, a higher mandatory coverage ratio favors individuals having relatively high longevity risks because they are not bound to the regulation and can enjoy the reduced premium. It may reduce the welfare of individuals having relatively low longevity risks, on the other hand, since the mandatory minimum coverage exceeds what they want to purchase.

These points are formally demonstrated as follows. The utility of a type-i individual is written as $v_i^* W^{1-\sigma}$, where

$$
v_i^* := \begin{cases}
\dfrac{1}{1-\sigma} \left(\dfrac{p^* + \rho_i^*}{\rho_i^*} \right)^{\sigma} & \text{if } \theta_i > \dfrac{p^*}{\delta} \left(\dfrac{1}{\alpha} - p^* \right)^{-\sigma} \\[3mm]
\dfrac{1}{1-\sigma} \{ (1 - p^*\alpha)^{1-\sigma} + \delta\theta_i \alpha^{1-\sigma} \} & \text{otherwise.}
\end{cases}
$$

The upper expression on the right-hand side corresponds to the case when the individual is not bound to the regulation. Wherever $p^*(\alpha)$ is differentiable, we have

$$
\frac{dv_i^*}{d\alpha} = \begin{cases}
-\dfrac{1}{\rho_i^*} \left(\dfrac{p^* + \rho_i^*}{\rho_i^*} \right)^{\sigma-1} \dfrac{dp^*}{d\alpha} & \text{if } \theta_i > \dfrac{p^*}{\delta} \left(\dfrac{1}{\alpha} - p^* \right)^{-\sigma} \\[3mm]
-\alpha^{1-\sigma} \left(\dfrac{1}{\alpha} - p^* \right)^{-\sigma} \dfrac{dp^*}{d\alpha} + \alpha^{-\sigma} \left[\delta\theta_i - p^* \left(\dfrac{1}{\alpha} - p^* \right)^{-\sigma} \right] & \text{otherwise.}
\end{cases}
$$

$$(14)$$

Since $dp^*/d\alpha < 0$ if the regulation binds only a part of the individuals, a marginal increase in α improves the welfare of individuals who are not bound to the mandatory minimum, whereas it may reduce the welfare of the rest. Look at the lower expression on the right-hand side of (14). The first term stands for the welfare gain from the reduced premium while the second represents the loss from being forced to purchase more coverage than they want.

Nevertheless, we can show that the introduction of minimum coverage improves the welfare of every individual unless the mandatory coverage ratio is too high. Since $dv^*/d\alpha$ is increasing in θ_i from (14), a Pareto improvement occurs if and only if the utility of a type-1 individual increases. Consider now the least-binding minimum coverage regulation, which sets a mandatory minimum infinitesimally larger than the coverage that a type-1 individual contracts in the *laissez-faire* equilibrium. Look at the lower expression on the right-hand side of (14) again to see how such a regulation affects the utility of a type-1 individual. While the first term is positive due to the reduced premium, the second is negative but negligibly small because it binds a type-1 individual to the least extent.[23]

11.5 Concluding remarks

This paper examined the long-term welfare consequences of pre-funding, coverage reduction, and privatization of a pay-as-you-go financed public pension program, taking account of their impacts on the cost of adverse selection in annuity markets. Let us briefly summarize the implications of the analysis.

Prefunding improves long-term welfare if the economic growth rate is lower than the interest rate, and thus the Golden Rule criterion survives in this respect. Concerning coverage reduction and privatization, however, its validity is lost since the replacement ratio of a public pension program affects the premium for private annuities. With adverse selection in annuity markets, a public pension program obtains endogenously produced economies of scale in the sense that a higher replacement ratio raises the premium for private annuities and hence strengthens the relative cost advantage of public pensions. From this point of view, coverage reduction may lead to the worst outcome among the three proposals since it fails to take advantage of such scale economies. In other words, a public pension program should maintain so large a replacement ratio as to make private annuities unnecessary for low-longevity-risk individuals if it is to continue to exist in society at all.

When amortizing the current unfunded pension obligations with taxes on future wage income, however, prefunding can leave no gains for future generations. Also, the abolishment of a pay-as-you-go financed public pension program cannot be optimal from the Rawlsian view of social welfare, no matter how small the economic growth rate is relative to the interest rate. When the Rawlsian social welfare function is employed, the replacement ratio must be so large as to induce the lowest-longevity-risk individuals to need no supplemental private annuity plans.

A minimum coverage regulation on private annuity contracts will have distinct welfare effects, depending on how it is institutionally enforced. With single contrast restriction the regulation favors low-longevity-risk individuals as well as a fully-funded public pension program, and otherwise it favors high-longevity-risk individuals by reducing the premium for private annuities. Such governmental interventions in annuity markets can be justified from the point of economic welfare as a policy device to reduce the cost of adverse selection.

Finally, let us provide two concluding remarks. First, the model simplifies the analysis by not assuming bequest motives, which makes it possible for us to concentrate on private annuities as a sole private means to finance after-retirement consumption. In reality, however, annuity markets are not very large and people save more in the capital market for retirement funds. One of the reasons is because annuities are less attractive to people who want to leave bequests to their children. Extending the model to incorporate bequest motives is left for the future research but it is not so straightforward since individuals come to differ not only in their survival probabilities but also in their inheritances. Second, as mentioned in the introduction, recent empirical studies show that transaction costs explain the estimated load factor of private annuities at least as much as adverse selection. From this chapter's point of view, we can argue that the presence of such costs weakens the case for small public pension programs and the single contract restriction is less costly as a means to enforce minimum coverage under privatization. Nevertheless, it is necessary to shed more light on the nature of transaction costs in annuity markets empirically as well as theoretically.[24]

Notes

1 In Japan, Hatta and Oguchi (1992) advocate prefunding of the pension program. For privatization proposals, see World Bank (1994), Samwick and Skinner (1997), and Feldstein (1998, Introduction) among others. Several privatization issues as well as country studies are covered by the articles in Feldstein (1998).

2 Samuelson (1958) and Aaron (1966) first proposed possible welfare improvements by intergenerational transfer and Samuelson (1975) later established the Golden Rule criterion. In the context of the recent public pension reform, Feldstein (1996) gives an excellent overview from the standpoint of this criterion.

3 See Stiglitz (1988) among others. Blinder (1988) provided an excellent survey as to why the government should be in the pension business.

4 Using the data of individual life annuities sold to men aged 65 in the US in 1995, Mitchell *et al.* (1997) estimate the cost of adverse selection to be approximately as large as 10 percent of the premium cost. For the empirical studies on the "money's worth" of private annuities, see also Friedman and Warshawsky (1988: 90) and Warshawsky (1988).

5 For example, see World Bank (1994), Samwick and Skinner (1997), and Feldstein (1998: Introduction).

6 In a related study, Eckstein *et al.* (1985) employed a Rothschild-Stiglitz-Wilson model considering two types of individuals, and showed that introducing a fully-funded public pension program achieves a Pareto improvement when the initial equilibrium is pooling. However, the pooling equilibrium they assumed does not pass the intuitive criterion regarding the rational belief formation off the equilibrium path.

7 With bequest motives, individuals have an incentive to save in the capital market. See Abel (1986) and Eichenbaum and Peled (1987).

8 It must be admitted that the supply strategy of firms assumed in the price-competition model is quite passive, and as Jaynes (1978) revealed, the assumption of costly monitoring is not sufficient to justify why firms compete only in premiums. In fact, if a firm unilaterally places a certain uniform restriction on sales to each individual, it can then obtain a positive profit when other firms are charging a unit premium without any quantity restrictions. Therefore, to justify why insurance companies engage in price competition without placing any restrictions on coverage levels, we need to assume more than the monitoring assumption; although such an investigation is well beyond the scope here and is left for future study.

9 The formal proof is as follows. For notational simplicity let us write α_i as $\alpha_i(p, \tau, \beta)$ in a functional form. Assuming the condition of (2), consider two combinations of τ and β, (τ^0, β^0) and (τ^1, β^1), such that $(\tau^0, \beta^0) \neq (\tau^1, \beta^1)$, $\tau^1 \geq \tau^0$, and $\beta^1 \geq \beta^0$. Their corresponding equilibrium premiums are $p^0 := p^*(\tau^0, \beta^0)$ and $p^1 := p^*(\tau^1, \beta^1)$. If $p^1 \leq p^0$, then, from the definition of the equilibrium premium, we must have

$$\sum_{i=1}^{h} (p^1 - R\theta_i)s_i\alpha_i(p^1, \tau^0, \beta^0) \leq 0 = \sum_{i=1}^{h} (p^1 - R\theta_i)s_i\alpha_i(p^1, \tau^1, \beta^1),$$

which yields

$$\sum_{i=1}^{k_1-1} (p^1 - R\theta_i)\alpha_i(p^1, \tau^0, \beta^0) + \sum_{i=k_1}^{h} (p^1 - R\theta_i)s_i\alpha_i(p^1, \tau^1, \beta^1)\Omega_i \leq 0,$$

where $\Omega_i := [\alpha_i(p^1, \tau^0, \beta^0) - \alpha_i(p^1, \tau^1, \beta^1)]/\alpha_i(p^1, \tau^1, \beta^1)$ and k_1 is the type of individual such that $\alpha_i(p^1, \tau^1, \beta^1) > 0$ if and only if $i \geq k_1$. We will show that this inequality never holds. With (2) being met, the first term on the left-hand side is non-negative because $p^1 > R\theta_i$ for $i \leq k_1$. As to the second term, on the other hand, because $\Omega_i = [\tau^1 - \tau^0 + \rho_i^1(\beta^1 - \beta^0)]/[1 - \tau^1 - \rho_i^1\beta^1]$ with $\rho_i^1 := (\delta\theta_i/p^1)^{-1/\sigma}$, Ω_i is strictly decreasing in θ_i, which assures that the second term is strictly positive as far as $k_1 < h$. Therefore, the above inequality never happens and $p^1 > p^0$ follows as far as at least two types of individuals demand annuities in equilibrium.

10 The associated transition problems are considered later.

11 Here we assume that the value of $dp^*/d\beta$ will not change very much with β.

12 The proof makes use of a revealed preference argument. Consider a type-i individual and let (C_1^{LF}, C_2^{LF}) be the consumption bundle he or she chooses at the *laissez-faire* equilibrium under the intertemporal budget constraint $C_1 + p^{LF}C_2 \leq W$. If a type-i individual chooses (C_1^*, C_2^*) with a public pension program introduced, $C_1^* = (1 - \phi\beta - p^*\alpha_i^*)W$ and $C_2^* = (\alpha_i^* + \beta)W$, from which it follows that $C_1^* + p^{LF}C_2^* = [1 + (p^{LF} - \phi)\beta + (p^{LF} - p^*)\alpha_i^*]W$. If $\beta > 0$ and $p^{LF} < \phi$, then $(p^{LF} - \phi)\beta + (p^{LF} - p^*)\alpha_i^* < 0$, which assures that $C_1^* + p^{LF}C_2^* < W$.

13 The proof is provided by a revealed preference argument again. Notice first that the Rawlsian social welfare is determined by the utility of a type-1 individual, since v_i^* is increasing θ_i. Second, as is already clear, $\beta = 0$ is Pareto optimal if $\phi > p^{LF}$ (see Note 12). Now suppose that $\phi \leq p^{LF}$. When

$\beta = [\phi + (\delta\theta_1/\phi)^{-1/\sigma}]^{-1}$, then $\alpha_1^* = 0$ and hence the consumption bundle a type-1 individual chooses in equilibrium is $(C_1^o, C_2^o) := \arg\max U_1$ subject to $C_1 + \phi C_2 \le W$. When β is given arbitrarily, on the other hand, a type-1 individual chooses $C_1^* = (1 - \phi\beta - p^*\alpha_1^*)W$ and $C_2^* = (\alpha_1^* + \beta)W$, which yield $C_1^* + \phi C_2^* = [1 - (p^* - \phi)\alpha_1^*]W \le W$ because $p^* > \phi$. When $\phi = p^{LF}$ and $\beta = 0$, a type-1 individual chooses (C_1^o, C_2^o) as well. Hence β^{OPT} is the optimal replacement ratio for type-1 individuals.

14　Because such savings in a public domain are not necessarily limited to the insurance industry and are more or less prevalent elsewhere, admitting the existence of such exogenous cost advantages, Blinder (1988) states that he is inclined to dismiss the economies of scale as a rationale for why the government should run a pension business.

15　The possibility and impossibility of a dynamic Pareto improvement by pre-funding are recently analyzed by Breyer (1989), Homburg (1990), Breyer and Straub (1993), and Brunner (1996) among others.

16　The proof is quite similar to that given in Note 13. When the replacement ratio is given by (13), then $\alpha_1^* = 0$ and the consumption bundle chosen by a type-1 individual earning a labor income W is $(C_1^o, C_2^o) := \arg\max U_1$ subject to $C_1 + \phi^{FF}C_2 \le [1 - (\phi^{PAYG} - \phi^{FF})\beta_1]W$. If β is given arbitrarily, on the other hand, he or she chooses $C_1^* = [1 - \phi^{FF}\beta - (\phi^{PAYG} - \phi^{FF})\beta_1 - p^*\alpha_1^*]W$ and $C_2^* = (\alpha_1^* + \beta)W$, which yields $C_1^* + \phi^{FF}C_2^* = [1 - (\phi^{PAYG} - \phi^{FF})\beta_1 - (p^* - \phi^{FF})\alpha_1^*]W$. Because $p^* > \phi^{FF}$ and $\phi^{PAYG} > \phi^{FF}$, it follows that $C_1^* + \phi^{FF}C_2^* < W$.

17　As in the previous analysis, β^{OPT} is large to the extent that it makes type-1 individuals need no supplementary private annuities.

18　Such a mandatory privately-managed program has been introduced in Chile and proposed by the World Bank (1994).

19　To enforce such a system it is assumed here that unlike insurance firms, the government can verify if individuals comply with the regulation. It is this informational advantage that allows a government to undertake this minimum coverage policy. It does not seem very difficult for the government to hold such an advantage by imposing a rule in which individuals must report to the government their respectively contracted amounts.

20　Of course, they will also make differences in terms of transaction costs for individuals as well as for the government.

21　In the Chilean reform, all covered workers must place 10 percent of monthly earnings in a single savings account with a regulated intermediary and when they become eligible to receive pension benefits, they can choose a sequence of phased withdrawals or an annuity. Although stated in a context of efficient fund management and asset allocation, Diamond (1996) argues that a single account regulation is not necessary and allowing diversification of individual accounts is a possible option.

22　The proof is as follows. Consider two levels of the mandatory coverage ratios, α^0 and α^1, such that $\alpha^1 > \alpha^0$, and denote the associated equilibrium premiums by $p^0 := p^*(\alpha^0)$ and $p^1 := p^*(\alpha^1)$. We also write α_i as a functional form, $\alpha_i = \alpha_i(p, \alpha)$. If $p^0 \le p^1$, then, from the definition of the equilibrium premium, we must have

$$\sum_{i=1}^{h} (p^0 - R\theta_i)s_i\alpha_i(p^0, \alpha^1) \le 0 = \sum_{i=1}^{h} (p^0 - R\theta_i)s_i\alpha_i(p^0, \alpha^0),$$

which yields

$$\sum_{i=1}^{h} (p^0 - R\theta_i)\alpha_i(p^0, \alpha^0)s_i\Omega_i \le 0,$$

where $\Omega_i := [\alpha_i(p^0, \alpha^1) - \alpha_i(p^0, \alpha^0)]/\alpha_i(p^0, \alpha^0)$. We will show that this inequality never happens when the mandatory coverage binds not all but some of the individuals. If we let k^j ($j = 0, 1$) be the type of individual such that $\alpha_i(p^0, \alpha^j) > \alpha^j$ if and only if $i \geq k^j$, then, $k^1 \geq k^0$ and Ω_i is reduced to

$$\Omega_i = \begin{cases} 0 & \text{if } i \geq k^1 \\ \alpha^1 - 1/(p^0 + \rho_i^0) & \text{if } k^1 > i > k^0 \\ \alpha^1 - \alpha^0 & \text{otherwise,} \end{cases}$$

where $\rho_i^0 = (\delta\theta_i/p^0)^{-1/\sigma}$. For $k^1 > i > k^0$, Ω_i is strictly decreasing in i_i. Therefore the above inequality never occurs and hence $p^0 > p^1$.

23 Formally, this is proved as follows. Let α_1^{LF} be the ratio of coverage to the labor income that a type-1 individual chooses at the *laissez-faire* equilibrium and denote the least-binding minimum coverage by $\alpha = \alpha_1^{LF} + \Delta\alpha$, where $\Delta\alpha$ is infinitesimal and positive. Concerning the utility of a type-1 individual, since the second term in the lower expression on the right-hand side of (14) tends to zero as $\Delta\alpha \to 0$, all we have to show is that $\lim_{\Delta\alpha \to 0}[p^*(\alpha) - p^{LF}]/\Delta\alpha < 0$. Because $p^*(\alpha)$ is decreasing in α (see Note 22), the sign automatically follows if $p^*(\alpha)$ is not continuous at $\alpha = \alpha_1^{LF}$. The sign also follows if $p^*(\alpha)$ is continuous, because invoking (1) and taking the partial derivative of π from the right, we have $\partial\pi/\partial\alpha = (p^{LF} - R\theta_1)s_1 > 0$.

24 As an empirical study, Mitchell (1998) presents an extensive analysis of the costs of administering a wide range of retirement programs.

References

Aaron, H. (1966) "The social insurance paradox," *Canadian Journal of Economics and Political Science* 32: 371–4.

Abel, A. (1986) "Capital accumulation and uncertain lifetimes with adverse selection," *Econometrica* 54: 1079–97.

Blinder, A. S. (1988) "Why is the government in the pension business?," in S. M. Wachter (ed.), *Social Security and Private Pensions: Providing for Retirement in the Twenty-First Century*, Lexington Books.

Breyer, F. (1989) " On the intergenerational pareto efficiency of pay-as-you-go financed pension systems," *Journal of Institutional and Theoretical Economics* 145: 643–58.

Breyer, F. and Straub, M. (1993) "Welfare effects of unfunded pension systems when labor supply is endogenous," *Journal of Public Economics* 50: 77–91.

Brunner, J. K. (1996) "Transition from a pay-as-you-go to a fully funded pension system: the case of differing individuals and intragenerational fairness," *Journal of Public Economics* 60: 131–46.

Diamond, P. A. (1977) "A framework for social security analysis," *Journal of Public Economics* 8: 275–98.

—— (1996) "Social security reform in Chile: two views," in P. Diamond, D. Lindeman, and H. Young (eds), *Social Security: What Role for the Future?*, Washington, DC: National Academy of Social Insurance.

Eckstein, Z., Eichenbaum, M., and Peled, D. (1985) "Uncertain lifetimes and the welfare enhancing properties of annuity markets and social security," *Journal of Public Economics* 26: 303–26.

Eichenbaum, M. S. and Peled, D. (1987) "Capital accumulation and annuities in an adverse selection economy," *Journal of Political Economy* 95: 334–54.

Feldstein, M. (1996) "The missing piece in policy analysis: social security reform," *American Economic Review*, Papers and Proceedings 86: 1–14.

—— (1998) *Privatizing Social Security*, Chicago: University of Chicago Press.

Friedman, B. M. and Warshawsky, M. (1988) "Annuity prices and saving behavior in the United States," in Z. Bodie, J. B. Shoven, and D. A. Wise (eds), *Pensions in the U.S. Economy*, Chicago: University of Chicago Press.

—— (1990) "The cost of annuities: implications for saving behavior and bequest," *Quarterly Journal of Economics* 105: 135–54.

Hatta, T. and Oguchi, N. (1992) "Changing the Japanese social security system from pay as you go to actuarially fair," in D. Wise (ed.), *Topics in the Economics of Aging*, Chicago: University of Chicago Press, 207–48.

Homburg, S. (1990) "The efficiency of unfunded pension schemes," *Journal of Institutional and Theoretical Economics* 146: 640–7.

Jaynes, G. D. (1978) "Equilibria in monopolistically competitive insurance market," *Journal of Economic Theory* 19: 394–422.

Mitchell, O. S. (1998) "Administrative costs in public and private retirement systems," in M. Feldstein (ed.), *Privatizing Social Security*, Chicago: University of Chicago Press.

Mitchell, O. S., Poterba, J. M., Warshawsky, M. J., and Brown, J. R. (1997) "New evidence on the money's worth of individual annuities," *American Economic Review* 89: 1299–318.

Pauly, M. V. (1974) "Overinsurance and public provision of insurance: the roles of moral hazard and adverse selection," *Quarterly Journal of Economics* 88: 44–62.

Rothschild, M. and Stiglitz, J. E. (1976) "Equilibrium in competitive insurance markets," *Quarterly Journal of Economics* 14: 629–49.

Samuelson, P. A. (1958) "An exact consumption-loan model of interest with or without social contrivance of money," *Journal of Political Economy* 66: 467–82.

—— (1975) "Optimum social security in a life-cycle growth model," *International Economic Review* 16: 539–44.

Stiglitz, J. E. (1988) *Economics of the Public Sector*, second edn, Norton.

Samwick, A. and Skinner, J. (1997) "Abandoning the nest egg? 401(k) plans and inadequate pension saving," in S. Schiever and J. Shoven (eds), *Public Policy Toward Pensions*, Cambridge, MA: MIT Press.

Warshawsky, M. (1988) "Private annuity markets in the United States: 1919–1984," *Journal of Risk and Insurance* 55: 518–28.

Wilson, C. (1977) "A model of insurance market with asymmetric information," *Journal of Economic Theory* 6: 167–207.

World Bank (1994) *Averting the Old Age Crisis: Policies to Protect the Old and Promote Growth*, New York: Oxford University Press.

12 Pensions contributions and capital accumulation under modified funded systems[1]

Toshihiro Ihori

Abstract

This chapter investigates dynamic implications of pension contributions and intergenerational transfers under modified funded systems. By incorporating interest groups' contributions to social security funds into the conventional overlapping generations model, the model explores the long-term effects of public spending, social security fund, and economic growth. Good economic conditions will not necessarily lead to high growth of pension funds. The pension fund is too little in terms of static efficiency (or compared with private consumption) but may be too much or too little in terms of the dynamic efficiency (or as the steady state level). We finally examine the normative role of taxes (and subsidies) on consumption and pension contributions.

12.1 Introduction

There has been much interest in the long-term macroeconomic and inter-generational redistribution effects of public pension reform. It is well recognized that pay-as-you-go systems are not attractive when the rate of economic growth declines. However, the change from pay-as-you-go financing to full funding is hard in terms of intergenerational equity, just as reducing the public debt-GDP ratio is hard. Researchers have investigated mechanisms under which a decentralized economy might successfully change from a public pay-as-you-go pension scheme to a private fully funded one. There have been several important attempts to investigate such pension reform. The standard analysis is by simulation studies using overlapping generation models based on Auerbach and Kotlikoff (1987). Recently, Cifuentes and Valdes-Prieto (1997) among others offer the output from a simulation model that describes the transition in detail, year by year. Mulligan and Sala-i-Martin (1999a,b) present a useful survey of various theories of social security. (See Hatta and Oguchi (1999) for the simulation study on Japanese pension reforms.)

Because most of the social security tax revenue from current workers goes directly to fund benefits for current retirees in unfunded systems, the social security system does not significantly increase government savings. Therefore, to the extent that social security reduces private saving, it will also tend to reduce the total amount of saving in the economy. However, time-series and cross-country estimates are inconsistent and fraught with conceptual difficulties. They offer little additional information on the relationship between social security and saving. This is partly because the actual system may not be regarded as the pure pay-as-you-go financing, especially in Japan.

It is true that pay-as-you-go and fully funded systems are two representative pension schemes, and hence it is useful to investigate and compare long-term implications of both systems in terms of intergenerational equity. However, the actual public pension system is a combination of both systems in some countries. In particular, the Japanese pension system is often called a "modified funded system" (see Appendix). It originally started as fully funded but changed mainly to pay-as-you-go financing. It accumulated a lot of funds in the funded system. There is no direct link between contributions and benefits in the unfunded system. In some countries such as Japan and the US, the social security sector still accumulates pension reserves. Thus the actual system is the one between unfunded and fully funded schemes in some countries.

The modified funded system may be regarded as a transition from full funding toward pay-as-you-go financing. Such a reform is painless in terms of intergenerational transfers, as it allows the authorities to spend the initial pension fund and it is always easy to find politically advantageous uses for newly found resources. A pension system can be immature because creation is recent. Most members of the baby boom generation are still working when the current ratio between pension expenditure and the contribution revenue is less than the steady-state ratio. In the US current projections suggest that the social security trust fund will begin to decline in 2021 and will be exhausted by 2032.[2]

Although the impact of social security on economic growth is the major concern emerging from policy discussion, the direct application of economic literature to the analysis of the dynamic property of modified funded system is limited. In other words, economic theory has not developed yet a satisfactory set of tools suitable for this kind of investigation.[3] In the analysis of long-term pension finance problems the formulation of two relevant variables, social security benefits and contributions, would crucially affect the result. The conventional simulation studies usually assume that both contributions and benefits are exogenously given. The benefit may well be regarded as exogenous and fixed for a long time. For example, in Japan the replacement ratio has been maintained at about 65 percent since mid-1970s. On the contrary, it seems more plausible to make contributions endogenous when investigating the long-term property of the system. Every five years the Japanese government adjusts old-age benefits and contributions based on the newest estimate of future population changes. There is little room to revise (or reduce) the replacement ratio due to the political pressure of existing elderly generations. Thus, the main political issue is to what degree the contributions should be raised.

We assume that the old-age benefit in real terms, which is represented by the replacement ratio, is a policy variable and hence exogenously given, while social security contributions are effectively determined by interest groups. All relevant interest groups (such as employees in the private sector, civil servants of the central government, local government employees, self-employed, firms' managers and so on) may agree with an increase in the total contributions. Namely, when facing fiscal crises of public pension systems, every interest group generally agrees to the increase in total contributions. But it would not necessarily imply that each interest group is willing to accept increases in its own contributions or cuts in its own privilege within the pension system. They would not easily agree with the allocation of increases in total contributions. This phenomenon may be called acceptance with the overall goal but objection to more specific arrangements and may be analyzed using the concept of non-co-operative Nash equilibrium.

This chapter examines both intragenerational and intergenerational conflicts under the modified funded system where public amenities are provided by pension fund accumulation. By incorporating voluntary contributions of interest groups to social security funds at Nash conjectures, our model can exhibit various types of dynamic properties of pension fund accumulation; among others convergence to a steady state would be most relevant. The larger the return on pension funds and the concern for public spending, the deeper accumulation of public spending, pension fund and physical capital would be likely to occur. Physical capital and pension contributions usually grow at the same time. An increase in benefits (or an increase in the replacement ratio) will reduce capital accumulation. However, good economic conditions of providing the public good will not necessarily lead to high economic growth at the second best solution. Namely, the public sector does not have a strong incentive to raise the productivity of providing public amenities. The pension fund is too little in terms of the static efficiency (or compared with private consumption) but may be too much or too little in terms of the dynamic efficiency (or as the steady state level). Consumption taxes or a subsidy to social security contributions would always be desirable even if the pension fund is over-accumulated. If the government can control the replacement ratio so as to realize the modified Golden Rule, it would attain dynamic efficiency.

Section 2 presents the analytical model of overlapping generations. Section 3 investigates dynamic properties of the model using a Cobb-Douglas example. Section 4 considers long-term implications of changes in some policy factors. Section 5 examines some normative aspects of public pension policy. This section also derives optimal taxes on consumption or subsidies on pension contributions. Finally Section 6 concludes the chapter.

12.2 Model

12.2.1 Analytical framework

We develop a standard model of two-period overlapping generations. An agent (or an interest group) i of generation t born at time t, considers itself young in period t, old in period $t+1$, and dies at time $t+2$. When young an agent of generation t supplies one unit of labor inelastically and receives wages w_t out of which the agent consumes c^1_{it}, provides social security contributions g_{it} (if $g_{it}>0$), conducts political activities a_{it}, and saves s_{it}. An agent receives capital income $(1+r_{t+1})s_{it}$ and pension benefits βw_{t+1} when old, which the agent then spends entirely on consumption c^2_{it+1}. There are no private bequests. r_t is the rate of interest in period t. There is no population growth and each generation has n identical individuals (or interest groups).

Thus, a member i of generation t faces the following budget constraints:

$$c^1_{it} = w_{it} - g_{it} - s_{it} - a_{it} \tag{1.1}$$

$$c^2_{it+1} = (1+r_{t+1})s_{it} + \beta w_{t+1} \tag{1.2}$$

where βw is old age benefits. β is the replacement ratio, old age benefits per average current wage income. His political activities a may determine g. For simplicity, we assume the following reduced form.

$$g_{it} = \lambda(A - a_{it}) \tag{2}$$

where $\lambda>1$. λA is the target contribution level set by the government but each interest group can reduce its own contribution by conducting political activities. In order to get fewer contributions to public pensions, more political activities are needed. If $1>\lambda$, it would not pay to conduct any positive political activities; $a=0$ and the contributor would contribute λA.

The contributor's lifetime utility function is written as

$$U^i_t = U^i(c^1_{it}, c^2_{it+1}, G_{t+1}) \tag{3}$$

where G is benefits from public amenities, which is pure public good. It is assumed for simplicity that the contributor is only concerned with public amenities in old age, G_{t+1}. Public amenities are beneficial only for the older generation.

The dynamic process of pension fund F or the budget constraint of the social security fund is written as

$$F_{t+1} = (1+b)F_t - n\beta w_t + \sum_{i=1}^{n} g_{it} \tag{4}$$

where b measures the autonomous improvement of the pension fund (the rate of return on the pension fund). It is assumed for simplicity that reserve fund is invested outside the model (to the world market or to public capital) if $b>0$, if $b=0$, is not invested, if $b<0$, is wasted (say, due to the inefficient bureaucratic system). Public pension funds may be regarded as public capital stock for improving public amenities. In such a case, if public capital depreciates, b could become negative. We assume $b<r$ for an interior solution since F provides public amenities as well as pecuniary returns. g_i may be regarded as voluntary provision of improving pension fund.

As stated before, the pension fund is also used for providing public amenities. We assume that benefits from public amenities increase with the pension fund.

$$G_t = eF_t \tag{5}$$

e is an exogenously given productivity coefficient.

Equations (4) and (5) summarize the modified funded system. There is no direct link between young-people's contributions and old-people's benefits as in the unfunded system. There is fund reserve accumulation as in the fully funded system. In Japan some of the pension funds are used for providing various benefits to current generation through FILP (Fiscal Investment and Loan Program) such as the improvement of public amenities or subsidies on housing loans. We could have in the steady state either type of public pension (pay-as-you-go system or a fully funded system) as a special case of (4). If $\beta w = g$ and $b=0$, (4) reduces to the unfunded system. If $\beta w = (1+r)g$, (4) reduces to the fully funded system.

Since there is no link between contributions and benefits and $1<\lambda$ in the modified funded system, each interest group does not have an incentive to paying contributions unless we incorporate the benefits from pension funds formulated by (5). Introducing G into the utility function is one plausible explanation why Japan has a considerable sized pension fund although there is no direct link between contributions and benefits. Alternatively, we could consider the situation where the government subsidizes the pension fund accumulation by transferring some revenue from taxes. In such a case, an increase in F means a reduction in public subsidies to the pension fund, which is beneficial to the interest group since the reduction in subsidies means an increase in public goods from the government budget constraint. Or, we may simply assume that the interest group has an altruistic preference over pension fund accumulation, so that F directly enters into the utility function.

Substituting (5) into (4), we may derive the dynamic process of G (and hence F) as

$$G_{t+1} = (1+b)G_t - en\beta w_t + e\sum_{i=1}^{n} g_{it} \qquad (6)$$

From (1), (2), and (6), the lifetime private budget constraint is given by

$$c_{it}^1 + \frac{1}{1+r_{t+1}} c_{it+1}^2 + qG_{t+1} = w_t + \frac{1}{1+r_{t+1}} \beta w_{t+1}$$

$$- n\beta w_t + \sum_{i \neq j} g_{it} + (1+b)qG_t + A \qquad (7)$$

where $q \equiv (1 - 1/\lambda)/e$. As in the standard model of voluntary provision of a pure public good, we will exclude binding contracts or co-operative behavior between the agents and will explore the outcome of non-co-operative Nash behavior.[4]

In this Cournot-Nash model, the right hand side of (7) means real income,

$$E_t^i \equiv w_t(1 - n\beta) + \frac{1}{1+r_{t+1}} \beta w_{t+1} + \sum_{i \neq j} g_{it} + (1+b)qG_t + A,$$

which contains actual disposable income,

$$w_t + \frac{1}{1+r_{t+1}} \beta w_{t+1},$$

degradation of pension fund by current old age benefits, $n\beta w_t$, the externalities from other agents' provision of pension contributions,

$$\sum_{i \neq j} g_{it},$$

and the previous level of pension fund inherited from the previous generation, $(1+b)qG_t$.

From (6) and (7) we have

$$\sum_{i=1}^{n} E_t^i = n(1 - \beta)w_t + \frac{1}{1+r_{t+1}} n\beta w_{t+1} + q(n-1)G_{t+1} \div q(1+b)G_t + nA \qquad (8)$$

Namely, add (7) from $i = 1$ to n and use (6). Then we will get (8).

$(n-1)G_{t+1}$, the third term in the right hand side of (8), captures externalities from $n-1$ persons' contributions within the same generation.

Let us then formulate the aggregate production function. The firms are perfectly competitive profit maximizers who produce output using the production function.

$$Y_t = F(K_t, n_t) \tag{9}$$

$F(\ )$ exhibits constant returns to scale. As for the standard first-order conditions from the firm's maximization problem in period t, we have

$$r_t = r(K_t) \tag{10}$$

$$w_t = w(K_t) \tag{11}$$

since n is exogenously given.

In an equilibrium agents can save by holding physical capital. We have

$$ns_t = K_{t+1} \tag{12}$$

The system may be summarized by these two equations.

$$nE[Q(K_{t+1}), q, U_t] = n(1-\beta)w(K_t) + Q(K_{t+1})n\beta w(K_{t+1}) +$$
$$q(n-1)E_3[Q(K_{t+1}), q, U_t] + q(1+b)E_3[Q(K_t), q, U_{t-1}] + nA \tag{13}$$

$$nE_2[Q(K_{t+1}), q, U_t] = K_{t+1}/Q(K_{t+1}) + n\beta w(K_{t+1}) \tag{14}$$

where $E(\ )$ is the expenditure function, which minimizes the left hand side of (8) as a function of $Q(K) \equiv 1/(1+r(K))$, q, and U. $E_3 \equiv \partial E/\partial q = G$ is the compensated demand function for G and $E_2 \equiv \partial E/\partial Q = c^2$ is the compensated demand function for c^2.

12.3 The Cobb-Douglas example

In order to demonstrate concrete results with respect to dynamic properties, let us assume that the utility function (3) is given as a Cobb-Douglas one. The qualitative results are almost the same in a more general production function.

$$U_t = (c_t^1)^{\alpha_1}(c_{t+1}^2)^{\alpha_2}(G_{t+1})^{\alpha_3} \qquad (\alpha_1 + \alpha_2 + \alpha_3 = 1) \tag{3'}$$

Then in this case we have

$$E_t = q\left(\frac{\alpha_1}{\alpha_3} + \frac{\alpha_2}{\alpha_3} + 1\right)G_{t+1} \tag{15.1}$$

$$c_t^1 = \frac{\alpha_1}{\alpha_3} q G_{t+1} \tag{15.2}$$

$$c_{t+1}^2 = \frac{\alpha_2}{\alpha_3} q (1 + r_{t+1}) G_{t+1} \tag{15.3}$$

From (2), (12), and (15.3) (14) may reduce to

$$nq\alpha G_{t+1} = K_{t+1} + \frac{1}{1 + r(K_{t+1})} n\beta w(K_{t+1}) \tag{16}$$

where $\alpha \equiv \alpha_2/\alpha_3$.
  From (16) we have

$$G_{t+1} = G(K_{t+1}; q, \beta, \alpha) \tag{17}$$

where

$$G'(K) = \frac{1}{nq\alpha} \{1 + A(K)\} > 0 \tag{18}$$

and

$$A(K) \equiv \frac{\beta\lambda(1-\lambda)n^\lambda K^{-\lambda}(1+n^\lambda K^{-\lambda})}{(1+(1-\lambda)n^\lambda K^{-\lambda})^2}.$$

From (18) we know

$$G'(\infty) = \frac{1}{nq\alpha}$$

and

$$G'(0) = \frac{1+\beta\lambda}{nq\alpha}.$$

It is also easy to show $G'' < 0$.
  G and K always move to the same direction, which implies a positive relation between G (or F) and K. Under the interdependence between the pension fund accumulation and public amenities, formulated as (4) and (5), an increase in public spending (or pension fund contributions) is consistent with economic growth. An increase in capital stock raises real income, stimulating the demand for public amenities. In order to have a larger amount of public amenities, it is necessary to raise the subsidy from the pension fund accounting. Thus, the agent is willing to pay more pension contributions, inducing deeper accumulation of pension fund. In

general we have the substitution effect as well. Namely, an increase in K raises $1/(1+r)$, the price of c^2, inducing a substitution from c^2 to G. This effect also produces deeper accumulation of pension fund. This analytical result may explain why public pension funds have rapidly been accumulated since 1960s in Japan.

Hence, considering (10), (11), (12.1), and (12.3), (13) may be rewritten as

$$\frac{qn}{\alpha_3} G(K_{t+1}) = n(1 - \beta)w(K_t) + \frac{n\beta}{[1 + r(K_{t+1})]} w(K_{t+1})$$

$$+ q(n - 1)G(K_{t+1}) + q(1 + b)G(K_t) + nA \qquad (19)$$

Or we have

$$q(\theta n + 1 - n\alpha)G(K_{t+1}) + K_{t+1} = n(1 - \beta)w(K_t)$$
$$+ q(1 + b)G(K_t) + nA \qquad (20)$$

where $\theta = (1 - \alpha_3)/\alpha_3$. (20) may be expressed as

$$K_{t+1} = \Phi(K_t) \qquad (20)'$$

which is the fundamental dynamic equation of the model.

Let us now investigate dynamics of (20) or (20)'. We have from (20)'

$$\Phi' = \frac{(1 + b)G' + (1 - \beta)q^{-1}n^\lambda K^{-\lambda}\lambda(1 - \lambda)}{(\theta n + 1 - n\alpha)G' - q^{-1}} \qquad (21)$$

The numerator when $K \Rightarrow \infty$

$$(\theta n + 1 - n\alpha)G' - \frac{1}{q} = \frac{1}{nq\alpha}(\theta n + 1)$$

is positive since $\theta > \alpha$ and hence $\theta n + 1 > n\alpha$. Thus, (21) is positive if $1 + b > 0$. We assume this.

The stability condition is

$$\Phi' = \frac{(1 + b)G' + (1 - \beta)q^{-1}n^\lambda K^{-\lambda}\lambda(1 - \lambda)}{(\theta n + 1 - n\alpha)G' - q^{-1}} < 1$$

Or, we have

$$\Delta \equiv (\theta n - n\alpha - b)G' - q^{-1} - (1 - \beta)q^{-1}n^\lambda K^{-\lambda}\lambda(1 - \lambda) > 0 \qquad (22)$$

$\theta n - b - n\alpha > 0$ is necessary for the stability condition (22). We know that $\Phi'(0) > 1$. We assume

$$\theta n - 2\alpha n - b > 0 \tag{22}$$

Then, we have that $\Phi'(\infty) < 1$. The system becomes dynamically stable. The larger the level of α_3 (the preference for public spending) and the lower the level of b (the rate of return on pension fund), it is more likely that the system would be stable.

12.4 Comparative statics

From (13) and (14) the steady state equilibrium may be summarized by the following two equations.

$$nE[Q(K), q, U] = n[1 - \beta + \beta Q(K)]w(K) \\ + q(n + b)E_3[Q(K), q, U] + nA \tag{23}$$

$$nE_2[Q(K), q, U] = \frac{1}{Q(K)}K + n\beta w(K) \tag{24}$$

Totally differentiating (23) and (24), we have

$$\frac{dU}{db} = \frac{1}{\Omega}qG\left(nE_{22}Q' - n\beta w' - \frac{Q - KQ'}{Q^2}\right) > 0 \tag{25.1}$$

$$\frac{dK}{db} = -\frac{1}{\Omega}nE_{2U}qG > 0 \tag{26.1}$$

where

$$\Omega \equiv [nE_U - q(n + b)G_U]\left[nE_{22}Q' - \beta w' - \frac{Q - KQ'}{Q^2}\right]$$

$$- nE_{2U}[(nE_2 - q(n + b)E_{32})Q' - n(1 - \beta + \beta Q)w' - n\beta wQ']$$

We know

$$nE_U - q(n + b)E_{3U} > 0, \; E_{2U} > 0. \; nE_{22}Q' - \beta w' - \frac{Q - KQ'}{Q^2} \; \text{is}$$

negative. And, the sign of $(nE_2 - q(n + b)E_{32})Q' - n(1 - \beta + \beta Q)$ $w' - n\beta wQ'$ is ambiguous. When Ω becomes negative, the sign of (25.1) becomes positive, which is intuitively plausible. Thus, we assume $\Omega < 0$. Hence, (26.1) becomes positive as well.

We also have

$$\frac{dU}{d\beta} = \frac{1}{\Omega}\left\{ nw(-1+Q)\left[nE_{22}Q' - \beta w' - \frac{Q-Q'K}{Q^2}\right]\right.$$

$$\left. - [(nE_2 - q(n+b)E_{32})Q' - n(1-\beta+\beta Q)w' - n\beta wQ']nw\right\} \quad (25.2)$$

$$\frac{dK}{d\beta} = \frac{nw}{\Omega}[nE_U - q(n+b)G_U - (-1+\theta)nE_{2U}] < 0 \quad (26.2)$$

$$\frac{dU}{dq} = \frac{1}{\Omega}\left\{ [bE_3 + q(n+b)E_{33}]\left[nE_{22}Q' - \beta w' - \frac{Q-Q'K}{Q^2}\right]\right.$$

$$- (-nE_{23})[(nE_2 - q(n+b)E_{32})Q' - n(1-\beta+\beta Q)w'$$

$$\left. - n\beta wQ']\right\} \quad (25.3)$$

$$\frac{dK}{dq} = \frac{n}{\Omega}[-E_{23}[nE_U - q(n+b)G_U] - E_{2U}(n+b)(E_3 + qE_{33})] \quad (26.3)$$

The effect of an increase in β or q (or e) on U is generally ambiguous. See Table 12.1. By setting (25.2) to be zero, we may implicitly derive the optimal level of β, the replacement ratio at the second best solution. An increase in β raises old-age consumption, which is desirable, while it reduces the effective income, the right-hand side of (23), which is undesirable. It should be stressed that an increase in q may raise welfare at the second best solution. Intuition is as follows. On the one hand, an increase in q raises private savings due to the substitution effect, which is beneficial. On the other hand, it reduces the benefits from contributions to pension funds, which is not beneficial. The overall effect is ambiguous.

As to the effect on capital accumulation, an increase in the rate of return on pension fund will raise accumulation of public spending, capital, and pension fund. An increase in the replacement ratio will reduce accumulation of capital. However, its effect on public spending and pension fund accumulation is ambiguous. These results are also intuitively plausible.

Table 12.1 Effect on welfare

	b	β	q
U	+	?	?

Table 12.2 Effect on accumulation of capital and pension fund

	b	β	q
K	+	-	?
G	+	?	?

The sign of (26.3) is ambiguous. On the one hand, an increase in q (or decrease in e) reduces the lifetime disposable income, producing the negative effect on capital accumulation and public spending. On the other hand, an increase in q will reduce voluntary contributions, producing more savings due to the substitution effect. This stimulates capital accumulation. Thus, the overall effect is ambiguous. In other words, an increase in the efficiency of providing the public amenity may not necessarily stimulate accumulation of capital, public spending, and pension fund. These results are summarized in Table 12.2.

There are no conflicts between the first best and second best situations when b changes; it is always desirable for b to increase. But there may exist a conflict between the first best and second best situations when e changes; an increase in e is desirable at the first best solution but is not always desirable at the second best solution. The public sector does not have a strong incentive to raise the productivity of providing public amenities although it should benefit the economy as the first best solution.

12.5 Normative aspects of public pension fund

12.5.1 Constrained first best

In order to investigate the normative aspect of the model, it is useful to derive the (constrained) first best solution. From (1), (2), (4), (5), and (9), the feasibility condition is given as

$$qG_{t+1} = (1+b)qG_t + Y_t + K_t - K_{t+1} - n(c_t^1 + c_t^2) \tag{27}$$

We assume that providing public amenities using the public pension system given as (4) and (5) is exogenously given and cannot be altered here. The government may choose $g(= \lambda A)$ and β but cannot choose b or e. Political activities α would be absent. In this sense, the first best investigated here is a constrained maximization solution. Otherwise, the normative role of pension fund could not be derived in the present formulation. Namely, in the fully controlled economy the government could attain the first best without relying on the public pension system.

We analyze the optimal path which would be chosen by a central planner who maximizes an intertemporal social welfare function expressed as the sum of generational utilities discounted by the social discount factor on future generations, ρ, which is between 0 and 1.

$$\max \sum_{t=0}^{\infty} \rho^t U(c_t^1, c_{t+1}^2, G_{t+1}) \qquad \text{subject to (27)}$$

In other words, the (constrained) first best problem is to maximize the Lagrange function

$$W = \sum_{t=0}^{\infty} \rho^t [nU(c_t^1, c_{t+1}^2, G_{t+1}) - \mu_t[qG_{t+1} - q(1+b)G_t - Y_t - K_t + K_{t+1}$$
$$+ n(c_t^1 + c_{t+1}^2)]\} \qquad (28)$$

where $\rho^t \mu_t$ is a Lagrange multiplier at time t.
    The first order conditions are as follows.

$$U_{1t} - \mu_t = 0 \qquad (29.1)$$

$$U_{2t+1} - \mu_{t+1}\rho = 0 \qquad (29.2)$$

$$nU_{3t+1} - q\mu_t + q(1+b)\rho\mu_{t+1} = 0 \qquad (29.3)$$

$$\mu_{t+1}(1+r_{t+1})\rho - \mu_t = 0 \qquad (29.4)$$

along with the transversality conditions

$$\lim_{t\to\infty}\rho^t\mu_t G_t = 0, \lim_{t\to\infty}\rho^t\mu_t K_t = 0$$

where $U_{1t} = \partial U_t/\partial c_t^1$, $U_{2t+1} = \partial U_t/\partial c_{t+1}^2$, and $U_{3t+1} = \partial U_t/\partial G_t +_1$.
    From these conditions we have

$$\frac{U_{3t+1}}{U_{1t}} = \frac{q(r_{t+1} - b)}{(1 + r_{t+1})n} \qquad (30.1)$$

$$\frac{U_{3t+1}}{U_{2t+1}} = \frac{q(r_{t+1} - b)}{n} \qquad (30.2)$$

The inequality $r > b$ is assumed to have an interior solution. From (30.1) and (30.2), we have

$$\frac{U_{3t+1}}{U_{1t}} + \frac{U_{3t+1}}{U_{2t+1}} < q + q(1 + r_{t+1}) \qquad (31)$$

Note that $n > 1$. Since in the competitive economy we always have

$$\frac{U_{3t+1}}{U_{1t}} = q, \tag{32.1}$$

$$\frac{U_{3t+1}}{U_{2t+1}} = q(1 + r_{t+1}), \tag{32.2}$$

inequality (31) means that $(c_t^1 + c_{t+1}^2)/G_{t+1}$ in the competitive economy is greater than in the first best economy since each agent does not fully recognize the total effect of voluntary contributions to public pension reserves. That is, the main reason for such under provision of G is that each group disregards a positive externality of cooperation with public pension schemes which spills over into all other groups in choosing its own contribution. (This is the conventional result in the literature. See Bliss and Nalebuff (1984) Bergstrom *et al.* (1986), and Boadway *et al.* (1989).) Public spending (or pension fund) divided by total consumption is too little in the modified funded system at the second best solution. In this sense, public spending (or pension fund) is too little and private consumption is too much in the competitive economy in terms of the static efficiency.

In terms of dynamic efficiency from (29.4) we have as the modified Golden Rule:

$$(1 + r)\rho = 1 \tag{33}$$

The first best solution may be summarized by (27), (30.1), (30.2), and (33).

Under the Cobb-Douglas utility function (3)′, (30.1), and (30.2) are rewritten as

$$\frac{\alpha_3 c^1}{\alpha_1 G} = \frac{q(r - b)}{(1 + r)n} \tag{30.1}′$$

$$\frac{\alpha_3 c^2}{\alpha_2 G} = \frac{q(r - b)}{n} \tag{30.2}′$$

Substituting these two equations into (27) and considering (33), we finally obtain the first best G, G_{FB}, as

$$G_{FB} = \frac{Y_{FB}}{\dfrac{q}{\alpha_3}\left[\dfrac{1}{\rho} - (1 + b)\right](\rho\alpha_1 + \alpha_2) - qb} \tag{34}$$

where Y_{FB} is output associated with the modified Golden Rule. The first best public spending is decreasing with q and increasing with ρ, b, and α_3.

These results are intuitively plausible. Considering (7), the first best pension fund is independent of q in this case.

In the standard overlapping generations growth model it is well known that capital may be over supplied in the competitive equilibrium. Capital may be too much in this model as well when the competitive steady state economy is on the inefficient path $((1+r)\rho<1)$. Also, (34) suggests that the steady-state level of public spending (or pension fund) may be too much if q is very high or ρ is very small. The pension fund at the second best solution may be increasing with q, while its steady state level at the first best solution is independent of q.

Let us compare the steady-state levels of public spending, G^* at the Nash solution, and G_{FB} at the first best solution. Remember that the public good at the second best solution is independent of ρ (and δ). If $r^*\geq\delta$, it is easy to see $G^*<G_{FB}$. However, if $r^*<\delta$, we cannot exclude the possibility of $G^*>G_{FB}$. Public goods at the non-co-operative Nash solution could be over provided. In other words, G^* given by (23), (24) could be higher than G_{FB} given by (34) if δ is large enough. If α_2 is large, we could have the same possibility.

In Figure 12.1 line AB represents the feasibility condition at the steady state where the modified Golden Rule (33) is satisfied.

$$n(c^1+c^2)-bG=Y_{FB}$$

Point F is the first best solution, while point N is the Nash equilibrium when $r^*=\delta$. The movement from F to N on the same budget line AB reflects the free-riding effect. As shown in Figure 12.1, G is too little at point N compared with point F.

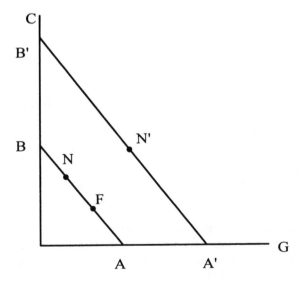

Figure 12.1 Steady state level of public spending

If $r^* < \delta$, we may draw Figure 12.1 where line A'B' represents the feasibility condition at the steady state in the competitive economy. A shift from line AB to line A'B' reflects the income effect. Thus, if the income effect dominates the free-riding effect, G^* at point N' could be greater than G_{FB} at point F. The higher the discount rate δ and the concern with future consumption α_2, it is more likely to have such a paradoxical case.

12.5.2 Optimal tax and subsidy policy

Finally, let us consider some tax and subsidy polices to attain the first best economy in the long run. As to the static efficiency, consumption taxes could attain the target. When consumption taxes are not available, a subsidy to social security contributions would be equivalent to taxing the second period consumption as well as the first period consumption.

Suppose that consumption taxes η^1, η^2, a subsidy to contributions τ and political activities a and a tax on interest income μ are available. We also assume that the total revenues from these taxes (or subsidies) are used for a lump sum transfer (or tax), T^1, T^2. Then, the budget constraints (1.1) and (1.2) are rewritten as

$$(1 + \eta^1)c_{it}^l = w_{it} - (1 - \tau)g_{it} - s_{it} - (1 - \tau)a_{it} - T^1 \tag{1.1}'$$

$$(1 + \eta^2)c_{it+1}^2 = [1 + (1 - \mu)r_{t+1}]s_{it} + \beta w_{t+1} - T^2 \tag{1.2}'$$

Then, considering (1)' and (2)', (32.1), and (32.2) are rewritten as

$$\frac{U_{3t+1}}{U_{1t}} = \frac{q(1 - \tau)}{1 + \eta^1} \tag{32.1}'$$

$$\frac{U_{3t+1}}{U_{2t+1}} = \frac{q[1 + (1 - \mu)r_{t+1}]}{1 + \eta^2} \tag{32.2}'$$

From (30.1), (30.2), and (32.1)', (32.2)', when $\eta^1 = \eta^2 = 0$ the optimal values of τ and μ are respectively given as

$$\tau^* = 1 - \frac{r - b}{(1 + r)n} > 0 \tag{35.1}$$

$$\mu^* = 0 \tag{35.2}$$

(35.1) and (35.2) show that a subsidy to contributions is optimal for attaining the static efficiency. In Japan public pension contributions are fully exempted from the income tax base. It actually subsidizes contributions. Furthermore, the government covers one-third of the total cost of the flat-rate basic benefits. This policy also subsidizes contributions. The above analysis suggests that such public subsidies may be justified to realize the static efficiency although the actual level of subsidies may not be optimal.[5] From (35.2) it is desirable not to tax interest income. Note that a tax on old-age benefits is not effective since it cannot affect the first order conditions of consumers in the modified funded system.

It might be difficult to subsidize political activities in addition to pension contributions. Alternatively, when $\tau = \mu = 0$, the optimal values of consumption taxes are respectively given as,

$$\eta^{1''} = \eta^{2''} = \frac{n + r(n-1) + b}{r - b} > 0 \tag{36}$$

The optimal consumption tax rates are uniform and positive.

As to the dynamic efficiency, intergenerational redistribution policy would be useful. Or if the government can control the replacement ratio so as to realize the modified Golden Rule, it would attain the dynamic efficiency. When physical capital is over-provided at the Nash equilibrium ($r^* \leq \delta$), the intergenerational transfer from the young to the old would be required. An increase in the replacement ratio could have this effect. Such a policy would reduce the lifetime disposable income, reducing savings. It would raise r^*, hence depressing voluntary provision of pension contributions, which is desirable in this case. Although a subsidy to pension contributions given by (35.1) may be rationalized in terms of static efficiency, it is desirable to depress voluntary contributions using the intergenerational transfer policy when capital is over-provided in the competitive economy. In such a case an increase in the replacement ratio would be desirable.

On the contrary, when capital is under-provided ($r^* > \delta$), the intergenerational transfer from the old to the young would be required. A decease in the replacement ratio would be desirable. Such a policy would allow better funding of the pension system. It seems that this case would be more relevant to Japan.

12.6 Conclusion

This chapter has developed a general equilibrium model of a modified pension system in which interest groups provide a social security contribution under the assumption that a part of the pension fund is used for providing public goods.

We have clarified how the relevant parameters would affect dynamic properties. Both the return on public pension fund and the amount of old-age benefits have important roles for dynamic properties. The larger the rate of rerun on the pension fund, the deeper accumulation of public spending, pension fund, and capital would be likely to occur at the competitive solution.

We have investigated the effect of contribution externalities on welfare during the growth process where both public spending and capital move in the same direction. An increase in capital stock raises real income, stimulating the demand for public amenities. In order to have a larger amount of public amenities, it is necessary to raise the pension fund accumulation. Thus, the agent is willing to pay more pension contributions, inducing deeper accumulation of pension fund.

An increase in the replacement ratio will reduce accumulation of capital although its effect on welfare is ambiguous. There are no conflicts between the first best and decentralized situations when the rate of return on pension fund changes. But there may exist a conflict between the first best and decentralized situations when the efficiency of public amenities changes. The public sector does not have a strong incentive to raise the benefit from public amenities although it benefits all generations at the first best solution.

Capital may be too much in the long run when the competitive steady-state economy is on the inefficient path. Also, the steady-state level of public spending and pension fund may be too much in the model although it is too little compared with consumption. As to attaining static efficiency, consumption taxes or a subsidy to social security contributions would be useful for correcting the free-riding behavior of interest groups. This is desirable even if pension fund is over-accumulated. If the government can control the replacement ratio so as to realize the modified Golden Rule, it would attain the dynamic efficiency. When capital is under-provided, the intergenerational transfer from the old to the young would be required. A decease in the replacement ratio would be desirable. Such a policy would give the pension system greater funding.

Appendix

The Japanese pension system

Let us briefly summarize public pension programs in Japan. Japan currently has six public pension programs covering different sectors of the population. Although each system has its own contribution and benefit structure, all systems are similar, operating largely like pay-as-you-go systems. Japan currently has a two-tier system of public pensions, the flat-rate tier; flat-rate basic benefits cover all residents including self-employed and unemployed. The second tier, earnings-related benefits apply only to employees.

The principal program for private sector employees is the Kosei-Nenkin-Hoken (KNH). Civil servants of the central government, local government employees, private school teachers and employees, and employees of agriculture/forestry/fishing organizations and unemployed are covered under the Kokumin-Nenkin (KN).

The average monthly earnings are calculated over the employee's entire period of employment, adjusted by a wage index factor, and converted to the current earnings level. At present, the KNH old-age benefits for the newly awarded model retiree (with an average salary earned for 37 years of employment) and his dependent spouse (full-time housewife) are about ¥220,092 per month in 1994, replacing 65 percent of average monthly earnings of currently active male workers. Consequently the current replacement rate to take-home pay or net income is about 80 percent.

Under the KNH, equal percentage contributions are required of employees and their employers. The contributions are based on the Hyojun-Hosyu-Getsugaku (HHG), the monthly standard earnings, graded into 30 levels currently raging from ¥92,000 to ¥590,000 per month. The total percentage currently in effect in 1997 is 17.35 percent.

The Japanese population has been relatively young and the public pension programs in Japan are still at an early stage of maturity. Both demographic and economic factors in the future will probably impose greater stresses on the programs. Japan now faces a serious aging problem due to higher life expectancy and declining fertility.

Substantial increases in the contribution rate of the KNH (and of the KN) will be required to support currently legislated benefits, provided the normal retirement age and old age benefits remain unchanged. Currently the KNH has a reserve fund of about ¥118.5 trillion (23 percent of GDP) in 1998. The funded reserve could mitigate future financial sufferings of the KNH. From the beginning KNH contributions have been accumulated in a reserve fund to be invested in public capital for the construction of highways, railways, bridges, airports, and other public projects, but these reserves will soon begin to diminish in real terms, and might disappear in the next fifteen years unless contributions are raised. The current reserve will no longer provide a substantial cushion for the KNH. See Takayama (1998) and Hatta and Oguchi (1999).

Notes

1 Earlier versions of the chapter were presented at the conference on Social Security Reform at University of Tokyo, September 6–7, 1999 as well as seminars at University of California, Irvine, Kyoto University, and Niigata University. I wish to thank Fumio Ohtake and other seminar participants.

2 Table III.B2 of the 1998 Annual Report of the Board of Trustees of the Federal Old-Age and Survivors Insurance and Disability Insurance Trust Funds reports projections for the assets of the combined OASI and DI Trust Funds.

3 Recently Abel (1999) develops a tractable stochastic overlapping generations model to analyze the equilibrium equity premium and growth rate of the capital stock in the presence of a defined-benefit social security system.

4 As for voluntary provision of public goods, see Shibata (1971), Warr (1983), and Bergstrom *et al.* (1986) among others.

5 It may not be realistic to subsidize political activities as well. The Japanese pension system does not necessarily subsidize political activities.

References

Abel, A. B. (1999) "The social security trust fund, the riskless interest rate, and capital accumulation," *NBER Working Paper* 6991.

Auerbach, A. and Kotlikoff, L. (1987) *Dynamic Fiscal Policy*, Cambridge: Cambridge University Press.

Bergstrom, T., Blume, L., and Varian, H. (1986) "On the private provision of public good," *Journal of Public Economics* 29: 25–49.

Bliss, C. and Nalebuff, B. (1984) "Dragon-slaying and ballroom dancing: the private supply of a public good," *Journal of Public Economics* 25: 1–12.

Boadway, R., Pestieau, P., and Wildasin, D. (1989) "Tax-transfer policy and the voluntary provision of public goods," *Journal of Public Economics* 39: 157–76.

Cifuentes, R. and Valdes-Prieto, S. (1997) "Transitions in the presence of credit constraints," in S. Valdes-Prieto (ed.), *The Economics of Pensions*, Cambridge: Cambridge University Press.

Hatta, T. and Oguchi, T. (1999) *Nenkinkaikakuron (Japanese Pension Reform)*, Nihonkeizai-shinbunsya, in Japanese.

Mulligan, C. B. and Sala-i-Martin, X. (1999a) "Social security in the theory and practice (I): Facts and political theories," *NBER Working Paper* 7118.

Mulligan, C. B. and Sala-i-Martin, X. (1999b) "Social security in the theory and practice (I): Efficiency theories, narrative theories, and implications for reform," *NBER Working Paper* 7119.

Shibata, H. (1971) "A bargaining model of the pure theory of public expenditures," *Journal of Political Economy* 79: 1–29.

Takayama, A. (1998) *The Morning After in Japan: Its Declining Population, Too Generous Pensions and a Weakened Economy*, Tokyo: Maruzen.

Warr, P. G. (1983) "The private provision of a public good is independent of the distribution of income," *Economics Letters* 13: 207–11.

Index